J.K. LASSER'S™

FINANCIAL BASICS FOR BUSINESS MANAGERS

Look for these and other titles from J.K. Lasser™—Practical Guides for All Your Financial Needs

J.K. Lasser's Pick Winning Stocks by Edward F. Mrkvicka, Jr.

J.K. Lasser's Invest Online by LauraMaery Gold and Dan Post

J.K. Lasser's Year-Round Tax Strategies by David S. De Jong and Ann Gray Jakabin

J.K. Lasser's Taxes Made Easy for Your Home-Based Business by Gary W. Carter

J.K. Lasser's Finance and Tax for Your Family Business by Barbara Weltman

J.K. Lasser's Pick Winning Mutual Funds by Jerry Tweddell with Jack Pierce

J.K. Lasser's Your Winning Retirement Plan by Henry K. Hebeler

J.K. Lasser's Winning With Your 401(K) by Grace Weinstein

J.K. Lasser's Winning With Your 403(b) by Pam Horowitz

J.K. Lasser's Strategic Investing After 50 by Julie Jason

J.K. Lasser's Winning Financial Strategies for Women by Rhonda Ecker and Denise Gustin-Piazza

J.K. Lasser's Online Taxes by Barbara Weltman

J.K. Lasser's Pick Stocks Like Warren Buffett by Warren Boroson

J.K. Lasser's The New Tax Law Simplified

J.K. Lasser's New Rules for Retirement and Tax by Paul Westbrook

J.K. Lasser's New Rules for Small Business Taxes by Barbara Weltman

J.K. Lasser's Investor's Tax Guide by Elaine Floyd

J.K. Lasser's Choosing the Right Long-Term Care Insurance by Ben Lipson

J.K. Lasser's Winning Ways to Save for College by Barbara Wagner

J.K. Lasser's Financial Basics for Business Managers by John A. Tracy

J.K. LASSER'S™

FINANCIAL BASICS FOR BUSINESS MANAGERS

John A. Tracy

John Wiley & Sons, Inc.

Published by John Wiley & Sons, Inc.
Published simultaneously in Canada.

This publication is designed to provide accurate and authoritative information in
regard to the subject matter covered. It is sold with the understanding that the
publisher is not engaged in rendering professional services. If professional advice
or other expert assistance is required, the services of a competent professional
person should be sought.

ISBN 0-471-09323-8

Printed in the United States of America

10 9 8 7 6 5 4 3 2 1

For Our Children—
Mary, John, Cris, Jackie,and Tage

Contents

0153588

Acknowledgments

I've been a Wiley author now for more than 25 years. I've had the very good fortune of working with several outstanding editors on my books. These men and women have helped me a great deal. My editor for this book, Dave Pugh, kept a careful eye on the development of the book. The staff at Cape Cod Compositors polished my clumsy prose and made excellent suggestions for improving the book. Many thanks to Dave—and all my past editors with Wiley.

J.K. LASSER'S™

FINANCIAL BASICS FOR BUSINESS MANAGERS

CHAPTER 1

Making Profit 101

Business Models and Profit Models

Making profit is no fluke. Keeping a business consistently on the profit side of the ledger is a demanding task. A well-thought-out business plan is essential. And developing a *business model* is particularly helpful. A business plan typically runs 20, 30, or more pages. A typical business model runs 20 or 30 words. It encapsulates the core strategy of the business plan in a short, crystal-clear statement. A business model has relatively few words but says a lot.

The business model provides a common touchstone for managers. If a tentative decision doesn't square with the business model, the manager would be veering off course. Moving ahead with the decision may be a good new direction to go. Perhaps not. In any case, the model serves as the strategic compass of the business. A business model is also very useful in communicating with employees, customers, creditors, lenders, and investors—to tell the story of the business in a few words.

In my business consulting experience and having served on several boards of directors, I've seen the critical importance of a well-crafted business model—whether a business is public or private, large or small, just starting up or well-established, a seller of products or services, and whether struggling or coasting along. Most businesses I've worked with had a fairly good business model—not always written in stone, but nevertheless one that was clear in the minds of its top-level managers. Of course a business model may change over time, after deep soul searching regarding which new directions to take and which new strategies the business should embrace.

As useful as it is, a business model has one inherent danger. You can get caught up in the rhetoric of a business model; you can too easily accept the model as a self-fulfilling prophecy. A business model may promise more than it can deliver in actual bottom-line results. It may be no more than wishful thinking. Keep in mind that a business model is written to be a persuasive explanation of how the business makes profit. As the adage says, the proof is not in the pudding but in the eating. In more modern terms, can a business walk the talk of its business model?

A business model, in other words, can be a very convincing theory that looks good on paper. The reality check is whether a business can actually translate the words into profit. A business also needs a *profit model* to put its business model into action. A business model focuses on marketing strategies, competitive advantages, quality standards, and so on. Mainly words. A profit model focuses on sales prices, costs, expenses, margins, and total profit. Mainly numbers. A profit model focuses on the essential data that determine the amount of profit for a period. A business model is more left brain. A profit model is more right brain. However, a good profit model should be like the business model in one key respect—short and to the point, having no more elements than absolutely necessary.

As a business consultant I would challenge a company's managers as follows. I understand your business model and I like it. But let's crank the numbers through your profit model and test whether your data actually yield enough profit or not. Often they would reply: What's a profit model? They would argue that their business model was their profit model. I would argue that a business model is like a map that plots the general directions to a destination. You still have to quantify the number of miles, gas mileage, average speed, number of passengers, and so on. In short, you must put some numbers on the main factors that drive profit.

Of course profit is the main financial objective of a business—or, I should say profit is one of its primary financial objectives. A business also has to generate **cash flow**. A business has to meet its payroll, pay its debts on time, pay dividends to its stockholders (if they demand dividends), have ready cash to invest for growth, and so on.

A business should operate in the black (make profit) and keep its cash balance in the black (keep cash at adequate levels). A business has to stay out of the red on both counts.

This book explains both profit models and cash flow models for managing a business. This first chapter examines how a business makes profit by introducing and explaining the basic profit model that fits a very broad range of businesses. The second chapter examines **cash flow from profit**. In most situations one dollar of profit in a period does not yield exactly one dollar of cash flow over the same period. A dollar of profit generates either more than a dollar, or less than a dollar of cash flow. Business managers should be very clear in their minds about this divergence between profit and cash flow.

Introducing the Profit Model

Figure 1.1 presents the basic profit model for a typical business. Note that it's *the* profit model instead of *a* profit model. The framework and factors of the profit model in Figure 1.1 apply to the large majority of businesses. In the example the business sells products. The values for the factors in the profit model can be easily adapted to fit a company that sells services rather than products. (Alternative business examples are discussed later.) The basic factors in the

FIGURE 1.1 Profit Model for Period

Line Number	Profit Factors	Values
1.	Sales Price	$100.00
2.	Less: Product Cost Expense	$60.00
3.	Equals: Gross Margin	$40.00
4.	Less: Unit-Driven Expenses	$5.50
5.	Less: Revenue-Driven Expenses	7.50%
6.	Equals: Unit Margin	$27.00
7.	Multiplied by: Sales Volume	100,000
8.	Equals: Contribution Margin	$2,700,000
9.	Less: Fixed Operating Expenses	$1,500,000
10.	Equals: Profit (before Other Expenses)	$1,200,000

profit model are the same across a very broad cross section of businesses. In short the profit model is generic, but the dollar amounts and the other measures for each factor vary significantly across industry sectors, and the data even can be quite different from company to company within one industry.

For instance, in the example the company adds a $40.00 mark-up to its $60.00 product cost to set the $100.00 sales price. So its **gross margin** (profit before other expenses) is 40 percent of sales price. In short, mark-up is gross profit. Many businesses need 50 percent or higher gross margin on sales to make an adequate profit (because their other expenses are high). In contrast, some businesses can make profit with a gross profit on sales of only 25 percent or less. As I write this, Apple Computer reported a 27 percent gross margin on sales, though I'm sure Apple would like to do better (and has done better in the past).

A profit model is like a Swiss army knife—an excellent tool for several different purposes. The profit model is very useful in developing a profit plan for the coming period, particularly for setting sales prices and expense targets. It's equally useful for analyzing actual results for the period just ended. In other words, the profit model is very helpful for analyzing how to reach profit goals for the coming period, and for comparing actual profit performance for the period against the goals for the period (or with the last period).

Time Period and Domain of Profit Model

By its very nature profit is the cumulative result over a period of time. One of the most important functions of business accounting is to measure profit performance and to prepare periodic financial statements that report the profit, cash flows, and financial condition of the business. Almost all businesses report quarterly financial statements to their outside shareowners and lenders. Measuring profit for a quarter-year is a rather short time period. Measuring profit for an entire year provides a much more reliable measure. One year is a natural time period for many businesses over which to measure profit performance. Thus, quarterly financial statements are treated as somewhat tentative until the annual financial statements are reported by a business. The timetable for financial reporting outside the business does not govern how often financial statements are prepared for the managers of a business, however.

Managers at all levels in a business organization receive internal financial reports that do not circulate outside the business. The scope of information in each manager's financial report encompasses his or her area of responsibility in the business organization. These internal financial reports contain a good deal of confidential information that must be shielded from the eyes of competitors. Internal financial reports to managers contain a lot of detail, mainly for control purposes. To control what's going on, managers have to keep their eyes on a lot of details, that's for sure. Furthermore, internal financial reports to many managers are needed weekly or monthly, so that things don't spin out of control before the manager is even aware of what's going wrong.

The profit model is designed not primarily for frequent control monitoring. The profit model is for decision-making analysis (and for review of actual profit performance). Managers need to keep a constant and close watch on many details to exercise control. In contrast, the profit model is extremely condensed. Also, control reports are needed frequently. The profit model is for a decision-based time period, which is usually longer than the relatively short time periods for which control reports are prepared. The right time period for the profit model depends mainly on how frequently managers set and reset *sales prices*. It's difficult to generalize about the time period of a profit model. Some companies publish list prices that they hold onto for as long as one year. Some companies bring out new models just once a year. Some companies set sales prices for part of a year, such as for the fall and spring seasons. Some retail businesses reset sales prices frequently (gas stations and grocery stores come to mind). Managers plan ahead for a certain time horizon, and the profit model should fit this time period.

A separate profit model is needed for each source of profit. The business needs to know each stream and creek that flows into the river of its sales and profit. Managers have to circumscribe and map out each **profit module** of the business. For instance, besides selling coffee by the cup a Starbucks store sells coffee beans, coffee machines, and many other items (including books and music). Managers need a separate profit model for each area of profit making. A business is a collection of many different sources of sales and profits—segments, territories, branches, product lines, stores, divisions, departments, and so on. Even smaller businesses usually consist of two or more disparate parts. Its managers should clearly identify each separate source of the business's sales and profit—called profit modules.

Identifying profit modules depends on the organizational structure of the business, how the company markets its goods and services, the geographical dispersion of the business, and several other factors. The bottom-line test is whether the profit module is focused enough for decision making—without a manager's having too many separate profit modules to deal with. The can't see the forest for the trees adage comes to mind. Though I would say that managers as forest rangers have to sort between different kinds of trees and put the trees into meaningful groves and stands. General Motors would not lump together its Saturn model line with its Cadillac line. I'm sure that Ford separates its Explorer line of SUV vehicles separately from its light trucks.

The profit model in Figure 1.1 includes fixed operating expenses (see line 9), which are deducted from contribution margin (line 8) for the period. Many fixed expenses can be coupled with the sales activity included in the profit model. A fixed amount spent for advertising the products whose sales are included in the profit model is one example. The rent cost for a warehouse that stores only products included in the profit model is included as a fixed operating expense. The fixed salaries of employees who work only in sales and supporting activities included in the profit model are included in the fixed operating expenses. All fixed expenses directly related to the sales activity should be included in the profit model.

Businesses have general fixed overhead costs that are very remote to any particular source of sales and profit. Examples include the general legal costs of the business, the annual compensation of the president and chief executive officer of the business, institutional advertising that does not mention any particular product or service sold by the business, the costs of the human resources department of the business, and many more. These indirect fixed costs cannot be directly matched to a particular source of sales. They can be allocated to profit sources according to some method, but this issue is put off until later in the book. In summary, profit in the profit model (Figure 1.1, line 10) is before unallocated company-wide overhead expenses, and before interest and income tax expenses. Interest and income tax expenses come into play at the company-wide level, and depend on how the business is financed and its income tax situation.

Running through the Profit Model Factors

Before beginning the line-by-line explanations of each factor in the profit model presented in Figure 1.1, it should be emphasized that the profit model is for a group of products that constitute an identifiable source of sales and profit. These groupings are called profit modules. In a retail department store a profit module could be men's or women's shoes. For Dell, Gateway, and Apple a profit module would be for laptop computers. For Ford one profit module may be for Explorers. The appropriate profit module depends on the judgment of managers and the nature of the business.

The point I wish to make here is that a profit module is for a mix of products and, therefore, the per unit values in the profit model (Figure 1.1) are averages for the period. The average sales price in the profit model depends on the sales mix, or proportions of products that constitute the profit module. The different products making up the profit module are sold at different sales prices. For example if only two products are included in the profit model and one-half are sold at $110.00 and one-half are sold at $90.00, then the average sales price is $100.00. If the sales mix shifts to a greater proportion of higher-priced units, then the average sales price would be higher, of course. Likewise, the average product cost and the other average unit amounts in the profit model depend on the mix of products included in the profit module.

In the rest of this section I explain briefly each of the factors in the profit model. Please refer to the corresponding line in Figure 1.1 as each factor is explained.

1. Sales Price

This is the average sales price over the period, net of any customer discounts, rebates, and allowances. In other words, the sales price is the actual amount received by the business that can be used to cover expenses and provide profit. Discounts, rebates, and allowances are accounted for and reported to managers, but the profit model focuses on the net sales price.

2. Product Cost Expense

If the business manufacturers the products it sells this is the production cost per unit; if the business is a retailer (or wholesaler), this is the purchase cost per unit. Product costs typically fluctuate during a period, so, the average product cost depends to some degree on which accounting method is being used. Chapter 13 explains the choice of product cost accounting methods.

3. Gross Margin

This is the profit per unit before any other expenses of making the sales are deducted; only product cost is deducted at this point. This preliminary, or first-line, measure of profit is also called **gross profit** Gross means that many other expenses are not yet deducted against sales revenue.

4. Unit-Driven Expenses

These are incremental costs that increase with each additional unit sold, such as shipping, handling, and packaging. These costs depend mainly on weight and/or size of product, not on sales value.

5. Revenue-Driven Expenses

These are incremental costs that increase with each additional dollar of sales revenue, such as commissions paid to salespersons based on a percent of sales amounts and credit card discounts paid by retailers to the bank that are based as a percent of sales amounts. Note that the percent is given in the profit model (7.50 percent of sales price in the example) so the dollar amount is $7.50 of the $100.00 sales price.

6. Unit Margin

This is an extraordinarily important amount; it's the amount of profit per unit after deducting from sales price the cost of the product sold and the variable expenses of making sales. *Warning:* Fixed operating expenses still have to be considered to determine total profit, as you see in Figure 1.1. But these fixed costs are considered in total, not on a per unit basis. In short, **unit margin** is profit per unit after all variable expenses are deducted from sale price but before fixed operating expenses are taken into account.

7. Sales Volume

This is the total number of units sold over a period, net of units returned by customers. On a more technical note, this quantity may be the total number of customers served (such as for a restaurant) or the total number of sales tickets or sales invoices for the period.

8. Contribution Margin

The margin from each unit sold contributes toward covering the total fixed operating expenses of the sales included in the profit model. A certain number of units must be sold just to cover the fixed operating expenses of the period. Once over this hump of fixed costs the additional units sold contribute toward profit.

9. Fixed Operating Expenses

Virtually every business makes costs commitments for the period that cannot be changed too much over the short run, such as rent, depreciation, salaries, and utilities. These fixed expenses provide the capacity to make sales and to carry on operations—by providing the space, people, and other things needed to operate. One of the toughest decisions managers have to make is how much capacity will be needed in the future, and whether to upsize or downsize the capacity of the business.

10. Profit (before Other Expenses)

This is the total amount of profit from sales before other expenses of the business are taken into account. These other expenses include the general, indirect fixed overhead costs of the business that cannot be matched with any particular source of sales, interest on the debt of the business, and income tax expense. Of course, a business has to take into account these other expenses when preparing the income statement for the business as a whole (which is discussed later in the chapter).

I could elaborate at length on each of the above profit model factors, but these brief explanations cover the essentials. Other aspects of the factors are expanded on as the need arises.

Basic Lessons from Profit Model

In this section the most important lessons from the profit model are explained. (Using the profit model to chart the ways for improving profit performance is explained in Chapters 6 and 7.) Please keep in mind that the definition of *profit* at this point in this discussion is before deducting the indirect fixed costs of the business that cannot be linked to the sales activity included in the profit model, and before deducting the company's interest and income tax expenses. In other words, the profit amount in the profit model (Figure 1.1, line 10) is not the final bottom-line profit of a business, which is reported in the company's income statement. This is explained in the income statement later in the chapter. (For a sneak preview of the income statement you can look ahead to Figure 1.3.)

Question: How did the business make $1.2 million profit?

The business sold products for a $100.00 average sales price and controlled its average product cost and its **variable expenses** of making sales so that its unit margin was $27.00. The company's 100,000 units *sales volume* generated $2,700,000 **contribution margin** (see line 8 in Figure 1.1). Deducting its $1,500,000 *fixed operating expenses* for the period leaves $1,200,000 million profit for the period. (Chapter 5 explains how to evaluate profit performance relative to sales revenue, assets used to make profit, and owner's equity capital invested in the business.)

CALCULATION OF PROFIT

$27.00 \times 100,000 = \$2,700,000$
$$-\$1,500,000 = \$1,200,000$$

Question: **At what sales volume would the business have just covered its fixed operating costs and made a zero profit for the period?**

By earning $27.00 unit margin and selling 100,000 units during the period (see lines 6 and 7 in Figure 1.1), the business garnered contribution margin that was $1,200,000 more than its fixed operating expenses for the period. This is the profit for the period, of course. Now, suppose the business had sold only 55,556 units. In this scenario the company's profit would have been exactly zero: [55,556 units sales volume $\times$ $27.00 unit margin = $1,500,000 contribution margin, which just equals its $1,500,000 fixed operating expenses for the period]. The calculation of this particular sales volume is: [$1,500,000 fixed operating expenses $\div$ $27.00 unit margin = 55,556 units (rounded)]. This zero profit scenario (or zero loss scenario, depending on your point of view) is called the **breakeven point**, or the **breakeven volume**. Subtracting the breakeven volume from actual sales volume reveals that the company sold 44,444 units in excess of its breakeven point. Sales volume would have to sink more than 44.4 percent before the business would slip into the loss territory, assuming its unit margin and total fixed operating expenses remain the same.

CALCULATION OF BREAKEVEN SALES VOLUME

$$\frac{\$1,500,000}{\$27.00} = 55,556$$

Question: **How does the company's sales volume for the period stack up against its fixed operating expenses for the period?**

Your attention is directed to lines 7 and 9 in the profit model (Figure 1.1)—sales volume and fixed operating expenses for the period. Virtually every business has fixed operating expenses, which cannot be easily reduced over the short run. The profit model includes the fixed costs that can be directly linked with the sales activity included in the profit module. In very rough terms there are three kinds of fixed operating expenses. A few are rock bottom costs necessary just to open the doors of the business—such as required annual licenses and inspections, minimum costs of telephone and utilities per period, a few employees that must be on the payroll, and so on.

Other fixed costs are the amounts spent on advertising and other marketing efforts to promote sales of products in the profit model. The third category of fixed operating expenses include all the cost commitments entered into by a business based on the sales volume its managers expect to achieve.

Managers make many fixed cost commitments for the coming period to provide the resources that are needed to carry on profit-making activities—the number of employees needed, the retail floor space needed, the warehouse storage space needed, and so on. These fixed operating expenses in the profit model provide the business with the personnel, space, equipment, and other things needed to sell 100,000 units during the period. Quite possibly the business could have sold more than 100,000 units given its level of fixed cost commitments for the period. Perhaps the business could have sold 125,000 units, for example, without having to have increased its fixed costs for the period.

Managers should make a rough estimate of the maximum sales volume that the business could sell based on its fixed operating costs for the period. In this example assume that the company had the capacity to sell 125,000 units. Now, assume that managers do not see any possibility of selling 125,000 units in the foreseeable future. In this situation, perhaps, the managers should bite the bullet and trim fixed costs to bring capacity in line with forecast sales.

Question: At what unit margin would the business have just covered its fixed operating expenses and made a zero profit for the period?

The company's total fixed operating expenses for the period were $1,500,000. Keeping sales volume at 100,000 units for the period, the business would have needed a minimum unit margin of $15.00 to earn total contribution margin of $1,500,000 to cover its total fixed operating expenses for the period: [$1,500,000 fixed operating expenses ÷ 100,000 units sales volume = $15.00 unit margin]. This scenario would have yielded a zero profit for the period. Of course, the goal is not to earn a zero profit. By comparing the actual $27.00 unit margin against the $15.00 *breakeven unit margin* managers determine how much cushion or reserve they have on the downside. Unit margins are always under downward pressure. Unit margins can slip due to cut sales prices, or because of increases in one or more of the three variable expenses of making sales—**product cost**, **unit-driven expenses**, or **revenue-driven expenses**.

CALCULATION OF BREAKEVEN UNIT MARGIN

$$\frac{\$1,500,000}{100,000} = \$15.00$$

Question: **How did the business make its $1.2 million profit?**

Wait a minute. Didn't we already answer this question? Yes, this is the same question again. It is answered in a different way here, a way that is more helpful in understanding profit sensitivity to changes in sales volume. As just calculated the company's breakeven volume is 55,556 units. The company actually sold 44,444 more units than its breakeven volume: [100,000 units sales volume – 55,556 breakeven sales volume = 44,444 units excess over breakeven].

One way to look at how the business made its profit is that 55,556 units of sales were needed to cover its fixed operating expenses, and once over this hump the additional units sold provided profit. According to this viewpoint, the company's profit is calculated as follows: [44,444 units sold in excess of breakeven × $27.00 unit margin = $1,200,000 profit].

Examples of this profit concept are retailers who depend on their busy seasons from Thanksgiving through Christmas, which makes or breaks their profit performance for the year. The thinking is that the units sold from the start of the year to Thanksgiving cover their annual fixed costs, and their profit depends on sales during their busy season.

CALCULATION OF PROFIT AS EXCESS SALES OVER BREAKEVEN VOLUME

$$100,000 - 55,556 = 44,444$$
$$\times \$27.00 = \$1,200,000$$

Question: **Does profit change by the same percent as a percent change in sales volume, unit margin, or fixed operating expenses?**

Intuitively what's your answer to this question? No fair sitting on the sidelines. What do you think? Time's up. The answer is a definite and unequivocal NO! Profit swings up or down more than the percent change in a profit factor. To illustrate this extremely important point from the profit model I change each factor by a favorable 10 percent. I look at each change singularly, which means the other profit factors are held the same. Suppose sales volume increases 10 percent, which is 10,000 units. Each additional unit sold earns an additional $27.00 unit margin, so profit improves $270,000. The profit improvement is 22.5 percent: [$270,000 additional contribution margin ÷ $1,200,000 baseline profit = 22.5% improvement].

The reason for this larger percent change in profit is not obvious. Recall that the company makes $1,200,000 profit because it sold 44,444 units in excess of its breakeven volume. The 10,000 additional units represent a 22.5 percent increase in the excess over breakeven sales volume: [10,000 units increase in sales volume ÷ 44,444 units over breakeven sales volume = 22.5%]. In other words, the units bringing in the profit (once fixed costs have been covered by the first 55,556 units sold) increase by 22.5 percent, so profit increases accordingly.

The bigger swing in profit relative to a smaller swing in total sales volume is referred to as **operating leverage**. The company's fixed costs provide a fulcrum point on which it can put its sales volume lever. The assumption is that sales volume could increase 10 percent, to 110,000 units, with no increase in total fixed operating expenses. (As assumed earlier, the level of fixed operating expenses for the period provided the business 125,000 units sales capacity.)

Suppose that the unit margin had been 10 percent better, or $2.70 higher than in the profit model: [$27.00 unit margin × 10% improvement = $2.70 gain]. The business sold 100,000 units, so the $2.70 unit margin improvement would have increased profit $270,000, the same amount as for the 10 percent sales volume gain.

Suppose total fixed operating expenses could have been improved (reduced) 10 percent. Shaving 10 percent off its fixed costs would have saved $150,000 on the expense side and added $150,000 on the profit side, and this equals a 12.5 percent improvement in profit: [$150,000 reduction in fixed operating expenses ÷ $1,200,000 profit = 12.5% increase in profit]. But be careful here. Reducing fixed operating expenses could cause a significant reduction in capacity. The business should make sure that it still had the number of people, the space, and the equipment needed to sell 100,000 units over the period (in this example). Cutting fixed costs 10 percent could cause much more than a 10 percent reduction in capacity.

Now for the bad news. To this point I have examined changes that improve profit performance. What would have happened if each factor in the profit model had moved 10 percent in the opposite direction? Profit would have plunged 22.5 percent if sales volume or if unit margin had decreased 10 percent. And profit would have dropped 12.5 percent if the company's fixed operating expenses had gone up 10 percent. The percent of change in profit is a two-edged sword: The swing in profit is as bad on the downside as it is good on the upside. The main lesson is that the percent change in profit is more volatile than a percent change in a factor driving profit.

CALCULATIONS OF PERCENT CHANGES IN PROFIT

10% Sales Volume Change: $10,000 \times \$27.00 = \$270,000/\$1,200,000$
$= 22.5\%$

10% Unit Margin Change: $\$2.70 \times 10,000 \quad = \$270,000/\$1,200,000$
$= 22.5\%$

10% Fixed Costs Change: $\$1,500,000 \times 10\% = \$150,000/\$1,200,000$
$= 12.5\%$

From the Profit Model to the Income Statement

The profit model is an excellent scaffold for constructing a profit plan for every profit module of a business. Managers set sales price targets, sales volume goals, and expense limits for achieving the profit objectives for the period. Of course, actual outcomes always deviate from the original plan, hopefully in positive directions for the most part. Shortly after the end of the period actual results are plugged into the profit model so that the manager can do a critical review of profit performance. Figure 1.2 reports the actual outcomes for the period just ended in comparison with the original plan for the example presented in Figure 1.1 earlier in the chapter.

Actual profit for the profit module turned out to be a little better than planned. If you were the manager having profit responsibility for this part of the business, you'd probably be reasonably pleased

FIGURE 1.2 Plan and Actual Profit Model for Period

	Plan	Actual
Sales Price	$100.00	$105.00
Product Cost Expense	$60.00	$63.00
Gross Margin	$40.00	$42.00
Unit-Driven Expenses	$5.50	$5.75
Revenue-Driven Expenses	7.50%	8.00%
Unit Margin	$27.00	$27.85
Sales Volume	100,000	102,000
Contribution Margin	$2,700,000	$2,840,700
Fixed Operating Expenses	$1,500,000	$1,568,000
Profit (before Other Expenses)	$1,200,000	$1,272,700

Tip

The income statement is one of the three primary financial statements comprising the hard core of a financial report. The other two financial statements are the statement of financial condition (also called the balance sheet) and the cash flows statement. The statement of financial condition summarizes the financial situation of the business at the end of the period. The cash flows statement summarizes its sources and uses of cash during the period. The financial statements released outside the business to its shareowners and lenders are called *external* financial statements. External financial statements conform to established financial disclosure standards and accounting methods called generally accepted accounting principles, or GAAP for short. These authoritative guidelines have been developed over many years to ensure adequate disclosure and a common core of consistent accounting methods, so that business investors and lenders are provided a reliable base of information about a business.

with the results. Techniques for the comparative analysis of actual outcomes against the profit plan are explained in Chapter 6. Here I want to build a bridge from the profit model example to the financial statement that reports profit performance. This profit report is the **income statement**.

As soon as possible after the close of its fiscal (accounting) year a business prepares the annual income statement that summarizes its sales revenue and expenses for the year. Subtracting expenses from sales revenue (plus any other income a business may have) gives the net profit or net loss for the year. The income statement is also called the **profit and loss statement** although a business has either a profit or a loss, but not both for the period.

An income statement is prepared for the business as a whole, as one comprehensive enterprise. Of course the top-level managers and directors of a business need to look at the business as a whole, in its entirety. Top-level managers also need to look at the separate pieces, segments, and components of the business. Mid-level and lower-level managers focus on their particular areas of responsibility. A separate profit model is needed for each profit module of the business, as argued earlier in the chapter. Even a smaller business may have 5 or 10 distinct sources of sales and profit.

Presenting the Income Statement

Figure 1.3 presents an income statement for the profit model example—as if the example is the entire company. I do this so you can fol-

FIGURE 1.3 Income Statement for Period

Sales Revenue	$10,710,000
Cost of Goods Sold Expense	$6,426,000
Gross Margin	$4,284,000
Selling and Administrative Expenses	$3,011,300
Earnings before Interest and Income Tax	$1,272,700
Interest Expense	$XXX,XXX
Earnings before Income Tax	$XXX,XXX
Income Tax Expense	$XXX,XXX
Net Income	$XXX,XXX

low the data from the profit model into the income statement. In other words, assume that the business sells only the products included in the profit model example. Assume also that all fixed operating expenses of the business are included in the profit model. The business does not have additional central office fixed costs that have to be brought into the income statement. (Typically, a business has some amount of headquarters costs that are not allocated or assigned to its different profit modules.) Note in the income statement that the company's earnings before interest and income tax is $1,272,700. This is the same actual profit amount shown on the last line in the profit model (see Figure 1.2).

The income statement reports two expenses not included in the profit model—*interest expense* and *income tax expense*. (In Figure 1.3 no specific amounts are shown for these two expenses.) The profit model ends with profit before interest and income tax expenses. Most businesses borrow money and pay interest on the amount borrowed. Interest is the financial cost of using debt capi-

Tip

External income statements sent to the shareowners of businesses report actual sales revenue, expenses, and profit, usually in comparison with the actual results of the previous period or two periods. The budgeted sales revenue and expenses for the year are not reported outside the business. For internal reporting to managers, on the other hand, actual sales revenue and expenses should be presented in comparison with the budgeted amounts for the period, so that managers can focus on significant deviations.

tal. Every business has to determine its annual taxable income, which is a rather complex calculation, to say the least. Many businesses do not pay income tax as a separate entity. Instead they are taxable income conduits; they pass through their annual taxable income to their owners, who must include their shares of the total taxable income of the business in their tax returns. Many business corporations have too many stockholders to qualify as a pass-through tax entity. Therefore, they have to pay income tax on their taxable income.

Take notice that the income statement presents *cumulative total amounts* of sales revenue and expenses for the period. The first, or top line in the income statement reveals that sales revenue was $10,710,000 for the period. In contrast the profit model focuses on the two variables that determine total sales revenue, which are the $105.00 average sales price and the 102,000 units sales volume for the period (see Figure 1.2). Total sales revenue is equal to: [$105.00 average sales price × 102,000 units sales volume = $10,710,000]. Managers need to know all three variables in this equation, not just the total amount. The profit model reveals that the average product cost was $63.00 per unit for the 102,000 units sales volume for the period. In contrast the income statement reports only the total $6,426,000 cost of goods sold expense. In short, the profit model focuses on the specific variables that drive profit, whereas the income statement focuses on the cumulative amounts of sales revenue and expenses for the period.

Note another difference between the income statement and the profit model. In the income statement all operating expenses, both variable and fixed, are lumped together. See in Figure 1.3 the $3,011,300 total amount for Selling and Administrative Expenses— a commonly used generic title for operating expenses. External income statements do not divide operating expenses into variable and fixed classes. So only one total amount is shown in Figure 1.3 for the company's operating expenses. Internal income statements reported to managers should separate between variable and fixed operating expenses, but in my experience internal accounting reports do not emphasize this key distinction between the fixed and variable behavior of expenses.

Because fixed operating expenses are not reported as a separate item in the income statement, the company's contribution margin for the period is not reported. (Refer to the profit model shown in Figure 1.2 for the contribution margin earned by the business.) Without knowing its total fixed operating expenses, we cannot determine the company's breakeven sales volume. In summary, the information boundaries of the income statement limit its usefulness for management analysis. The profit model provides the additional specific information that managers need in making decisions and in reviewing profit performance.

Running through the Income Statement

In this section the elements of the income statement are explained briefly. Please refer to Figure 1.3 as each line is explained.

Sales Revenue

The top line of the income statement equals total revenue, or gross income from sales of products and services over the period. The amount is net of any sales discounts, rebates, and product returns. So, the amount is also called *net sales revenue*. Sales returns, rebates, and other discounts and allowances are recorded and reported to managers so that they can keep an eye on these sales revenue offsets. Annual sales revenue is the most popular measure of the size of a business, although total assets and number of employees also are used to express the size of a business.

Cost of Goods Sold Expense

This amount is the total cost of all products sold to customers over the period. Fluctuations in unit product costs (which are typical) force a business to choose between alternative accounting methods to record this major expense. Different accounting methods yield somewhat different expense amounts, a topic discussed in Chapter 13.

Gross Margin

This amount equals profit before other expenses are deducted. Gross margin is also called gross profit. Most businesses have developed benchmark ratios for their gross margins that are necessary to make a satisfactory bottom-line profit. In the example the company's gross margin ratio is 40 percent: [$4,284,000 ÷ $10,710,000 sales revenue = 40%]. Gross margin ratios vary widely industry to industry, and product line to product line within a business. Gross margins of 20 percent or less are rare. Some products are sold at extraordinarily high gross margins of 75 percent or more because the business has very high expenses of selling the products or very high fixed costs (such as research and development expenditures).

Selling and Administrative Expenses

This figure is the amount of all variable and fixed operating expenses for the period. Two or more lines of these expenses may be reported in an income statement, classified by function (marketing, research and development, administration, etc.), or by object of expenditure (salaries, property taxes, office expenses, etc.).

Earnings before Interest and Income Tax (EBIT)

This profit measure is the residual amount after deducting the cost of products sold and all operating expenses from sales revenue. The idea is to show profit before two other types of expenses are subtracted, that is, the cost of debt (the interest paid on borrowed money) and the income tax levy on the business.

Interest Expense

It's possible that a business has no interest-bearing liabilities. But most businesses borrow money. A business has a contractual obligation to pay interest, even if the business suffers a loss before interest expense is considered. Interest is the first take out from EBIT, and interest expense is deductible to determine taxable income.

Earnings before Income Tax

Because of the complexities of the income tax law and because a business has many options under the income tax law, a business's actual taxable income for the year usually is different from the pretax earnings figure in its income statement. Without going into technical matters here, I'll simply mention that in these situations an accounting manipulation is recorded so that the income tax expense amount reported in the income statement is consistent with the amount of earnings before income tax reported in the income statement.

Income Tax Expense

A business legally organized as a partnership does not pay federal income tax as a separate entity. A business legally organized as a limited liability company can elect to pay no income tax itself. A corporation with no more than 75 stockholders can elect to be treated as an S corporation that does not pay income tax. These types of businesses pass-through their annual taxable income to their owners. A regular corporation pays federal income tax on its annual taxable income. If the corporation distributes some of its aftertax profit to its shareowners, the cash distributions are taxable in their hands as dividend income.

Net Income

This is the so-called **bottom-line** profit earned for the year (or other period). A business may record one or more nonrecurring, extraordinary losses or gains in the period—such as uninsured losses, asset write-offs, legal damages assessed against the business, selling off a major part of the business at a large gain, and so on. These unusual losses or gains, net of their related income tax effects, are reported separately from the ordinary ongoing sales revenue and expenses of the business. Net income from continuing operations is reported on one line, and these extraordinary gains and losses are added or subtracted to arrive at the bottom-line net income. Publicly owned businesses also report their net income, or earnings per share of stock.

No two income statements are exactly alike in every respect. Figure 1.3 presents the basic format and content of a typical income statement. But I can tell you, having read thousands of income statements over the years, that I've seen many variations and idiosyncrasies from business to business and even by the same business from year to year.

Summary

- Profit is not by happenstance; a business must craft a clear-cut strategy to reach its profit objectives.

- A business should develop a well-thought-out and thorough business plan that clearly points the way to reaching its profit objectives.

- A business should encapsulate its strategy and business plan into a pithy statement of very few words, which is called a business model.

- The profit model is the quantitative counterpart to the business model; the profit model focuses on the relatively few decisive factors that drive profit.

- The profit model is an essential analysis tool that helps managers in making decisions and in reviewing actual profit performance.

- The income statement reports the profit performance of a business for a period. This financial statement focuses on total amounts of sales revenue and expenses for the period. In contrast, the profit model focuses on the key variables that managers have to decide on and to reach the profit objectives of the business.

Summary Review Exercise

Facts: For this exercise the business has three profit modules. The data for the three profit models are given next. The business had $428,500 total central office fixed overhead costs for the year, none of which was allocated to its three profit modules. The company's total interest expense for the year was $795,000. To simplify, assume that the company's taxable income for the year is the same amount as its earnings before income tax in the income statement. The income rate is 35 percent on its taxable income.

Required: Complete the three profit modules for the year, and prepare the company's income statement for the year. Use the following templates. The answers are given on the next page.

Profit Models	Module A	Module B	Module C
Sales Price	$45.00	$103.25	$225.00
Product Cost Expense	$31.75	$46.65	$158.50
Gross Margin			
Unit-Driven Expenses	$2.75	$7.85	$15.75
Revenue-Driven Expenses	4.60%	9.15%	12.50%
Unit Margin			
Sales Volume	425,000	115,000	38,500
Contribution Margin			
Fixed Operating Expenses	$1,685,500	$2,057,250	$1,568,000
Profit before Other Expenses			

INCOME STATEMENT

Sales Revenue	
Cost of Goods Sold Expense	_____
Gross Margin	
Selling and Administrative Expenses	_____
Earnings before Interest and Income Tax	
Interest Expense	$795,000
Earnings before Income Tax	
Income Tax Expense	_____
Net Income	_____

FIGURE 1.4 Profit Model Answers

	Module A	Module B	Module C
Sales Price	$45.00	$103.25	$225.00
Product Cost Expense	$31.75	$46.65	$158.50
Gross Margin	$13.25	$56.60	$66.50
Unit-Driven Expenses	$2.75	$7.85	$15.75
Revenue-Driven Expenses	4.60%	9.15%	12.50%
Unit Margin	$8.43	$39.30	$22.63
Sales Volume	425,000	115,000	38,500
Contribution Margin	$3,582,750	$4,519,802	$871,063
Fixed Operating Expenses	$1,685,500	$2,057,250	$1,568,000
Profit before Other Expenses	$1,897,250	$2,462,552	($696,938)

FIGURE 1.5 Income Statement Answers

INCOME STATEMENT	
Sales Revenue	$39,661,250
Cost of Goods Sold Expense	$24,960,750
Gross Margin	$14,700,500
Selling and Administrative Expenses	$11,466,135
Earnings before Interest and Income Tax	$3,234,365
Interest Expense	$795,000
Earnings before Income Tax	$2,439,365
Income Tax Expense	$853,778
Net Income	$1,585,587

CHAPTER 2

Profit and Cash Flow

Can you imagine trying to run a business and not keeping track of your cash receipts and disbursements? Every business must keep close tabs on its cash inflows and outflows, and its cash balance, of course. However, simple checkbook accounting is not nearly adequate for a business. Every business needs to keep accounts for its liabilities, inventories of products held for sale, receivables, long-term operating assets, shareowners' equities, and so on. All the same, cash flows are the heartbeat of every business and must be managed very carefully. Running out of money can stop a business in its tracks.

Business Cash Sources and Uses

The cash receipts and cash disbursements of a business can be sorted into four basic categories. For each cash source there is an opposing cash use. Figure 2.1 summarizes these fundamental types of cash flows through a business.

I should make a couple of quick comments here. First, the amount of money distributed to shareowners from profit each year depends heavily on whether the business needs money to grow. Rapidly expanding businesses typically pay no cash distributions from their

FIGURE 2.1 Business Cash Flow Sources and Uses

Cash Sources	Cash Uses
• From Shareowners Money is invested in the business by its shareowners at the inception of the entity, and from time to time thereafter when the business needs more capital.	• To Shareowners Money is distributed to its shareowners from profit; and, the business may return capital to them if the business no longer needs all the money invested by them.
• From Lenders Money is borrowed on the basis of interest-bearing debt instruments.	• To Lenders Debt principal is paid off or paid down at the due dates (or perhaps before).
• From Investments Cash proceeds are received from the disposals of assets other than inventory (i.e., the products held for sale to customers).	• To Investments Money is invested in long-term operating assets, and in nonoperating assets (such as marketable securities).
• From Sales Money is received from customers for sales of products and services to them, which is called sales revenue. (A business also may have cash income from investments or from one-time gains from nonrecurring transactions.)	• To Expenses Money is spent for products sold to customers, and for its operating expenses, interest expense, and income tax expense. (A business also may pay out cash for an extraordinary loss.)

profit. Second, disposing of operating assets such as machinery, equipment, and vehicles at the end of their useful lives does not bring in much cash flow. These assets have little salvage value when a business is done with them. In contrast, liquidating investments in marketable securities or other assets can be on occasion a major source of cash.

From Startup to Sustainable Sales Revenue

When starting a business, its founders raise money from owners and lenders. It's not easy to persuade people to invest their hard-earned dollars in a brand new business venture, and to convince financial institutions to loan money to an untested business. The first time a corporation raises capital by issuing stock (ownership) shares to the public is called its *initial public offering,* or IPO.

A business uses the initial capital it raises to invest in various assets it needs for making sales and carrying on its operations. Also money is needed to provide a day-to-day working cash balance. A business cannot operate with a zero balance in its checking account. The founders also must determine how much additional money will be needed to subsidize the operating expenses of the business until it builds a large enough base of customers that provides a steady stream of cash inflow from sales revenue. With little or no cash inflow from sales a business can race through a lot of money in a hurry. The speed of hemorrhaging cash is referred to as the **cash burn rate**.

To succeed, a new business needs to reach a sustainable level of sales revenue before it runs out of money. Many startups don't make it, as you know. Once it reaches a sustainable sales level, a business depends on making profit for its primary source of cash. Profit is the cash flow mainspring for successful businesses.

Over a year the cash inflow from sales revenue of a business should be more than its cash outflow for expenses—unless the business has unusually low cash inflow from sales revenue or unusually large cash outflow for expenses. Managers need to know how much cash flow is provided from profit; they need to know exactly how much cash inflow from sales exceeds the cash outflow for expenses.

Profit and Cash Flow: Two Different Measures

One of the most important functions of business accounting is to measure **profit** period by period. One year is the benchmark time period for profit measurement, which is a time period long enough such that the accountant can make final decisions regarding the amounts of sales revenue and expenses that properly belong in the period (as well as any extraordinary gains or losses that should be recorded). Profit is measured for shorter periods. For example publicly owned business corporations report profit to their shareowners every quarter (three months). Privately owned businesses also determine profit quarterly, and perhaps monthly. However, measuring profit over periods shorter than one year is fraught with several accounting problems. Estimates and arbitrary allocations have to be made that cause the profit number for the shorter period to be more tentative and provisional, and not as conclusive as the annual profit number.

It should be mentioned that the word profit is shunned in most business financial reports. Businesses generally use the terms **net income**, **earnings**, or **net earnings** for the bottom-line profit reported in their income statements. Whatever terminology is used profit and cash flow from profit are two different measures. It's extremely important to distinguish between these two financial measures. Both measures are very important, but different.

Note please: Cash flow from profit also is commonly called **operating cash flow**, and in the statement of cash flows (presented later in the chapter) it is labeled **cash flow from operating activities**. The terms are used interchangeably. I favor the term cash flow from profit because it seems more descriptive than the other two. More strictly one should say cash inflows from sales minus cash outflows for expenses. But this is too much of a mouthful, don't you agree?

Accrual Basis of Profit Accounting

The profit or loss for a period of time equals the total sales revenue for the period (plus any gains or other income during the period) minus total expenses for the period (and minus any unusual losses recorded during the period). If sales revenue is more than expenses, the business makes a profit; if expenses exceed sales revenue, the business suffers a loss. Sales revenue and expenses are recorded according to the **accrual basis of accounting**.

Sales revenue is recorded when a sale is made, which means when the products are delivered to the customer or when the service for the customer has been completed by the business. The customer owes the business for the products or services received. The customer may pay immediately, or customers may be given credit in which case they don't pay the business until sometime later. Expenses are recorded according to the *matching principle*. Some costs can be directly matched with their sales revenue, such as the cost of goods sold to customers, the sales commissions paid to salespersons that are a percent of sales revenue, the costs of delivering products to customers, and some other costs.

However, many costs of operating a business cannot be matched with particular sales. These costs are recorded as expenses to the period in which the business benefits from the cost. For example, the rent paid on building space is expensed to the month for which the rent applies. Employee salaries are expensed to the week or month during which the employees work. Property taxes are expensed to the year in which the business has use of the property. The cost of long-lived operating assets that are used several years such as delivery trucks, machines, tools, buildings, and computers are apportioned to the periods they are used in the operations of the business.

The accounting profession has developed many authoritative accounting standards, rules, methods, and procedures for recording sales revenue and expenses—which are a major part of the official collection of generally accepted accounting principles (GAAP). Nevertheless, in actual practice accountants have a good deal of latitude in interpreting and applying these guidelines for recording sales revenue and expenses (and for recognizing gains and losses). The amount of profit reported by a business is not just a matter of counting beans. Accountants are called bean counters, as you probably have heard. Chapter 13 explains the alternative profit accounting methods among which a business must select, and the nature of profit accounting in general.

Recording sales revenue and expenses depends on the judgment, experience, and most of all the integrity of the accountant. Even though an independent CPA firm audits its financial statements, a business may later restate its sales and expenses for the year. I just read a news item in the *New York Times* about a company that originally reported $12.6 million profit on $205 million sales revenue for the year, but later issued revised financial statements that revealed that it had suffered a $33.7 million *loss* on sales revenue of only $151 million. This doesn't happen often, thank goodness, but it does happen.

You probably know how much attention is given to the profit or loss reported by a business. Without a doubt the profit (or loss) performance of a business is its most closely watched measure of financial performance. The market value of the ownership shares of a business depends on its past profit performance and its profit prospects, more than any other factor. The second most watched financial performance measure of a business is its cash flow from profit.

Cash Flow from Profit

Cash flow from profit for a period equals the total of cash inflows during the period from sales (plus cash received from gains and other income) minus the total cash outflows during the period for expenses (and minus cash paid out for any unusual losses during the period). Note that this measure of cash flow does not include cash inflows from money invested by shareowners, nor money borrowed from lenders, nor money received from disposals of investments. And this measure does not include cash outflows for money paid to shareowners, nor payments to lenders on debt owed to them, nor cash expenditures on investments. In short, cash flow from profit is restricted to the cash inflows and outflows of the sales and expenses activities of a business, which are called **operating activities**.

The difference between accrual-basis profit accounting and cash flow is demonstrated by comparing the sales revenue for a period and the cash inflow during the period from sales. To illustrate, suppose a business recorded $12.0 million sales revenue for the year just ended. This is the amount of sales made and billed to customers during the year. The business extends credit to its customers (in contrast to retailers that sell only for cash or for credit card payment at the time of sale). Not all of its $12.0 million sales made this year were collected by the end of the year. The last month of sales were not collected by the end of the year, which is $1.0 million of accounts receivable at year-end. Therefore, you might surmise that cash inflow from sales was $11.0 million for the year.

What about the carryover of accounts receivable at the start of the year? These receivables from sales made last year were collected during the early part of the year. Assume that the opening balance of accounts receivable from last year's sales was $900,000. Thus, cash inflow from sales during this year equals $11.9 million: ($11.0 million cash collections from sales made during the year plus $900,000 cash collections from sales made last year). The $12.0 million is the correct amount for sales revenue that is used to measure profit for the year. The $11.9 million is the correct amount of cash inflow from sales to measure cash flow for the year. Two different measures—for two different purposes!

Every business manager should understand that the profit recorded for the period (based on accrual-basis accounting methods for recording sales revenue and expenses) does not simultaneously generate a cash increase of the same amount. I can't emphasize this point enough. In my experience I've talked with many business managers who read the bottom line of an income statement and jump to the conclusion that this profit number equals the cash increase during the period. In fact the cash flow from profit can be much more or much less than the amount of profit. It's even possible that cash may have *decreased* when a business reports profit, which is called **negative cash flow**.

Cash Flows from Sales Revenue and for Expenses

To explain cash flows I continue with the business example introduced in the exercise at the end of Chapter 1. Figure 2.2 presents the company's income statement for the year and its cash flows from sales revenue and for expenses during the year. Expenses are shown with parentheses in Figure 2.2—to emphasize that they are deducted from sales revenue and to be consistent with how cash flows are shown. Note also in Figure 2.2 that **depreciation expense** is separated from the larger, catchall account for selling and administration expenses. Depreciation is a unique expense, which is discussed later in the chapter at some length.

You might take a moment and focus on the differences in the right column of Figure 2.2. The income statement amounts of sales revenue and every expense differ from their corresponding cash flow

FIGURE 2.2 Income Statement Compared with Cash Inflow from Sales Revenue and Cash Outflows for Expenses

	Income Statement	Cash Flows	Differences
Sales Revenue	$39,661,250	$39,315,000	($346,250)
Cost of Goods Sold Expense	($24,960,750)	($25,776,230)	($815,480)
Gross Margin	$14,700,500		
Selling & Administrative Expenses	($10,697,685)	($10,554,885)	$142,800
Depreciation Expense	($768,450)	$0	$768,450
Earnings before Interest and Income Tax	$3,234,365		
Interest Expense	($795,000)	($773,550)	$21,450
Earnings before Income Tax	$2,439,365		
Income Tax Expense	($853,778)	($912,428)	($58,650)
Net Income, Cash Flow from Profit, and Net Difference	$1,585,587	$1,297,907	($287,680)

amounts. A negative difference is shown with parentheses. A negative difference means that cash inflow was less than sales revenue or that cash outflow was more than the expense. A negative cash flow difference means that the company's cash balance decreased. A positive difference means that cash outflow was less than the expense. A positive cash flow difference means that the company's cash balance increased. (If the business's cash collections from sales had been higher than its sales revenue for the year, the difference would have been positive.)

From the information in Figure 2.2 observe the following points.

• The business collected less cash during the year from customers than its sales revenue for the period.

• The business spent more cash during the year to purchase and manufacture products than the cost of goods sold.

• The business paid out less cash during the year for two of its expenses than the amounts of the expenses in the income statement (selling and administrative expenses, and interest expense).

• The business paid more money during the year to the IRS than income tax expense in its income statement.

Finally, the business had no cash outlay for the depreciation expense reported in its income statement. In previous years cash was invested in the assets being depreciated. Part of the original cost invested in these assets was written off and charged to depreciation expense for the year. But recording depreciation expense does not involve any cash outlay.

The cash flows and differences shown in Figure 2.2 are explained in the following sections. If you think you have a good grasp on the cash flows from sales and for expenses and why the cash flows differ from the sales revenue and expense amounts reported in the income statement, you could skip ahead to the section Interpreting Cash Flow From Profit. I would recommend, however, that you at least peruse the Depreciation Cash Flow section before jumping ahead.

Sales Revenue Cash Flow

Figure 2.2 shows that the cash flow difference for sales revenue is a *negative* $346,250. During the year the business received $346,250 less cash collections from customers than its sales revenue for the year. Many retailers make sales for cash or accept credit cards that are converted into cash the same day. The business in this example, however, makes sales *on credit*. It offers all of its customers 30 days to pay for their purchases. The company offers a discount from the invoice price for prompt payment. But most customers wait a month or more to pay for their purchases.

The revenue from a sale on credit is recorded immediately. The **accounts receivable** asset account is increased to record the sale instead of cash. Later, when cash is received from customers, the cash account is increased and the accounts receivable account is decreased. The business's sales for the year just ended increased substantially over the previous year, and this sales growth caused its accounts receivable to increase. The company's accounts receivable balance at the end of the year was $346,250 higher than at the start of the year. The business collected the beginning balance (the carryover from last year's sales) but did not collect the ending balance (the carryover to next year from credit sales made during the year just ended).

Note: In this and the following discussion there are frequent references to increases and decreases in the business's assets and liabilities, such as the accounts receivable increase in this section. These changes are determined from the accounts of the business. The accountant (me) looks in the account and determines the increase or decrease during the year by comparing the ending balance with the beginning balance of the account. A manager does not do this look

> ### Tip
>
> Managers should know the reason for an increase in accounts receivable. As a general rule this asset increases with increases in sales revenue. But the asset may increase for other reasons. An increase could be due to more liberal credit terms being offered to customers. Or more customers may be taking longer to pay. If accounts receivable had *decreased*, say $300,000, then the cash flow difference would have been a *positive* $300,000. The business would have collected $300,000 more cash than its sales revenue for the year.

up; the accountant digs out this information for the manager. I do not present a list of the assets and liabilities of the business with their beginning and ending balances. You can look ahead to Figure 5.2 in Chapter 5 that presents the comparative balance sheet for the business, which reports the beginning and ending balances of its assets and liabilities.

Compared with the company's total sales revenue of about $40 million the negative $346,250 cash flow difference may seem trivial. But compared with its $1,585,587 net income for the year, the cash flow difference is significant. The difference put a big dent in cash flow from profit. Cash flow from profit would have been more than net income for the year if accounts receivable had not increased during the year.

Cost of Goods Sold Expense Cash Flow

The first expense deducted from sales revenue in the income statement, which is the largest one, is cost of goods sold expense. (Refer to Figure 2.2 again.) The business, like most businesses that sell products, delivers products out of its inventory when sales are made to customers. The business has the products on hand in its warehouses, ready for immediate shipment to its customers. It does not back order products for future delivery. In short, the business has a stockpile of products waiting to be sold. The average holding period before sale is about three months. The cost of products purchased or manufactured by the business is recorded in its *inventories* asset account. The cost of products sold is removed from the asset account and charged to the cost of goods sold expense account.

When a business maintains its inventories at a constant level, the cash outflow for products manufactured and purchased is about equal to the cost of goods sold expense for the year. However, even in this steady state case inflation can drive up the cost of inventories. When a business increases its inventories, its cash outlays for products during the year can be substantially more than its cost of goods sold expense for the year. In Figure 2.2 the cash flow difference for cost of goods sold expense is a *negative* $815,480. This is the main culprit causing cash flow from profit to be less than profit for the year.

The business increased its inventories of products held for sale $815,480 during the year. The company experienced significant sales growth over last year, and top-level managers decided to increase the company's inventory level to support the higher volume of sales. Accordingly, the business manufactured and purchased more products than it sold during the year. The company's total cash outlays for the manufacture and purchases of products were $815,480 higher than the cost of goods sold.

Actually, the company's ending cost balance of inventories was $1,098,750 higher than at the start of the year. The company's accounts payable for inventory also increased $283,270 during the year. In terms of cash flow the increase in accounts payable offsets part of the inventory increase. The net effect of the two increases on cash flow equals $815,480: ($1,098,750 inventories increase minus $283,270 payables increase). Sales growth requires inventory growth in most cases, which crimps cash flow.

Selling and Administrative Expenses Cash Flow

Selling and Administrative Expenses is a catchall category that includes quite a variety of different expenses—advertising and other marketing costs; salaries of executives, office staff, managers, and maintenance personnel; legal fees; office expenses; telephone expenses; and so on. For management control purposes these various

Tip

Managers should pay close attention to an increase in inventories. Is the inventory increase consistent with the company's sales growth increase? Or did the company increase its inventory holding period? Did the business build up the inventory levels of some products that have not sold very well?

If inventory had decreased, say $500,000, then the cash flow difference would have been a *positive* $500,000. This means the business would have made cash outlays $500,000 less than the cost of products sold during the year. Part of its inventories would have been liquidated, or converted into cash. However, decreasing inventory when sales are increasing usually is not possible.

expenses are reported in detail to the managers having responsibility for the expenses. Often a budget target is set for each major expense category, and variances from budget have to be pre-approved by the appropriate manager. The concern here is with cash flow from profit. Was the total of cash payments for these expenses exactly the same amount as the expense? As you may suspect, the answer is no.

Some selling and administrative expenses are *prepaid*. Two examples are insurance policy premiums that are paid in advance of the coverage period, and office and maintenance supplies that are bought and paid that won't be used until later. When purchased the costs of these items are recorded in an asset account called prepaid expenses. The costs are released to expense gradually over the weeks benefited by the costs. For instance one-sixth of a six-months insurance policy is charged to each month of coverage. As office and maintenance supplies are used, an appropriate amount of cost is removed from the prepaid expenses asset account and charged to expense.

In summary, cash outflow takes place before these expenses are recorded. An increase in a company's prepaid expenses asset account means that more money was paid out during the period than was recorded to expense. An increase in prepaid expenses therefore causes a negative cash flow difference; the company's cash balance is lower.

In contrast to prepaid expenses, a fair amount of a business's total operating expenses for the year are *unpaid* at the end of the year. Businesses don't have to pay certain operating costs until a month or so after recording these expenses. The full amounts of the expenses are recorded according to the accrual basis of accounting—in order to match the costs to the period benefited by the costs. Unpaid expense balances are recorded in two liability accounts—**accounts payable** and *accrued expenses payable*.

Increases in these two liability accounts during the year cause positive cash flow effects. Using round numbers here, suppose the beginning balances were $1,850,000 and the ending balances were $2,000,000. The business paid the beginning balances but avoided paying the ending balances. The net effect on cash is that the business's cash balance was $150,000 higher than it would have been if there had been no increase in its accounts payable and accrued expenses payable.

Collecting together the increase in prepaid expenses (which causes a negative cash flow effect) and the increases in accounts payable and accrued expenses payable (which have positive cash flow effects), the net cash flow difference for the company's selling and administrative expenses is a positive $142,800. (See Figure 2.2.) This cash flow difference usually is small relative to the cash flow differences for sales revenue (caused by a change in accounts receivable) and for the cost of goods sold expense (caused by changes in the company's inventories and accounts payable for inventories).

If the cash flow difference for selling and administrative expenses had been fairly sizable, say over $500,000 in this example, such a large difference would be worth investigating. For example, the business may have recorded an unusually large amount in its accrued expenses payable liability account for future warranty and guarantee work that was caused by a product recall.

Depreciation Cash Flow

The amount of depreciation expense recorded for the period equals a fraction of the original cost of the long-term assets used by a business in making sales and carrying on its operations. These long-term resources include buildings, leasehold improvements, warehouse shelving, forklift trucks, machinery and equipment of many kinds, delivery trucks, computers, copiers, and office furniture.

Long-term operating assets are referred to informally as **fixed assets**, because they are relatively fixed investments of a business over several years in assets that are not held for sale. These assets wear out and lose their economic usefulness over time. Therefore, each year is charged with a portion of the original cost of a company's fixed assets—in order to recognize the using up and wasting away of these economic resources that, as one wag put it many years ago, are on their inevitable journey to the junkyard.

The business in the example recorded $768,450 depreciation expense for the year just ended (see Figure 2.2). The cost value of the fixed assets was decreased this amount (by increasing the accumulated depreciation offset account that is deducted from the original cost of the assets). There's no question that allocating the cost of fixed assets over the years of their use is the correct way to record the expense of using the resources. The exact method of allocation is an issue that accountants disagree on. Nonetheless, the theory of apportioning the cost of fixed assets over their useful lives by recording deprecation expense to each year is indisputable.

The cash flow difference equals the full amount of the depreciation expense because recording depreciation expense does not require any cash outlay. The cash outlay occurred when the fixed assets were purchased and paid for. When depreciable assets are bought or constructed, the business invests cash in these long-lived operating assets, which are reported in the **property, plant, and equipment** asset account. As mentioned earlier, these long-term operating resources also are referred to as fixed assets, which is a shorter and informal moniker.

As the business uses its fixed assets, it does not have to pay for them again. If you paid cash for a new car, you don't have to pay again for the car as you drive it. The depreciation expense for the year is a real expense, but it is unique because the expense was paid for in previous years—going back many years for some fixed assets. To repeat: Depreciation expense is not a cash outlay in the year recorded. The cash outlay occurred years earlier. (If the business had rented all of its fixed assets instead of owning them, then rent expense is a cash outlay during the period.)

There is another very important reason for singling out depreciation expense, which after all is just one of many expenses of a business. A part of the cash inflow from sales reimburses a business for the use of its fixed assets during the year. A business recoups part of the capital invested in its fixed assets through the cash inflow from sales during the year. Consider, for instance, a taxicab owner setting fares high enough to recover the cost of the cab over the several years of driving the cab. Every time the taxi driver collects a fare a small time share is sold to the passenger as it were.

Likewise the business in the example sold-off $768,450 of its fixed assets to its customers during the year—not literally of course, but by setting its sales prices high enough to recover this amount of the original cost of its fixed assets. In summary, the business converted $768,450 of the original cost invested some years ago in its fixed assets back into cash during the year. In this way a business gradually

Tip

A business may invest in long-term intangible operating assets, such as patents that have several years' useful life to the business. The cost of intangibles is *amortized,* which means the total cost is allocated to expense over the predicted economic useful life of the intangible asset. Amortization is just like depreciation, although amortization methods for income tax are different from depreciation methods. In any case, amortization expense is treated the same as depreciation in cash flow analysis. (By the way don't confuse the amortization of an intangible asset's cost with the amortization of a loan, which refers to the pay-off schedule on the debt's principal balance.)

liquidates the investment in its fixed assets over the several years of using these economic resources.

Interest Expense Cash Flow

Interest on debt accrues day by day, even though interest is not paid at the end of the loan period on short-term debt, and is paid quarterly or semiannually on long-term debt. The full amount of interest is recorded as expense for the year, whether or not all the interest was actually paid by the end of the year. In the example the business had interest payable at the start of the year, which was paid in the early part of the year. The beginning balance of unpaid interest was $100,000. At the end of the year the business had $121,450 interest payable, which is $21,450 higher than the beginning balance of this liability. Unpaid interest is recorded in the *accrued expenses payable* liability account.

Interest expense is $795,000 for the year (see Figure 2.2). Unpaid interest at year-end was $121,450, which means the business avoided cash outlay of this amount. But the business paid the $100,000 beginning balance. So the net cash avoidance is $21,450, which is shown as a positive difference in Figure 2.2. As an aside, what if the cash flow difference in this example had been a positive $795,000? This would mean that *none* of the year's interest expense had been paid by the end of the year. The business would be in dire straits if it couldn't pay interest on its debt.

Income Tax Expense Cash Flow

The federal income tax law dictates that a business corporation that pays income tax as a separate entity must estimate its taxable income for the present year and make installment payments during the year so that by the end of the year virtually 100 percent of its income tax on its annual taxable income will have been paid. Well, this is the theory. There are many provisions and loopholes in the income tax law such that a corporation may not pay 100 percent of its income tax by the end of the year. I'm sure you understand that the federal income tax code is very complex—and state income tax laws are not much less complicated. Accountants are income tax law professionals; they determine the taxable income of the business, how much income tax is due, and when it should be paid.

At the start of the year the business had a carry forward $135,150 balance in its *income tax payable* liability account. This was the portion of its previous year's income tax that had not been paid by the end of the previous year. The business paid this amount during the year. During the year just ended the business paid $777,278 of its

$853,778 income tax for the year. It still owes the IRS $76,500 on its income tax for the year. The business paid the IRS a total of $912,428 during the year: ($135,150 final payment on last year's income tax plus $777,278 on the most recent year's income tax). So the cash outlay for income tax during the year was $58,680 higher than the income tax expense for the year, which has a negative cash flow effect (see Figure 2.2 again).

Interpreting Cash Flow from Profit

So what's the bottom line regarding cash flow from profit? The business earned $1,585,587 net income for the year but its cash flow from profit is $1,297,907, as shown in Figure 2.2. Its operating cash flow equals 82 percent of profit: ($1,297,907 cash flow from profit ÷ $1,585,587 net income = 82%). You may ask whether 82 percent is within a normal range for this ratio. Well, I don't know of any benchmarks or norms for this ratio. Stock analysts and other finance professionals hardly ever mention this particular ratio.

In my view a 20 percent, or even a 30 percent operating cash flow shortfall relative to net income should not set off fire alarm bells in most situations. However, if operating cash flow were less than 50 percent of a company's net income for the year, I certainly would take a closer look and pinpoint the main reasons for such a large deficit of cash flow from profit. In their annual corporate financial reports businesses do *not* comment on the difference between their net income and operating cash flow for the year. Personally, I think that the CEO should explain the main reasons for the difference between these two important measures of financial performance.

Stock analysts, investment managers, and business finance professionals have not reached a consensus regarding how to interpret cash flow from profit (operating cash flow). Nevertheless, it's clear that they use operating cash flow as a second measure of profit, or as a reference point against which a company's accounting measure of profit is compared. Operating cash flow is treated as the alter ego of net income. Large differences between operating cash flow and bottom-line profit could be the tip-off that the net income reported by a business is on shaky ground and should be questioned. In this way operating cash flow serves as a red flag on profit.

For example, suppose a business reported $50 million sales revenue for the year and its accounts receivable increased $20 million during the year, which causes a $20 million negative cash flow effect for the period. One obvious question is: Why does the business have such a large amount of uncollected sales revenue at the end of the year? Perhaps the company shipped products to customers that they didn't really order. The customers accepted delivery because the business told them, off the record, that they wouldn't have to pay for the products for several months. In this situation the company records sales revenue prematurely and overstates its profit for the year. (As you may have guessed, this example is based on an actual case.) In summary, very low operating cash flow compared with net income could very well signal a cause for concern about the company's profit accounting.

Operating cash flow is frequently referred to as **free cash flow**. The term *free* means that the business is free to do as it wishes with its operating cash flow for the year—pay cash dividends to share-owners, pay down debt, invest in new fixed assets, or whatever. The counterview is that a company's operating cash flow for the year is not entirely free for any use that a business might have in mind. The argument is that the depreciation cash flow recovery during the year should be earmarked, or reserved for purchasing new fixed assets (real estate, machinery, equipment, etc.). A going business must replace and update its long-term operating assets, and a growing business needs to increase its investments in fixed assets. Depreciation cash flow is the natural place to look for money to buy new fixed assets. From this viewpoint the cash flow from depreciation should be tagged for replacing and expanding its fixed assets.

On the other hand, money is *fungible*. Once deposited in a company's checking account money loses its lineage. A checking account has just one total balance, of course; a bank doesn't keep separate trails for each source of a company's cash deposits (from sales, from borrowing, etc.). All sources of cash are blended together into one pool of money. Managing the financial affairs of a business requires a global approach that includes all cash sources and uses. You can't isolate just one source or one use without looking at the big picture. Therefore, a summary of cash flows is needed that goes beyond cash flow from profit and includes the business's other sources of cash during the year, as well as what the business did with its cash inflow during the year.

Statement of Cash Flows

External financial reports by businesses include three primary financial statements, one of which is the **statement of cash flows**. The basic idea of this statement is to disclose where a business got its money during the period and what it did with its money. In the far distant past a financial statement similar to the statement of cash flows was prepared that was called the "where got, where gone" statement. I've always liked this name, though it has fallen out of use. The modern day statement of cash flows has superseded it—though not for the better (if you will permit me an editorial comment).

Threefold Nature of the Statement of Cash Flows

Figure 2.3 presents the statement of cash flows for the business example, as you would see it in the external financial report of the business. This framework for the statement follows generally accepted accounting principles (GAAP). The statement of cash flows is structured into three sections—(1) **operating activities**; (2) **investing activities**; and, (3) **financing activities**. These categories are not binding for internal management reporting. A business may find that

FIGURE 2.3 Statement of Cash Flows for Business Example

Statement of Cash Flows	
Cash Flows from Operating Activities	
Net Income	$1,585,587
Changes in Operating Assets and Liabilities	
Accounts Receivable	($346,250)
Inventories	($1,098,750)
Prepaid Expenses	($52,875)
Depreciation Expense	$768,450
Accounts Payable	$356,550
Accrued Expenses Payable	$143,845
Income Tax Payable	($58,650)
Cash Flow from Operating Activities	$1,297,907
Cash Flows from Investing Activities	
Investment in Property, Plant, & Equipment	($3,186,250)
Proceeds from Disposals of Property, Plant, & Equipment	$265,480
Cash Used in Investing Activities	($2,920,770)
Cash Flows from Financing Activities	
Net Increase in Short-term Debt	$485,000
Increase in Long-term Debt	$1,650,000
Issuance of Capital Stock Shares	$185,000
Cash Dividends to Stockholders	($450,000)
Cash from Financing Activities	$1,870,000
Cash Increase during Year	$247,137
Cash Balance at Beginning of Year	$2,098,538
Cash Balance at End of Year	$2,345,675

other classifications and formats are more useful. In particular I favor the format shown in Figure 2.2 for reporting cash flow from profit to managers. The following remarks address the three groupings of cash flows in the statement of cash flows included in the *external* financial reports of a business.

The statement of cash flows starts with a section that reports the derivation of cash flow from profit for the period, which is labeled Cash Flows from Operating Activities. Operating activities are the profit-making transactions and events of a business (i.e., the sales revenue and expenses of a business). A business may have income from other sources such as rental of property that it doesn't currently use, interest and dividends from investments in securities, and so on. Any regular, ongoing source of income is included in the operating activities of a business.

The main examples of investing activities are purchases to replace and expand fixed assets, and the acquisition of intangible assets (such as patents, trademarks, secret processes, etc.). These outlays are referred to as **capital expenditures** because they are relatively long-term commitments and usually involve large amounts of money.

Businesses make other types of long-term investments, such as purchases of other corporations' stock shares as part of joint ventures and strategic alliances. A business may invest in marketable securities, for short or long periods. The investing activities section of the cash flow statement includes cash inflows from disposals of investments, such as selling fixed assets that reached the end of their useful lives to the business, and proceeds from liquidating investments in marketable securities.

Financing refers to dealings with the sources of capital to a business, (i.e., shareowners and lenders). Financing activities include raising money from debt and equity sources, and the return of capital to these sources. This section of the statement of cash flows also includes cash dividends paid to the shareowners of the business. When a corporation buys back some of its outstanding capital stock shares, the cash outlay is included in this section of the cash flows statement. In this example, the business did not buy back any of its stock shares. Just the opposite; it issued additional stock shares for cash to key executives according to their management stock purchase plans.

A company's cash flow from operating activities, or cash flow from profit, often does not provide all the money it needs for replacing and expanding its fixed assets, for adding to the company's working capital balance, for distributions from profit to shareowners, and for other purposes. A business, therefore, may raise additional money from its shareowners or lenders, or sell some of its assets. A comprehensive statement of all cash sources and uses is needed to pull everything together in one place, which is precisely the purpose of the statement of cash flows.

Reading the Statement of Cash Flows

Please refer to Figure 2.3 as we walk through the following analysis of the company's cash flows for the year. *Warning:* This is how I would read the statement, not necessarily how other persons would read the statement of cash flows.

The business spent $3,186,250 for purchases of new fixed assets during the year. The company realized $265,480 from disposals of old assets no longer needed. So the net amount of cash expenditure for fixed assets was $2,920,770. Where did the business get this money? The first place I looked is its cash flow from profit. However, cash flow from profit was far less than the money invested in its fixed assets:

$2,920,770 capital expenditures during year (net cash outlay)
– $1,297,907 operating cash flow (see Figure 2.3)

= $1,622,863 cash flow deficit for capital expenditures

The business increased its short-term borrowings $485,00 and its long-term borrowings $1,650,000, which together provided more than enough to cover the money needed for capital expenditures:

$2,135,000 increases in short-term and long-term debt
– $1,622,863 cash flow deficit for capital expenditures

= $ 512,137 cash available for other uses

The company issued additional capital stock shares to key executives of the business, under terms of their stock purchase plans. (I read this in a footnote to the financial statements). This was not a major source of cash; the primary purpose is to encourage key executives to accumulate an ownership stake in the business. The issuance of stock shares brought in $185,000 cash flow, so the business had a total of $697,137 cash flow at its disposal ($512,137 cash from above + $185,000 = $697,137). The business paid $450,000 cash dividends from profit to its shareowners, which did not exhaust the cash at its disposal. Thus, its cash balance increased $247,137: ($697,137 – $450,000 cash dividends = $247,137 increase in cash balance).

The cash dividend decision is not an easy one. If I were on the board of directors, I might have argued that the business should not have borrowed as much, say $450,000 less than it did, and it should not have paid cash dividends to stockholders. Of course, the stockholders may demand some cash income on their investment in the business. As it is, cash dividends equal only 28 percent of net income for the year and just 35 percent of operating cash flow for the year. I might also question the increase in the company's cash balance. The business could have borrowed less and have allowed its cash balance to remain at the same level. Borrowing money is serious business. A company *must service its debt*; it must make interest payments as they come due and be in a position to pay debt principal when it comes due (or be able to persuade its lenders to roll over the debt).

A Typical Statement of Cash Flows Example

Figure 2.4 presents the statement of cash flows reported recently by Hewlett-Packard Company, which I downloaded from its web site. This is a fairly typical example of what you find in external financial reports of publicly owned corporations. The usual statement of cash flows bulges with information. Thirty lines of information are reported in H-P's cash flows statement! Whether the average capital stock investor has the time and ability to read and understand the statement of cash flows is a good question. I don't think so. In my view the statement of cash flows needs to be condensed and simplified so that the reader can quickly grasp the overall picture of cash flows through the business.

Summary

If a business sells on credit, carries an inventory of products for sale, buys on credit, or records depreciation expense, then its cash flow from profit during a period is bound to be higher or lower than the amount of its profit for the period. Almost all businesses do one or more of these things. Many businesses do all of these things.

The chapter explains how each of these features of operating a business affects its cash flow from profit. Profit is measured on the accrual basis of accounting, which is correct and which is required by generally accepted accounting principles. But cash flow from profit is figured on the cash basis of accounting. Both measures of financial performance are extremely important, but different.

Cash flow from profit equals the increase or decrease in cash (as the case may be) during a period that is driven by the sales and expense activities of a business. Cash flow from profit is an indispensable source

FIGURE 2.4 Statement of Cash Flows for Hewlett-Packard Company

Condensed Consolidated Statement of Cash Flows
Hewlett-Packard Company and Subsidiaries

For the years ended October 31 (In millions)	2000	1999	1998
Cash flows from operating activities:			
Net earnings from continuing operations	$3,561	$3,104	$2,678
Adjustments to reconcile net earnings from continuing operations to net cash provided by operating activities			
Depreciation and amortization	1,368	1,316	1,377
Gains from divestitures	-212	—	-27
Deferred taxes on earnings	-689	-171	-1,101
Tax benefit on employee stock options	495	289	157
Changes in assets and liabilities			
Accounts and financing receivables	-1,312	-1,637	-1,100
Inventory	-845	-171	630
Accounts payable	1,544	751	61
Taxes on earnings	175	-639	1,200
Other current assets and liabilities	-282	330	731
Other, net	-343	-76	154
Net cash provided by operating activities	3,460	3,096	4,760
Cash flows from investing activities:			
Investment in property, plant and equipment	-1,737	-1,134	-1,584
Disposition of property, plant and equipment	420	542	260
Purchases of investments	-1,131	-1,015	-4,059
Maturities and sales of investments	1,004	1,063	4,834
Net proceeds from divestitures	448	35	89
Other, net	-130	-119	-148
Net cash used in investing activities	-1,126	-628	-608
Cash flows from financing activities:			
(Decrease) increase in notes payable and short-term borrowings	-1,297	2,399	-734
Issuance of long-term debt	1,936	240	223
Payment of long-term debt	-474	-1,047	-573
Issuance of common stock under employee stock plans	748	660	467
Repurchase of common stock	-5,570	-2,643	-2,424
Dividends	-638	-650	-625
Net cash used in financing activities	-5,295	-1,041	-3,666
Net cash provided by (used in) discontinued operations	965	-62	488
(Decrease) increase in cash and cash equivalents	-1,996	1,365	
Cash and cash equivalents at beginning of period	5,411	4,046	3,072
Cash and cash equivalents at end of period	$3,415	$5,411	$4,046

See Accompanying Notes to Condensed Consolidated Financial Statements.

of cash for every business—for continuing its operations, for providing money needed to grow the business, and for making cash distributions from profit to its shareowners.

Accomplishing the profit objective of the business does not automatically mean that its cash flow is under control. To control cash flow from profit, managers need to be aware of the differences between cash collections from sales and sales revenue for the period, and cash payments for expenses and expenses for the period. The chapter presents an innovative cash flow report for managers that focuses on these differences.

The statement of cash flows summarizes and reports the three types of cash flows of a business. Cash flow from profit is referred to as cash flow from operating activities in the statement of cash flows, instead of cash flow from profit. The other types of cash flows of a business are from its *investing* and *financing* activities. The statement of cash flows is one of the primary financial statements included in the annual and quarterly external financial reports by businesses to their outside shareowners and lenders. This statement discloses where the business got its money during the period, and what it did with the money.

The cash flow from profit (operating activities) may be grossly different from the amount of profit reported by a business. This gap may be evidence of suspicious accounting methods used by the business to measure profit. A business can cook its books in recording profit, but it is much more difficult to rig its cash flows. In any case, the reasons for a large difference between cash flow and profit should be identified. The rest of the statement, which reveals the investing activities and financing activities of the business during the period, exposes vital information regarding whether the business is building for the future, or is hunkering down for the time being.

CHAPTER 3

Assets for Making Profit

Business managers need a tool for understanding and analyzing the pathway to profit. Chapter 1 introduces a profit model that identifies the key variables that drive profit. The profit model focuses on the critical factors that managers have to be in command of to attain the profit objectives of the business. These key factors include sales prices, unit costs, and unit margins, as well as contribution margin and fixed expenses. This information is highly confidential and for the eyes of managers only. The information is not circulated outside the business.

The *income statement* is the means for reporting the profit performance of a business to its outside shareowners and lenders. The income statement does not reveal the sensitive information that is the heart and soul of the profit model. Instead, the income statement reports summary information—total sales revenue, total amounts for a few classes of expenses, and bottom-line profit (called net income, or earnings by most businesses). Figures 1.3 and 1.5 in Chapter 1 show examples of income statements.

This chapter identifies and explains the various assets required in making profit. The annual income statement is the point of reference. The profit model occupies center stage again in Chapters 6 and 7, which delve into how a business can improve its profit performance.

Sizing Up Total Assets

Figure 3.1 presents an abbreviated income statement for a company's most recent year. Actual income statements include more information about expenses and do not stop at the earnings before interest and income tax line of profit. Interest and income tax expenses are deducted to arrive at bottom-line net income. However, the condensed and truncated income statement shown in Figure 3.1 is just fine for the purpose at hand.

Note: This business example is a hypothetical but realistic composite, which is based on reading many financial reports over the years. Any specific business you select will differ in one or more respects from the example. Other businesses are smaller or larger than the one in the example; their annual sales revenue is lower or higher than in the example. The business in the example sells products, and therefore it has cost of goods sold expense. Other businesses sell services instead of products, and they don't have this expense. But the example serves as a good general-purpose template that has broad applicability across many lines of businesses.

Two Key Questions

Brick by brick this chapter builds the foundation of assets the business used to make sales of $52.0 million and to squeeze out $3.9 million profit (EBIT) from its sales revenue. Let me immediately put a question to you: What amount of total assets would you estimate that the business used in making annual sales of $52.0 million? Annual sales divided by total assets is called the **asset turnover ratio**. Indirectly, therefore, what I'm asking you is: What do you think the asset turnover ratio might be for the business?

The turnover ratios of businesses that manufacture and sell products tend to cluster in the range between 1.5 and 2.0. In other words, their annual sales revenue equals one and one-half to two times total

FIGURE 3.1 Abbreviated Income Statement Example

(Amounts in Millions of Dollars)	
Sales Revenue	$52.0
Cost of Goods Sold Expense	$31.2
Gross Margin	$20.8
Operating Expenses	$16.9
Earnings before Interest and Income Tax (EBIT)	$3.9

assets for these kinds of businesses. To keep the arithmetic easy to follow in the following discussion, assume that the total assets of the business in the example are $26.0 million. So its asset turnover ratio is 2.0: ($52.0 million annual sales revenue ÷ $26.0 million total assets = 2.0). An asset turnover ratio of 2.0 is on the high side, but I'll stick with it in the first part of the chapter.

The second question is this: Where did the business get the $26.0 million invested in its assets? The money for investing in assets comes from two different sources—*liabilities* and **owners' equity**. This point is summarized in the well-known **accounting equation**:

Assets = Liabilities + Owners' Equity

The accounting equation is the basis for double-entry bookkeeping. The *balance sheet* takes its name from the balance between assets on one side and liabilities plus owners' equity on the other side of the accounting equation. The balance sheet is the financial statement that reports a business's assets, liabilities, and owners' equity accounts; it is explained later in the chapter.

Return on Assets

The $26.0 million total assets of the business is the amount of capital it used to earn $3.9 million earnings before interest and income tax, or EBIT. Dividing EBIT by total assets gives the rate of **return on assets (ROA)** earned by the business. In the example the business earned a 15.0 percent ROA for the year: ($3.9 million EBIT ÷ $26.0 million total assets = 15.0%). Is this ROA just adequate, fairly good, or very good? Well, relative to what benchmark, or point of reference?

The business has borrowed money for part of the total $26.0 million total capital invested in its assets. The average annual interest rate on its debt is 8.0 percent. Relative to this annual interest rate the company's 15.0 percent ROA is more than adequate. Indeed, the favorable spread between these two rates works to the advantage of the owners of the business. The business borrows money at 8.0 percent and manages to earn 15.0 percent on the money. Chapter 4 explores the very important issue regarding debt versus owners' equity sources of capital to finance the assets of a business, and the advantages and risks of using debt capital.

This chapter deals mainly with the types and the amounts of assets needed to make profit. Also, the noninterest-bearing operating liabilities of businesses are included in the discussion. These short-term payables occur spontaneously when a business buys inventory on credit, receives money in advance for future delivery of products or services to customers, and delays paying for expenses. Payables arising from these sources are called **spontaneous liabilities**. In contrast, borrowing money from lenders and raising money from shareholders are anything but spontaneous. Persuading lenders to loan money to the business is a protracted process, as is getting people to invest money in the business as shareowners.

Assets and Sources of Capital for Assets

Continuing the example just introduced, the business has several different assets that at year-end add up to $26.0 million, as discussed. One of its assets is inventories, which are products being held by the business for sale to customers. These products haven't been sold yet, so the cost of the products is held in the asset account and will not be charged to expense until the products are sold. The cost of its inventories at year-end is $7.2 million. Of this amount $2.4 million hadn't been paid for by the end of the year. The company hadn't paid by year-end for this amount of its inventories. The business has an excellent credit rating. Its suppliers give the business a month to pay for purchases from them.

In addition to the amounts it owes for inventory purchases, the business also has short-term $2.6 million of liabilities for unpaid operating expenses at year-end. Of its $16.9 million of operating expenses for the year (see Figure 3.1) $2.6 million had not been paid by the end of the year. Both types of liabilities—payables for purchases of inventory on credit and for unpaid operating expenses—are short-term, noninterest-bearing obligations of the business. These are called **operating liabilities**, or spontaneous liabilities (as mentioned before). The total of these two short-term operating liabilities is $5.0 million in the example.

To summarize, the company's total assets, operating liabilities, and sources of capital for investing in its assets is shown in Figure 3.2.

In Figure 3.2 note that the $5.0 million of operating liabilities is deducted from total assets to determine the $32.5 million amount, which is the total capital needed for investing in its assets. Operating liabilities are subtracted from total assets because these creditors of the business do not charge interest (unless the company delays too long in paying these liabilities). If the business had paid all of its operating liabilities by year-end, then its cash balance would have been $5.0 million lower and its total assets would have been $21.0 million. (I should mention that the business probably would not have had enough cash to pay all of its operating liabilities before the end of the year.) A company's cash balance benefits from the *float*, which is

FIGURE 3.2 Summary of Company's Assets, Operating Liabilities, and Sources of Capital

(Dollar Amounts in Millions)			
Total Assets	$26.0	Short-term and long-term debt	$7.5
Less: Operating Liabilities	$5.0	Owners' equity	$13.5
Capital Needed for Assets	$21.0	Capital from debt and owners' equity	$21.0

the time period that goes by until the company pays its short-term operating liabilities. It's as if the business gets a $5.0 million interest-free loan from its creditors.

Debt versus Equity Sources of Capital

The $21.0 million of its assets ($26.0 million total assets minus the $5.0 million of its operating liabilities) is the amount of money that the business had to obtain from three general sources: (1) the business borrowed money; (2) the business raised money from shareowners; and, (3) the business retained a good part of its annual earnings instead of distributing all of its annual profits to shareowners. These three sources of capital have provided the $21.0 million invested in its assets. Of this total capital $7.5 million is from short-term and longer-term debt sources of capital. The rest of the company's total capital is from owners' equity, which consists of the amounts invested by shareowners over the years plus the accumulated *retained earnings* of the business. Figure 3.2 does not separate between the capital invested by shareowners versus the cumulative amount of retained earnings of the business—only the total $13.5 million for owners' equity is shown in Figure 3.2.

Interest is the cost of using debt capital, of course. In contrast a business does not make a contractual promise to pay shareowners a predetermined amount or a percent of distribution from profit each year. Rather the cost of equity capital is an *imputed* cost, equal to a sought-after amount of net income that the business should earn annually relative to the owners' equity employed in the business. The owners' equity is $13.5 million of the company's $21.0 million total capital. Shareowners expect the business to earn annual net income on owners' equity that is higher than the interest rate on its debt. Shareowners take more risk than lenders. Assume, therefore, that the business's objective is to earn a 15.0 percent or higher annual net income on owners' equity. In the example net income should be at least $2,025,000: ($13.5 million owners' equity × 15.0% = $2,025,000 net income goal).

A company's actual earnings before interest and income tax (EBIT) for a year may not be enough to pay interest on its debt capital, pay income tax, and achieve its after-tax net income objective relative to owners' equity. What about this example, for instance? The business made $3.9 million EBIT, as reported in Figure 3.1. The annual interest rate on its debt was 8.0 percent, as mentioned earlier. So its annual interest expense was $600,000 ($7.5 million total debt times 8.0 percent annual interest rate = $600,000).

So the business made $3.3 million earnings after interest and before income tax. Its income tax rate is 34 percent of this amount. Thus, its income tax is $1,122,000 and its net income, or earnings after interest and income tax is $2,178,000. The business achieved of its goal to earn 15.0 percent or better of net income on owners' equity: ($2,178,000 net income ÷ $13,500,000 owners' equity = 16.1%). The shareowners may be satisfied with this 16.1 percent return on their capital, or they may insist that the business should do better.

Chapter 4 explores the strategy of using debt to enhance net income performance (as well as the risks using debt capital, which a business may or may not be willing to take). The rest of this chapter focuses on the assets and operating liabilities that are driven by the profit-making activities of a business. A large chunk of a company's balance sheet (statement of financial condition) consists of these assets and operating liabilities.

Connecting Sales Revenue and Expenses With Their Assets and Operating Liabilities

Figure 3.3 shows the lines of connection from sales revenue and expenses to their respective assets and operating liabilities. The business example introduced above is continued in this section. The assets and operating liabilities shown in Figure 3.3 are explained briefly as follows:

- Making sales on credit causes a business to record accounts receivable.
- Acquiring and holding products before they are sold to customers causes a business to record inventories.
- The costs of some operating expenses are paid before the cost is recorded as an expense, which causes a business to record prepaid expenses.

FIGURE 3.3 Assets and Operating Liabilities Driven by Sales Revenue and Expenses

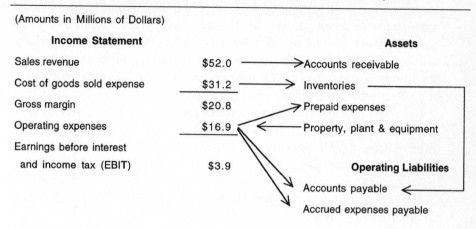

(Amounts in Millions of Dollars)

Income Statement		Assets
Sales revenue	$52.0	→ Accounts receivable
Cost of goods sold expense	$31.2	→ Inventories
Gross margin	$20.8	Prepaid expenses
Operating expenses	$16.9	Property, plant & equipment
Earnings before interest and income tax (EBIT)	$3.9	**Operating Liabilities**
		Accounts payable
		Accrued expenses payable

- Investments in long-term operating resources, called property, plant, and equipment causes a business to record depreciation expense, which is included in operating expenses.

- Inventory purchases on credit causes a business to record accounts payable.

- Many expenses are recorded before they are paid that cause a business to record its unpaid expense amounts in either an accounts payable account or an accrued expenses payable account. These two payables are called operating liabilities.

Accounts Receivable

No dollar amounts (also called *balances*) are shown for the assets and operating liabilities in Figure 3.3. The amounts depend on the policies and practices of the business. The amount of the accounts receivable asset depends on the credit terms offered to the company's customers, whether most of the customers pay their bills on time, and how many customers are delinquent. For example, assume the business offers its customers one-month credit, which most take, but the company's actual collection experience is closer to five weeks on average because some customers pay late. In this situation the balance of its accounts receivable would be five weeks of annual sales revenue, or $5.0 million at the end of the year: ($52.0 million annual sales revenue $\times$ $^5/_{52}$ = $5.0 million accounts receivable).

Inventories

The amount of the company's inventories asset depends on the company's holding period—the time from acquisition of products until the products are sold and delivered to customers. Suppose that on average, across all products sold, the business holds products in inventory for 12 weeks until sold. In this situation the company's year-end inventory would be $7.2 million: ($31.2 annual cost of goods sold expense $\times$ $^{12}/_{52}$ = $7.2 million). At the end of the year recent acquisitions of inventory had not been paid for, because the company buys on credit from the sources of products.

Thus, see the line of connection in Figure 3.3 from the inventories asset to accounts payable. Assume, for instance, that about one-third of its ending inventories had not been paid for. As the result the year-end accounts payable would be about $2.4 million from inventory purchases on credit. The total amount of accounts payable also includes the amount of unpaid expenses of the business at the end of the year for which the business has been billed by its vendors.

Operating Liabilities

For most businesses a sizeable amount of its operating expenses that have been recorded during the latter part of a year are not paid by the end of the year. At the end of the year the business has unpaid bills from its utility company for gas and electricity, from its lawyers for work done during recent weeks, from the telephone company, from maintenance and repair vendors, and so on. A business records the amounts it has been billed for (received an invoice for) in the accounts payable operating liability account. A business also has a second and equally important type of operating liability, which may be larger than accounts payable. A business has many expenses that accumulate, or accrue over time that it does not receive bills for, and to record these creeping expenses a business uses a second type of operating liability account that is discussed next.

In my experience business managers and investors do not appreciate the rather large size of *accruals* for various operating expenses. Many operating expenses are *not* on a pay-as-you-go basis. For example, accumulated vacation and sick leave benefits are not paid until the employees actually take their vacations and sick days. At year-end the company calculates profit sharing bonuses and other profit sharing amounts, which are recorded as expense in the period just ended even though they will not be paid until some time later. Product warranty and guarantee costs should be accrued and charged to expense so that these follow-up costs are recognized in the same year that sales revenue is recorded—to get a correct matching of sales revenue and expenses to measure profit. In summary, a surprising number of expense accruals are recorded.

Expense accruals are recorded in a separate account, labeled *accrued expenses payable* in Figure 3.3, because they are quite different from accounts payable. For one thing an account payable is based on an actual invoice received by the vendor, whereas accruals have no such hard copy that serve as evidence of the liability. Accruals depend much more on good faith estimates of the accountants and others making these calculations. Suppose the business in the example knows from experience that the balance of this operating liability tends to be about five weeks of its annual total operating expenses.

This ratio of accrued expenses payable to annual operating expenses is based on the types of accruals that the company records, such as accrued vacation and sick pay for employees, accrued property taxes, accrued warranty and guarantee costs on products, and so on. The five weeks reflects the average time between when these expenses are recorded and when they are eventually paid, which can be quite a long time for some items but rather short for others. Thus, the year-end balance of the company's accrued expenses payable liability account is about $1.6 million: ($16.9 million annual operating expenses $\times$ $5/_{52}$ = approximately $1.6 million).

Prepaid Expenses and Fixed Assets Depreciation

Chapter 2 examines profit and cash flow, and discusses that a business has to prepay a few of its operating expenses. I won't repeat that discussion here but simply piggyback on the discussion and point out that a business has an asset account called *prepaid expenses*, which holds the prepaid cost amounts that have not charged off to expense by the end of the year. Usually the amount of the prepaid expenses asset account is relatively small—although, if the ending balance were large compared with a company's annual operating expenses, this strange state of affairs definitely should be investigated. Indeed, the accountant should anticipate that the business manager would notice an unusually large balance in the prepaid expenses and provide an explanation without waiting to be asked for it.

One of the operating expenses of a business is depreciation. This is a very unique expense, especially from the cash flow point of view (as Chapter 2 discusses at some length). I do not separate depreciation expense in Figure 3.3, although I do show a line of connection from the company's fixed assets account (property, plant and equipment) to operating expenses. As I explain in Chapter 2 the original cost of fixed assets is spread over the years of their use according to an allocation method. (Chapter 13 examines the different depreciation methods used by accountants.)

What about Cash?

A business has one other asset not shown in Figure 3.3 nor mentioned so far—*cash*. Every business needs a working cash balance. Recall that in the example the company's annual sales revenue is $52.0 million, or $1.0 million per week on average. But the actual cash collections in a given week could be considerably less or much more than the $1.0 million average. A business can't live hand to mouth and wait for actual cash collections to arrive before it writes checks. Employees have to be paid on time of course, and a business can't ask its creditors to wait for payment until it collects enough money from its customers.

In short, a business maintains a minimum cash balance as a safety buffer to fall back on. Many businesses keep a rather large cash balance, part of which is invested in safe, short-term marketable debt securities that the business earns interest income from. The average cash balance of a business relative to its annual sales revenue may be very low or fairly high. Cash balance policies vary widely from business to business. If I had to guess the cash balance of the business in the example, I would put it at around two or three weeks of annual sales revenue, or about $2.0 to $3.0 million. But I wouldn't be surprised if its cash balance were outside this range.

There's no doubt that every business needs to keep enough cash in its checking account (or on hand in currency and coin for cash based businesses such as grocery stores and gambling casinos). But precisely how much? Every business manager would worry if cash were too low to meet the next payroll. Some liabilities can be put off for days or even weeks, but employees have to be paid on time. Beyond a minimum, rock bottom cash balance amount to meet the payroll and to provide at least a bare bones margin of safety, it is not clear how much additional cash balance a business should carry. It's somewhat like your friends: Some may have only $5.00 to $10.00 in walking-around money on them; others could reach in their billfold or purse and pull out $500.00.

Unnecessary excess cash balances should be avoided. Excess cash is an unproductive asset that doesn't pay its way toward meeting the company's cost of capital, that is, the interest on debt capital and the net income that should be earned on equity capital. For another thing excess cash balances can cause managers to get lax in controlling expenses. If money is there in the bank, waiting only for a check to be written, it is more of an incentive to make unnecessary expenditures and not to scrutinize expenditures as closely as needed. Also, excess cash balances can lead to greater opportunities for fraud and embezzlement.

Yet, having a large cash balance is a tremendous advantage in some situations. The business may be able to drive a hard bargain with a major vendor by paying cash up front rather than asking for the normal credit terms. There are many such reasons for holding a cash balance over and above what's really needed to meet payroll and to provide for a safety buffer for the normal lags and leads in the cash receipts and cash disbursements of the company. Frankly, if this were my business I would want at least three weeks' cash balance.

An executive of a leading company said he kept the company's cash balance lean and mean to keep its managers on their toes. There's probably a lot of truth in this. But if too much time and effort go into managing day-to-day cash flow, then the more important strategic factors may not get managed well.

Figure 3.3 does not present a complete picture of the company's financial condition. Cash is missing, as just discussed, and the sources of the company's capital are not shown. It's time therefore to fill in the remaining pieces for the statement of financial condition of a business, otherwise known as the balance sheet.

Balance Sheet
(including Tether Lines With Income Statement)

Figure 3.4 presents the income statement and balance sheet (statement of financial condition) for the business example introduced in the review exercise at the end of Chapter 1. Please note that this is a different example from that used earlier in this chapter. I have not presented a complete and formal balance sheet before in the book, so I should point out a few features of this financial statement. (In passing I should mention that businesses also include a statement of cash flows in their financial reports, which Chapter 2 examines.)

Figure 3.4 displays lines of connection, or tether lines from sales revenue and expenses in the income statement with their corresponding assets and operating liabilities in the balance sheet. These lines are not actually shown in financial reports, as you probably know. I include the lines in Figure 3.4 to remind you that the profit-making activities of a business drive a good part of its balance sheet. Managers could insist that these lines of connection be shown in their internal accounting reports, to remind them of the relationships between sales revenue and expenses and their respective assets and operating liabilities.

FIGURE 3.4 Balance Sheet With Income Statement

Income Statement		Balance Sheet	
		Assets	
		Cash	$2,345,675
Sales Revenue	$39,661,250 ⟶	Accounts Receivable	$3,813,582
Cost of Goods Sold Expense	$24,960,750 ⟶	Inventories	$5,760,173
Gross Margin	$14,700,500	Prepaid Expenses	$822,899
Operating Expenses	$10,697,685	Total Current Assets	$12,742,329
Depreciation Expense	$768,450	Property, Plant, & Equipment	$20,857,500
Earnings before Interest and Income Tax	$3,234,365	Accumulated Depreciation	($6,785,250)
Interest Expense	$795,000	Cost Less Accumulated Depreciation	$14,072,250
Earnings before Income Tax	$2,439,365	Total Assets	$26,814,579
Income Tax Expense	$853,778	**Liabilities & Owners' Equity**	
Net Income	$1,585,587	Accounts Payable	$2,537,232
		Accrued Expenses Payable	$1,280,214
		Income Tax Payable	$76,500
		Short-term Debt	$2,250,000
		Total Current Liabilities	$6,143,946
		Long-term Debt	$7,500,000
		Total Liabilities	$13,643,946
		Capital Stock	$4,587,500
		Retained Earnings	$8,583,133
		Total Owners' Equity	$13,170,633
		Total Liabilities and Owners' Equity	$26,814,579

A balance sheet is known more formally as a *statement of financial condition*. This financial statement summarizes the major types of assets owned by a business on the one hand, and the claims against its assets on the other hand. These claims are divided into two basic classes—liabilities and owners' equity. The basic components of a balance sheet are encapsulated in the accounting equation:

Assets = Liabilities + Owners' Equity

For the example shown in Figure 3.4 the accounting equation for the business is:

$26,814,579 Assets = $13,643,946 Liabilities + $13,170,633 Owners' Equity

Instead of the horizontal format of the accounting equation (assets on the left side, liabilities and owners' equity on the right side) the balance sheet in Figure 3.4 is presented in the vertical, or report format (assets above, liabilities and owners' equity below). The account titles and other details of the balance sheet shown in Figure 3.4 are commonly used, but every business makes minor variations in terminology and presentation details.

Classified But Not Secret

The balance sheet shown in Figure 3.4 is called a *classified* balance sheet, meaning that the accounts are grouped into certain classes and are listed in a certain order.

Except in certain specialized industries current assets are listed first, starting with cash and followed by receivables and inventories. Accounts receivable and inventories are converted into cash within one *operating cycle*, which refers to the sequence of purchasing or manufacturing products, holding products awaiting sale, selling products for cash or on credit, and finally collecting receivables from credit sales. **Current assets** should not include assets that would take longer than one year to convert into cash (except in very unusual situations). Typically, accounts receivable are collected in a month or so, and inventories are sold in one, two, or three months (or longer in some industries).

Current liabilities come due for payment in the short-term, which means one year or less. Accounts payable will be paid in a month or so in most situations; some accrued expenses take longer to pay. Short-term notes payable (or other debt instruments) that will come due in the next year plus any amounts of long-term debt that will come due within the next year are included in current liabilities. Owner's equity is divided between *paid-in capital*, which is the total money shareowners have invested in the business over the years, and *retained earnings* which is the cumulative amount of net income that the business has earned but has not distributed to its shareowners.

In external financial reports most businesses separate between their accounts payable and accrued expenses payable, as shown in Figure 3.4. Income tax payable is usually reported on a separate line. Be warned, however, that specific account titles for accrued expenses payable vary quite a bit from business to business. Furthermore, some businesses group together their accounts payable and accrued expenses payable and report only one total amount for both types of these short-term operating liabilities. In their internal reports managers of a business should insist on the classification for current liabilities that best meets their needs for control purposes and for analysis of the company's financial condition.

Reading the Balance Sheet

For analyzing the financial condition and performance of a business it is useful to put operating liabilities by themselves in one group and to put short-term and long-term debt together in another group. The purpose is to separate between the noninterest-bearing liabilities of a business and its interest-bearing debt. As discussed earlier, operating liabilities arise spontaneously in purchasing inventories on credit and in recording expenses that are not paid immediately. Its creditors do not charge interest on these liabilities of the business.

Also it's useful to round off the amounts reported in a business's income statement and balance sheet. In fact larger businesses round off the figures reported in their external financial statements, although practice is not uniform in this respect. Figure 3.5 presents the balance sheet of the business in a slightly modified format that separates between operating liabilities and interest-bearing debt. The figures in the income statement and balance sheet in Figure 3.5 are rounded to the nearest $.1 million. The lines of connection from the income statement to the balance sheet accounts are not shown in Figure 3.5, because they are not shown in financial reports (but you should keep these invisible lines in mind, of course).

FIGURE 3.5 Financial Statements for Analyzing Financial Condition and Performance

(Dollar Amounts in Millions)

Income Statement		Balance Sheet	
		Assets	
		Cash	$2.3
Income Statement		Accounts Receivable	$3.8
Sales Revenue	$39.7	Inventories	$5.8
Cost of Goods Sold Expense	$25.0	Prepaid Expenses	$0.8
Gross Margin	$14.7	*Total Current Assets*	$12.7
Operating Expenses	$10.7	Property, Plant, & Equipment	$20.9
Depreciation Expense	$0.8	Accumulated Depreciation	($6.8)
Earnings before Interest and Income Tax	$3.2	*Cost Less Accumulated Depreciation*	$14.1
Interest Expense	$0.8	*Total Assets*	$26.8
Earnings before Income Tax	$2.4	**Liabilities & Owners' Equity**	
Income Tax Expense	$0.8	Accounts Payable	$2.5
Net Income	$1.6	Accrued Expenses Payable	$1.3
		Income Tax Payable	$0.1
		Total Operating Liabilities	$3.9
		Short-term Debt	$2.2
		Long-term Debt	$7.5
		Total Debt	$9.7
		Capital Stock	$4.6
		Retained Earnings	$8.6
		Total Owners' Equity	$13.2
		Total Liabilities and Owners' Equity	$26.8

Demands on Current Assets

The modified balance sheet format (Figure 3.5) makes it easier to compare the company's operating liabilities that have to be paid in the short-term with the company's cash balance and other current assets. The short-term operating liabilities for all practical purposes are paid from the company's present cash balance and from converting its accounts receivable and inventories into cash during the short-term. The business has $12.7 million current assets compared with $3.9 operating liabilities at the end of its most recent fiscal year (see Figure 3.5). Its current assets are $8.8 million more than the company's operating liabilities at year-end. The excess of current assets over operating liabilities is a good indicator of the business's ability to pay its short-term trade creditors and still have cash for other purposes, in particular to pay its short-term debt when it comes due at maturity.

Many businesses do not actually pay off their short-term notes payable at maturity. Rather they roll over these notes payable as they become due; new notes payable replace the old notes payable. Of course this depends on the willingness of the lender to renew the loans to the business. In the worst case scenario the business cannot roll over any of its short-term debt, and must pay off all of its notes payable. The excess of its current assets over its operating liabilities is an important indicator of whether the business could weather the storm and pay off its short-term debt, or might face a serious financial squeeze in the short-term.

In short, the business appears to be in good shape to pay its operating liabilities and its short-term debt if need be. The business has $8.8 million excess of current assets over its operating liabilities, and these sources of near-term cash flow should be adequate to pay off its $2.2 million short-term debt at maturity if it comes to that. The only flies in the ointment would be if the business could not collect its accounts receivables soon enough, or could not sell its products being held in inventory soon enough.

Sources of Capital and Earnings on Equity Capital

The balance sheet layout shown in Figure 3.5 makes it easy to determine the amount of capital that the business has raised over the years to invest in its assets. The company had $26.8 million total assets at the end of its most recent fiscal year. Subtracting its $3.9 million operating liabilities gives $22.9 million, which is the amount of capital the business has raised from debt and equity sources. It's always important to ask where a business got the money to invest in its assets. Interest-bearing debt supplied $9.7 million, or 42 percent of the company's $22.9 million total capital; owners' equity supplied the other $13.2 million, or 58 percent. This mix of capital sources is a little debt heavy, which is not necessarily bad. The advantages and disadvantages of debt are examined in Chapter 4.

For the year just ended the business earned 12.0 percent net income on its owners' equity: ($1.6 million net income ÷ $13.2 million owners' equity = 12.0%). A 12.0 percent return on equity capital isn't too bad, although the business and its shareowners probably want to do better. Evaluating financial performance is explained in Chapter 5.

Is Anything out of Kilter?

In closing let us revisit two key connections between the income statement and the balance sheet—sales revenue and accounts receivable, and cost of goods sold expense and inventories. Business managers and investors should always closely watch these two links, mainly to see if either is out of kilter or has changed drastically from previous periods. Please refer to Figures 3.4 and 3.5 for reference in the following discussion. Calculations are not shown, to speed up the discussion.

In the example the business sells to other businesses and almost all of its sales are on credit. The business does not collect cash from its sales immediately, in other words. The business records sales revenue by increasing accounts receivable, and then waits a month or so before collecting cash from its customers. At year-end the company's accounts receivable balance equals about 10 percent of its annual sales revenue. This indicates that the business waits about 10 percent of a year, or about 36 days to collect its receivables. Put another way about 10 percent of its annual sales revenue had not been collected at year-end.

Are 36 days reasonable? Suppose the business offers its customers 30 days credit, and that some of its customers are slow payers that take longer than 30 days to pay the business. In this situation 36 days does not seem unreasonable. However, there could be too many past due customer accounts that need some form of encouragement or prodding to pay up. A business does not reveal in its external financial report the portion of its year-end total accounts receivable that is past due—although I have seen this information in financial reports of privately owned businesses. For internal reporting, managers definitely should insist on an *aging analysis* of their accounting receivable. I'm on the board of directors of a business and we get this information every period.

When a customer's account becomes seriously past due and it becomes unlikely that the business will ever collect the amount, an entry is made to write off the amount owed to the business. The accounts receivable asset is decreased and the **bad debts** expense is increased. This expense is never reported separately in external financial statements to lenders and shareowners. But it goes without saying that bad debts are one of the revenue-driven expenses in the profit model (see line 5 in Figure 1.1). Based on its experience a business can forecast with fairly good accuracy what percent of its credit sales will turn out to be uncollectible and have to be written off as bad debts.

The second critical linkage between the income statement and balance sheet is cost of goods sold expense with inventories. In the example the business sells products. The business buys some products from manufacturers, and manufactures itself some of the products it sells. When products are purchased the cost of the products is entered as an increase in the inventories asset account, and the operating liability account called accounts payable is increased the same amount. When the purchase invoice is paid later, cash is decreased and the liability account is decreased. The cost of purchased products remains in the inventories asset account until the goods are sold at which time the asset account is decreased by the cost of the products sold, and the cost of the goods sold expense account is increased the same amount.

Accumulating the costs of manufacturing products and recording these costs in the inventories account is much more complicated than recording the purchase cost of products. In both cases, however, the cost of products remains in the inventories asset account until the goods are sold, at which time the cost of goods sold is removed from the asset account and recorded in the expense account. The inventories asset account usually is one of the largest asset accounts of businesses that sell products.

At year-end the cost of the company's inventories equals about 23 percent of its annual cost of goods sold expense. This indicates that the business holds products in stock (in inventory) about 23 percent of a year, or 84 days on average before products are sold and delivered to customers. Put another way, if sales continue at the same level into next year, the business has enough products in inventory to provide for the next 84 days of sales. Managers should compare this ratio for the most recent period against previous periods. A substantial increase or decrease should be analyzed.

Are 84 days reasonable? Average inventory holding periods vary widely from industry to industry. For retail grocery store chains 84 days is definitely too high; they turn their inventory over every two or three weeks. Other retail businesses, on the other hand, hold inventory for as long as six months before sale. For many businesses 84 days is not untypical, especially for manufacturers. There could be some products in inventory that have been sitting on the shelves for several months. Generally speaking, the longer products have been held in inventory, the less likely they will be sold at normal prices or may not be sold at all.

Products should not be held in inventory any longer than necessary. Holding inventory is subject to several risks and requires several costs. Products may become obsolete, or may be stolen, or may be damaged, or even misplaced. Products have to be stored, usually have to be insured, and may have to be guarded. These costs are one of the unit-driven expenses in the profit model (see line 4 in Figure 1.1). The higher the sales volume, the higher the quantity of inventory and thus the higher are these inventory holding costs.

Generally accepted accounting principles (GAAP) require that the cost of products that cannot be sold or will have to be sold below cost have to be written down and charged to an expense. The business decreases the inventories account and increases the cost of goods sold expense, or a different expense account. Most businesses that sell products record inventory write-downs. However a business does not disclose in its external financial report the amount of its inventory write-down during the year. If the inventory write-down amount were very large, the business should disclose the amount of the loss and the general reasons for the write-down. For internal reporting managers should insist on an aging analysis of their inventories that clearly identifies slow-moving products.

Summary

A business needs assets to make profit. Therefore a business must raise capital for the money to invest in its assets. The seed capital comes from shareowners; they may invest additional money in the business from time to time after the business gets off the ground. Most businesses borrow money on the basis of interest-bearing debt instruments, such as notes payable. Profitable businesses retain part or all of their annual earnings to supplement the money invested in the business by their shareowners.

The balance sheet, or statement of financial condition reports the debt and equity capital sources of a business and the assets in which the business has invested. Several different types of assets are listed in the balance sheet. The balance sheet also reports the operating liabilities of a business that are generated by its profit-making activities and not from borrowing money. Operating liabilities are noninterest-bearing payables of a business, which are quite different from its interest-bearing debt obligations.

The relationships of sales revenue and expenses reported in a company's income statement with the assets and operating liabilities reported in its balance sheet are not haphazard. Far from it! Sales revenue and the different expenses in the income statement match up with particular assets and operating liabilities. Business managers, lenders, and investors should understand these critical connections between the components of the income statement and the components of the balance sheet. In particular, the amount of accounts receivable should be reasonable in comparison with annual sales revenue, and the amount of inventories should be reasonable in comparison with annual cost of goods sold expense.

In short, the balance sheet of a business should jive with and resonate with its income statement. These two financial statements are presented separately in financial reports, but business managers, lenders, and investors understand the interlocking nature of these two primary financial statements.

CHAPTER 4

Capital Strategies

This chapter picks up where Chapter 3 leaves off and examines in more depth the two basic sources of capital to business—debt and owners' equity. Every business must make a fundamental decision regarding how to finance the business, which refers to the mix or relative proportions of debt and equity. By borrowing money a business enlarges its equity capital, so the business has a bigger base of capital to carry on its profit-making activities. More capital generally means a business can make more sales, and more sales generally means more profit. Using debt in addition to equity capital is referred to as **financial leverage**. Leverage means that the equity capital base is used as a lever to borrow money. The chapter explains the gain or loss resulting from financial leverage, which often is a major contributor to bottom-line profit.

It's possible, I suppose, to find a business that is so antidebt that the only liabilities it has are normal operating liabilities, that is, accounts payable and accrued expenses payable. These short-term liabilities arise spontaneously in making purchases on credit and from delaying the payment of certain expenses until sometime after the expenses have been recorded. A business can hardly avoid operating liabilities. But a business doesn't have to borrow money. It could possibly raise all the capital it needs from shareowners and from retaining all or a good part of its annual earnings in the business. In short a business theoretically could rely entirely on equity capital sources and have no debt at all—but this way of financing a business is very rare indeed.

A New Business Example

Chapter 3 explains the various assets needed by a business that sells products on credit, and the operating liabilities that are part and parcel of its profit-making process. The attention of this chapter shifts to the other side of the balance sheet, that is, the capital sources tapped for money to invest in assets. Figure 4.1 presents the very condensed balance sheet and the abbreviated income statement for a new business example. The income statement is truncated at the earnings before interest and income tax line. The two financial statements in Figure 4.1 are telescoped into a few lines. In this chapter we don't need all the details that are actually reported in these two financial statements. (See Figure 3.4 for a balance sheet and the solution to the exercise at the end of Chapter 1 for an income statement.)

To support its $18.5 million annual sales the business used $11.5 million total assets. Operating liabilities provided $1.5 million of its assets. (Operating liabilities are explained in Chapter 3.) In Figure 4.1 the company's operating liabilities are deducted from its total assets to get a very important figure—*capital invested in assets*. The business had to raise $10.0 million capital from debt and owners' equity. The business borrows money on the basis of short-term and

FIGURE 4.1 Condensed Financial Statements

Balance Sheet		Income Statement	
Assets used in making profit	$11,500,000	Sales revenue	$18,500,000
Operating liabilities (accounts payable and accrued expenses payable)	($1,500,000)	All operating expenses	($16,700,000)
Capital invested in assets	$10,000,000	Earnings before interest and income tax expenses (EBIT)	$1,800,000
Debt and equity sources of capital	$10,000,000		

long-term notes payable. The business built up its owners' equity from money invested by shareowners plus the cumulative amount of retained earnings over the years (undistributed net income year after year).

Once Again Quickly: Assets and Operating Liabilities

I won't repeat the entire discussion in Chapter 3. You are just reminded here that a business that sells products on credit needs four main assets in making profit: cash, accounts receivable, inventories, and long-lived resources, such as land, buildings, machinery, and equipment that are referred to as fixed assets (or more formally as property, plant, and equipment). Chapter 3 goes into the characteristics of each asset, and how sales revenue and expenses are connected with these assets. Chapter 3 also explains how expenses drive the operating liabilities of a business. To determine the amount of capital raised by a business its operating liabilities are deducted from its total assets. It is important to be very clear about these payables of a business and why they are deducted from assets.

In the process of making profit a business generates certain short-term, noninterest-bearing liabilities that are inseparable from its profit-making transactions. One example is a purchase of products on credit. The inventories asset account is increased and the accounts payable liability account is increased the same amount. This liability will be paid a month or so later. Employees accumulate vacation and sick pay entitlements that are recorded as expense each pay period. These obligations of the business are not paid until employees take vacation and their sick days. Until then the accrued expenses payable account stays on the books as a liability. These payables of a business are called spontaneous liabilities because operating activities, not borrowing money, causes them.

Accounts payable are called *trade credit*; these sources of credit do not charge interest unless the business is very late in paying the bill. The business does not borrow money from its vendors. The business convinces its vendors and suppliers to sell products to the business on the strength of its credit reputation and good name. Consider again the purchase of products on credit by a business. Assume the business holds products in inventory for three months on average before the items are sold to customers. Assume the business doesn't pay the liability from the purchase until one month later. Thus the accounts payable liability finances the first month of holding inventory. But the business must raise capital from debt or equity sources to finance inventory for the second and third months. Of course, inventory is just one asset of several that a business needs to operate. A business needs to raise capital for its accounts receivable, for its day-to-day working cash balance, and for its fixed assets. In the example the business has managed to raise $10.0 million capital.

Capital Structure of Business

The capital a business needs for investing in its assets comes from two basic sources—debt and equity. Managers must convince lenders to loan money to the company, and must convince sources of equity capital to invest their money in the company. Both debt and equity sources of capital demand to be compensated for the use of their capital. Interest is paid on debt and is reported in the income statement as an expense, which like all other expenses is deducted from sales revenue to determine bottom-line net income. In contrast no charge or deduction for using equity capital is reported in the income statement.

Rather, net income is reported as the reward or pay-off on equity capital. In other words profit is defined from the shareowner's point of view, not from the total capital point of view. Interest is viewed not as a division of profit to one of the two sources of capital of the business. Instead interest is treated as an expense and profit is defined to be the residual amount after deducting interest.

Sometimes the owners' equity of a business is referred to as its **net worth**. The fundamental idea of net worth is this:

Net Worth = (Assets – Operating liabilities – Debt)

Net income increases the new worth of a business. The business is better off from earning net income because its net worth increased by the net income amount. Suppose another group of investors stands ready to buy the business for a total price equal to its net worth. This offering price, or market value of the business, increases by the amount of net income. Cash distributions of net income to shareowners decreases the net worth of a business because cash decreases with no decrease in the operating liabilities or debt of the business. The amounts of cash distributions from net income are reported in the statement of cash flows, which is explained in Chapter 2. (Dividends are also reported in a separate **Statement of Changes in Owners' Equity** accounts, if this particular schedule is included in a financial report.) In this chapter cash dividends take a back seat. Dividends are important to the shareowners of a business; the topic is examined in Chapter 5.

The valuation of a business is not so simple as someone buying the business for an amount equal to its net worth. Business valuation usually takes into account the net worth reported in its balance sheet, but many other factors play a role in putting a value on a business. The amount the buyer is willing to offer for a business can be considerably higher than the company's net worth based on the figures reported in the company's most recent balance sheet. The valuation of a privately owned business is quite a broad topic, which is beyond the scope of this book. Likewise, the valuation of stock shares of publicly owned business corporations is a far-reaching topic beyond the confines of this book.

At its most recent year-end the business had $10.0 million invested in assets to carry on its profit-making operations (total assets less its operating liabilities). Suppose that debt has provided $4.0 million of the total capital invested in assets and owners' equity has supplied the other $6.0 million. Collectively these capital sources are referred to as the **capitalization** or the **capital structure** of the business. Be careful about the term capitalization: similar terms mean something different. The terms **market capitalization**, **market cap**, or **cap** for short refer to the total market value of a publicly traded corporation, which is equal to the current market price per share of stock times the total number of stock shares outstanding (in the hands of stockholders).

A perpetual question that's not easy to answer concerns whether a business is using the optimal, or best capital structure. Perhaps the business in the example should have carried more debt. Maybe the company could have gotten by on a smaller cash balance, say $500,000 less—which means that $500,000 less capital would have been needed. Perhaps the business should have kept its accounts receivable and inventory balances lower, which would have reduced the need for capital. Every business has to make tough choices between debt versus equity, asking shareowners for more money versus retaining earnings, and working with a lean working cash balance versus a larger and more comfortable cash balance. The answers to these questions are seldom easy and clear cut.

Basic Characteristics of Debt

Debt may be very short-term, which generally means six months or less, or be long-term, which generally means 10 years or longer—or for any period mutually agreed on between the business and its lender. (A recent *New York Times* article commented on the increasing trend of debt issues with 50-year maturities, and mentioned one issue with a 999 years maturity date.) The term debt means *interest bearing* in all cases. Interest rates can be fixed over the life of the debt contract or can be subject to change usually at the lender's option. On short-term debt interest usually is paid at the end of the loan period. On long-term debt interest usually is paid monthly or quarterly (sometimes semi-annually).

A key feature of debt is whether the principal of the loan (the amount borrowed) is amortized over the life of the loan, instead of being paid at the end of the loan period. In addition to paying interest the business (who is the borrower, or debtor) may be required to make payments periodically that reduce the principal balance of the debt—instead of waiting until the final maturity date to pay off the entire principal amount at one time. For example, a loan may call for equal quarterly amounts over five years. Each quarterly payment is calculated to pay interest and to reduce a part of the principal balance so that at the end of the five years the loan principal will be paid off. Alternatively, the business may negotiate a *term* loan. Nothing is paid to reduce the principal balance during the life of a term loan; the entire amount borrowed (the principal) is paid at the maturity date of the loan.

The lender may demand that certain assets of the business be pledged as *collateral*. The lender would have the right to take control of the property in the event the business defaults on the loan. Real estate (land and buildings) is the most common type of collateral, and these types of loans are called *mortgages*. Inventory and other assets also serve as collateral on some business loans. Debt instruments such as bonds may have very restrictive covenants (conditions), or may be quite liberal and nonbinding on the business. Some debt is convertible into equity stock shares, though generally this feature is limited to publicly held corporations whose stock shares are actively traded. The debt of a business may be a private loan, or debt securities may be issued to the public at large and be actively traded on a bond market.

Lenders look over the shoulders of the managers of the business. Lenders do not simply say "Here's the money and call us if you need more." A business does not exactly have to bare its soul when applying for a loan, but the lender usually demands a lot of information from the business. If a business defaults on a loan, such as not making an interest payment on time or not being able to pay off the loan at maturity, the terms of the loan give the lender legally enforceable options that in the extreme could force the business into bankruptcy. If a business does not comply fully with the terms and provisions of its loans, it is more or less at the mercy of its lenders, which could cause serious disruptions or even force the business to terminate its operations.

Basic Characteristics of Equity

One person may operate a business as the sole proprietor and provide all the equity capital of the business. A *sole proprietorship* business is not a separate legal entity; it's an extension of the individual. Many businesses are legally organized as a *partnership* of two or more persons. A partnership is a separate entity or person in the eyes of the law. The general partners of the business can be held responsible for the liabilities of the partnership. Creditors can reach beyond the assets of the partnership to the personal assets of the individual partners to satisfy their claims against the business. The general partners have *unlimited liability* for the liabilities of the partnership. Some partnerships have two classes of partners—general and limited. Limited partners escape the unlimited liability of general partners but they have no voice in the management of the business.

Most businesses, even relatively small ones, favor the corporate form of organization. A corporation is a legal entity separate from its individual owners. A corporation is a legal entity that shields the personal assets of the owners (the stockholders or shareowners) from the creditors of the business. A business may deliberately defraud its creditors and attempt to abuse the limited liability of corporate shareowners. In this case the law will pierce the corporate veil and hold the guilty individuals responsible for the debts of the business.

The corporate form is a practical way to collect a pool of equity capital from a large number of investors. There are literally millions of corporations in the U.S. economy. In 1997 the Internal Revenue Service received more than 4.7 million tax returns from business corporations. Most were small businesses. More than 860,000 business corporations had annual sales revenue of more than $1.0 million, however.

Other countries around the globe have the equivalent of corporations, although the names of these organizations as well as their legal and political features differ from country to country. A recent development in the United States is the creation of a new type of business legal entity called a *limited liability company* (LLC). This innovative business entity is a hybrid between a partnership and a corporation; it has characteristics of both. Most states have passed laws enabling the creation of LLCs.

Corporations issue capital stock shares; these are the units of equity ownership in the business. A corporation may issue only one class of stock shares, called *common stock* or **capital stock**. Or a corporation may issue both *preferred stock* and common stock shares. Preferred stock shareholders are promised a certain amount of annual cash dividend per share. (The actual payment of the dividend is contingent on the corporation's earning enough net income and having enough cash on hand to pay the dividend.) A corporation may issue both voting and nonvoting classes of stock shares. Some corporations issue two classes of voting shares that have different voting power per share, for example, one class has 10 votes per share and the other only 1 vote per share.

Debt bears an explicit and legally contracted rate of interest. Equity capital does not. Nevertheless, equity capital has an imputed or implicit cost. Management must earn a satisfactory rate of earnings on the equity capital of the business to justify the use of this capital. Failure to do so reduces the value of the equity and makes it more difficult to attract additional equity capital (if and when needed). In extreme circumstances the majority of stockholders could vote to dissolve the corporation and force the business to liquidate its assets, pay off its liabilities, and distribute the remainder to the stockholders.

The equity shareholders in a business (the stockholders of a corporation) take the risk of business failure and poor performance. On the optimistic side, the shareowners have no limit on their participation in the success of the business. Continued growth can lead to continued growth in cash dividends. And the market value of the equity shares has no theoretical upper limit. The lower limit of market value is zero (the shares become worthless)—although corporate stock shares could be *assessable*, which means the corporation has the right to assess shareholders and make them contribute additional capital into the organization. Almost all corporate stock shares are issued as nonassessable shares, although equity investors in a business can't be too careful about this.

Return on Investment

I was a stockholder in a privately owned business a few years ago. I owned 1,000 shares of common stock in the business and served on its board of directors. One thing really hit home. I came to appreciate first hand that we (the stockholders) had a lot of money invested, and we expected the business to do well with our money. We could have invested our money elsewhere and received interest income or earned some other type of return on our alternative investment. Management was very much aware that their responsibility was to improve the value of our stock shares over time, which requires that the business earn a good return on our investment in the business.

The basic measure for evaluating the performance of capital investments is the **return on investment (ROI)** ratio, which always is expressed as a percent. To calculate ROI the amount of return is divided by the amount of capital invested:

Return ÷ Capital Invested = ROI%

ROI is always for a period of time, one year unless clearly stated otherwise. *Return* is a generic term and means different things for different investments. For investments in marketable securities return includes cash income received during the period and the increase or decrease in market value during the period. The ROI on an investment in marketable securities is negative if the decrease in market value is more than the cash income received during the period.

Market value is not a factor for some investments. One example is an investment in a certificate of deposit (CD) issued by a financial institution. Return equals just the interest earned. A CD is not traded in a public market place and has no market value. The value of a CD is the amount the financial institution will redeem this instrument for at the maturity date, which is the face value on which interest is based. In the event that the financial institution doesn't redeem the CD at full value at maturity, the investor suffers a loss that could wipe out part or all of the interest earned on the CD. (It should be noted that CDs issued by most financial institutions—banks, credit unions, and savings and loan associations for the most part—are guaranteed to a maximum limit of $100,000 by an agency of the federal government, which provides a base amount of protection.)

Real estate investments may or may not include market value appreciation in accounting for annual earnings, depending on whether market prices of the real estate properties can be reliably estimated or appraised at the end of each period. If market value changes are not booked, the return on a real estate investment venture is not known until the conclusion of the investment project.

Evaluating the investment performance of a business uses three different measures: (1) *Return on Assets (ROA)*; (2) *Interest Rate*; and (3) **Return on Equity (ROE)**. Figure 4.2 illustrates the calculations of these three key rates of return for the business introduced above. The example assumes that the business has $4.0 million debt capital and $6.0 million equity capital. (Different mixes of debt and equity capital are examined later.) The definitions for each rate of return follow:

FIGURE 4.2 Rates of Return on Assets, Debt, and Equity

Earnings before interest and income tax (EBIT)	$1,800,000	÷	Assets less operating liabilities	$10,000,000	=	Return on 18.0% assets (ROA)
Interest expense	($300,000)	÷	Debt	$4,000,000	=	7.5% Interest rate
Income tax expense @ 40% of taxable income	($600,000)		Government			
Net income	$900,000	÷	Owners' equity	$6,000,000	=	Return on 15.0% equity (ROE)

- **ROA** = (Earnings before interest and income tax expenses, or EBIT) ÷ (Assets less operating liabilities)
- **Interest rate** = (Interest expense) ÷ (Interest bearing debt)
- **ROE** = (Net income) ÷ (Owners' equity)

Figure 4.2 is a *capital structure model* that can be used to analyze alternative scenarios, such as a different debt to equity ratio, or a higher or lower ROA performance, and a different interest rate. Figure 4.2 is the printout of a relatively simple personal computer worksheet. Different numbers can be easily plugged into the appropriate cell for one or more of the variables in the model, in order to see how net income and the ROE would be affected. Alternative scenarios are examined later in the chapter using the capital structure model.

Sales revenue less all operating expenses equals earnings before interest and income tax, or EBIT for short. As shown in Figure 4.2 EBIT is divided three ways: (1) *interest* on debt capital; (2) *income tax* keeping in mind that interest is deductible to determine taxable income; and (3) residual *net income*. In other words, the debt holders get a chunk of EBIT (interest), the federal and state governments get their chunks (income tax), and what's left over is profit for the shareowners of the business (net income). Note that the ROA rate and the interest rate are before income tax, whereas ROE is after income tax. The income tax factor is in the middle of things in more ways than one.

Pivotal Role of Income Tax

In a world without income taxes EBIT would be divided between the two capital sources—interest on debt and net income for the equity owners (the stockholders of a corporation). But in the real world income tax takes a big bite out of earnings after interest. In the example the combined federal and state income tax rate is set at 40 percent of taxable income. As you probably know, interest expense is deducted from EBIT to determine taxable income: ($1,800,000 EBIT − $300,000 interest) = $1,500,000 taxable income; and ($1,500,000 taxable income × 40 percent combined federal and state income tax rate = $600,000 income tax).

The following question might be asked: Should income tax be considered a return on government capital investment? The federal and state governments do not directly invest capital in a business, of course. In a broader sense, however, government provides what can be called public capital. Government provides public use facilities (highways, parks, schools, etc.), political stability, the monetary system, the legal system, and police protection. In short government provides the necessary infrastructure for carrying on business activity, and government collects for this through income tax (as well as from other taxes).

Technical Notes on Income Tax

The company example uses a 40 percent combined federal and state income tax rate, which is realistic. However, the taxation of business income varies considerably from state to state. Also under the current federal income tax law, corporate taxable income starting at $335,000 up to $10,000,000 is taxed at a 34 percent rate. Annual taxable incomes below $335,000 are taxed at lower rates, and above $10,000,000 at a slightly higher rate. In the example the assumption is that the business is a corporation and is taxed as a domestic C or regular corporation.

A corporation with 75 or fewer stockholders may elect to be treated as an S corporation. An S corporation pays no income tax itself; its annual taxable income is passed through to its individual stockholders in proportion to their share ownership. Business sole proprietorships, partnerships, and limited liability companies are also tax conduits; they are not subject to income tax as a separate entity but pass their taxable income through to their owner or owners who have to include their shares of the entity's taxable income in their personal income tax returns. Individual situations vary widely as you know.

Corporations may have net loss carry-forwards that reduce or eliminate taxable income in one year. There is also the alternative minimum tax (AMT) to consider, saying nothing of a myriad of other provisions and options (loopholes) in the tax law. It's very difficult to generalize. The main point is that in a given year in a given situation the taxable income of the business may not result in a normal amount of income tax.

Under the federal income tax law (U.S. Internal Revenue Code) interest on debt is deductible to determine annual taxable income. Cash dividends paid to stockholders—which can be viewed as the equity equivalent of interest on debt—are *not* deductible to determine taxable income. This basic differentiation in the tax law has significant impact on the amount of EBIT needed to earn a satisfactory ROE on the equity capital of a business.

The business in the example needs to earn just $300,000 EBIT for its $300,000 interest. The $300,000 EBIT minus $300,000 interest leaves zero taxable income and thus no income tax. In contrast, to earn $900,000 *after-tax* net income on equity, the business needs $1,500,000 EBIT: [$900,000 net income ÷ (1 – 40% income tax rate)], or ($900,000 ÷ .6), which equals $1,500,000 EBIT. Income tax takes $600,000 of the $1,500,000 EBIT, leaving $900,000 net income after income tax.

Suppose, for the moment, that interest were not deductible to determine taxable income. In this imaginary income tax world the business would need $500,000 EBIT to cover its $300,000 interest. Income tax at the 40 percent rate would be $200,000 on this $500,000 EBIT leaving $300,000 after tax to pay interest. The business would need $500,000 EBIT for interest and $1,500,000 EBIT for net income, for a total of $2,000,000 EBIT. The business would have had to earn a 20.0 percent ROA rate in this situation. But since interest is deductible the business needed to earn only 18.0 percent ROA to pay interest and to generate 15.0 percent ROE for its shareowners.

Return on Equity (ROE)

In the example the business is organized as a corporation. The company's shareowners invested money in the business for which they received shares of capital stock issued by the business. Keep in mind that the stockholders could have invested this money elsewhere. The business over the years retained a good amount of its annual net income instead of distributing all its annual net income as cash dividends to its stockholders. The total owners' equity capital of the business from both sources is $6.0 million. This amount includes the paid-in capital invested in the business by its stockholders and the cumulative amount of retained earnings.

Stockholders' equity capital is at risk; the business may or may not be able to earn an adequate net income for its stockholders every year. For that matter the company could go belly up and go into bankruptcy. In bankruptcy proceedings stockholders are paid last, after all debts and liabilities are settled. There's no promise that cash dividends will be paid to stockholders even if the business earns net income. Net income was $1.6 million for its most recent year and only $400,000 was distributed as cash dividends. (The statement of cash flows reports the total amount of cash dividends to stockholders during the year). Cash dividends are used to calculate the **dividend yield ratio**, which is discussed in Chapter 5. The ROE ratio does not consider what portion (if any) of the business's annual net income was distributed as cash dividends. The entire net income figure is used to compute the ROE rate for the year.

In the example (see Figure 4.2) the company's ROE was 15.0 percent for the year, which is not terrific but not too bad. This comment raises a larger question regarding which yardstick is most relevant. Theoretically, the $6.0 million owners' equity in the business could be pulled out and invested somewhere else to earn a return on the best alternative investment. Should the company's ROE be compared with the rate of return that could be earned on a riskless and highly liquid investment, such as short-term U.S. Government securities? Surely not. Everyone agrees that a company's ROE should be compared with *comparable* investment alternatives that have the same risk and liquidity characteristics as stockholders' equity.

The rate of return on the most relevant alternative, or the next best investment alternative is called the *opportunity cost of capital*. To avoid a prolonged discussion, simply assume that the stockholders want the business to improve on its 15.0 percent ROE performance. This implies that their opportunity cost of capital is higher than 15.0 percent at least in the minds of the stockholders. Of course the company should maintain its ROE and do even better if possible. One reason why its ROE is as good as it is is that the company had a nice gain from financial leverage.

Financial Leverage

As it was mentioned at the start of the chapter, piling debt on top of equity capital is called financial leverage. Using debt capital in addition to equity capital leverages the equity capital base of a business. For this reason using debt is also called *trading on the equity*. The main advantage of debt is that a business has more capital to work with and is not limited to the amount of equity capital that a business can muster. The larger capital base can be used to crank out more sales, which should yield more profit. Of course, this assumes that the business can actually make profit from using its capital.

Using debt also has another important potential advantage. If a business borrows money at an interest rate that is lower than its

ROA rate, it makes a financial leverage gain. The idea is to borrow at a relatively low rate and earn at a relatively high rate and keep the difference. In Figure 4.2 note that the company earns 18.0 percent ROA but paid only 7.5 percent interest rate on its borrowed capital. (The business has several loans and pays different interest rates on each loan; the 7.5 percent is its composite average interest rate.) You don't have to be a rocket scientist to figure out that paying 7.5 percent on money you can earn 18.0 percent on is a good deal.

In the example debt provides 40 percent of the capital invested in assets ($4.0 million of the total $10.0 million). Thus, 40 percent of the company's EBIT is attributable to its debt capital: ($1.8 million EBIT × 40%) = $720,000. But the business paid only $300,000 interest expense for the use of the debt capital. Therefore, its gain is the excess, or $420,000: ($720,000 debt's share of EBIT − $300,000 interest = $420,000 financial leverage gain). Another way to compute the gain from financial leverage is to multiply the 10.5 percent *spread* between the 18.0 percent ROA earned by the business and its 7.5 percent interest rate times the amount of its debt: (10.5% spread × $4.0 million debt = $420,000 financial leverage gain before income tax).

A financial leverage gain adds to the share of EBIT attributable to equity capital. Figure 4.3 illustrates how important the financial leverage gain is in the company's profit performance for the year. Using debt provides additional earnings for the equity investors in the business. The shareowners earn EBIT on their capital in the business and also get the overflow of EBIT on debt capital after paying interest. In the example financial leverage gain contributes a good share of the earnings for shareowners as shown in Figure 4.3. The financial leverage gain adds 39 percent on top of EBIT earned on equity capital: ($420,000 financial leverage gain ÷ $1,080,000 EBIT on equity capital = 39%).

In analyzing profit performance, managers should separate two components of earnings before income tax: (1) the financial leverage gain; and (2) the EBIT earned on owners' equity capital. As shown in Figure 4.3 the company's $1,500,000 earnings before income tax consists of $420,000 financial leverage gain plus the $1,080,000 pretax EBIT on equity capital. Therefore, a good part of the company's pretax profit is sensitive to the interest rate on its debt (and the ratio of debt to equity, which is examined later). If its interest rate had been 18.0 percent (an unreasonably high interest rate these days) the financial leverage gain would have been zero.

The business, by using a moderate amount of debt capital, enhanced the earnings for its owners. Professor Ron Melicher, my long-time colleague at the University of Colorado, calls this the

FIGURE 4.3 Components of Earnings for Equity

$1,800,000 EBIT	X	40%	Debt percent of total capital =	$720,000	Debt share of EBIT
				($300,000)	Interest
				$420,000	Financial leverage gain
$1,800,000 EBIT	X	60%	Equity percent of total capital =	$1,080,000	Equity share of EBIT
				$1,500,000	Earnings for equity before income tax

earnings multiplier effect. I very much like this term to describe the effects of financial leverage. The financial leverage multiplier effect cuts both ways however. A percentage drop in the company's ROA causes earnings for equity to drop by a larger percentage. Figure 4.4 presents a range of ROA rates for the business and the financial leverage gain and loss for each ROA scenario.

Figure 4.4 illustrates that interest is a *fixed* financial expense (for a given amount of debt of course, and assuming constant interest rates). As explained earlier, interest is a contractual obligation and is payable regardless of the ROA performance of a business. The fixed nature of interest is another reason that the term leverage is used. Chapter 1 explains the leverage effect of fixed operating expenses on the profit performance of a business. Figure 4.4 demonstrates the leverage impact of the fixed interest expense of the business.

For instance, look at the percent improvement in earnings before income tax from the 5.0 percent to the 7.5 percent ROA level, which is a step-up of 50 percent in the ROA rate. The earnings amount increases 125 percent from $200,000 to $450,000. The percent increase in earnings is larger than the percent increase in ROA—although the earnings increase percent diminishes as ROA moves higher and higher. Managers are very concerned about the percent improvement in earnings, of course. So managers should understand the multiplier effect of financial leverage gain on earnings for equity shareowners.

FIGURE 4.4 Financial Leverage Effects for Different ROA Rates

Return on Assets (ROA) Rate	EBIT on Debt Capital @ ROA Rate	Interest on Debt @ 7.5%	Financial Leverage Gain (Loss)	EBIT on Equity Capital @ ROA Rate	Earnings before Income Tax	Percent Change
0.0%	$0	($300,000)	($300,000)	$0	($300,000)	
2.5%	$100,000	($300,000)	($200,000)	$150,000	($50,000)	–83%
5.0%	$200,000	($300,000)	($100,000)	$300,000	$200,000	n/a
7.5%	$300,000	($300,000)	$0	$450,000	$450,000	125%
10.0%	$400,000	($300,000)	$100,000	$600,000	$700,000	56%
12.5%	$500,000	($300,000)	$200,000	$750,000	$950,000	36%
15.0%	$600,000	($300,000)	$300,000	$900,000	$1,200,000	26%
17.5%	$700,000	($300,000)	$400,000	$1,050,000	$1,450,000	21%
20.0%	$800,000	($300,000)	$500,000	$1,200,000	$1,700,000	17%
22.5%	$900,000	($300,000)	$600,000	$1,350,000	$1,950,000	15%

Why not borrow to the hilt in order to maximize financial leverage gain? Well, for one thing the amount of debt that can be borrowed is limited. Lenders will lend only so much money to a business, relative to its assets and its sales revenue and profit history. Once a business hits its borrowing capacity, more debt is not available, or interest rates and other lending terms become prohibitive. Furthermore, there are several disadvantages of debt.

The deeper lenders are into the business, the more restrictions lenders impose on the business, such as limiting cash dividends to shareowners and insisting that the business maintain minimum cash balances. Lenders may demand more collateral for their loans as the debt load of a business increases. Also there is the threat that the lender may not renew the loans to the business. Some businesses end up too top heavy with debt and can't make their interest payments on time or can't pay their loans at maturity and the lender is not willing to renew the loan. These businesses may be forced into bankruptcy in an attempt to work out their debt problems.

In short, using debt capital has many risks. Interest rates change over time and the ROA rate earned by a business could plunge, even below its interest rate. Even relatively small changes in the ROA and interest rates can have a substantial impact on earnings. It's no surprise that many businesses are quite debt averse and decide on low levels of debt even though they could carry more debt. The company in the example uses a fair amount of debt; using more or less debt would have caused more or less financial leverage gain. These alternative scenarios are examined next.

Exploring Alternative Capital Structure Scenarios

The business example examined in the chapter to this point is not the only possible scenario, of course. To conclude the chapter three alternative scenarios are presented which are basic variations on the moderate debt example.

No Debt and All Equity

Suppose that the company in the example had used no interest-bearing debt—none at all. This presumes that the stockholders could have and would have supplied $4.0 million additional capital, or that the business could have accumulated this much additional retained earnings over the years. This may not have been possible, of course. In any case all the capital needed for its assets come from owners' equity in this scenario. Figure 4.5 shows the outcomes for this no debt/all equity alternative state of affairs.

The company's total capital invested in assets and its ROA rate are kept the same, so the company's EBIT is the same—$1.8 million. With no interest to pay, the company's taxable income equals its EBIT. At the 40 percent rate its income tax would be $720,000. So net income would be $1,080,000, which is higher than the company's $900,000 net income in the original example (see Figure 4.2). However, owners' equity would have been $4.0 million higher. So ROE would be considerably worse in this scenario—only 10.8 percent (see Figure 4.5)—instead of the respectable though not spectacular 15.0 percent ROE in the original example. By using no debt the business would pass up the opportunity to earn $420,000 financial leverage before tax for its owners.

Heavy Debt and Light Equity

The opposite scenario to the no debt case is one in which a business loads up on debt, convinced of its ability to earn a ROA higher than

FIGURE 4.5 No Debt and All Equity Capital

Earnings before interest and income tax (EBIT)	$1,800,000	÷	Assets less operating liabilities	$10,000,000	=	18.0%	Return on assets (ROA)
Interest expense	$0	÷	Debt	$0	=	n/a	Interest rate
Income tax expense @ 40% of taxable income	($720,000)		Government				
Net income	$1,080,000	÷	Owners' equity	$10,000,000	=	10.8%	Return on equity (ROE)

the interest rate on its debt. In this scenario a business takes advantage of financial leverage to the fullest extent possible. How large a percent of the total capital invested in assets are lenders willing to go? This is not easy to answer in general. Figure 4.6 shows a scenario in which 80 percent of the total capital is supplied from debt. For the vast majority of businesses 80 percent debt would be the maximum limit they could borrow, and perhaps too high as a matter of fact. For this example the interest rate is held at 7.5 percent for comparison with the other scenarios, but in actual practice such a heavy debt load would surely drive up the interest rate lenders would demand.

In this heavy debt scenario ROE would balloon to 36.0 percent, which needless to say is quite an improvement over the 15.0 percent ROE in the original example (see Figure 4.2). Financial leverage gain contributes a much larger share of the earnings before tax for equity, as shown in Figure 4.7. In fact the $840,000 financial leverage gain is more than twice the EBIT on equity capital. Note also that the after-tax 36.0 percent ROE rate is double the company's pretax 18.0 percent ROA rate in this heavy debt scenario, which shows the impact that highly leveraged capital structures can produce.

Solving for Debt to Equity Ratio

In the original example the business earns 15.0 percent ROE, which is not spectacular but acceptable for many businesses. Now suppose the business forecasts that its ROA for the coming year will drop to 12.0 percent. Remember that ROA is a before-tax rate and that ROE is an after-tax rate. The business could attempt to shift its mix of debt and equity capital in order to maintain its 15.0 percent ROE. The capital structure model is used to solve for the amounts of debt and equity to make ROE come out 15.0 percent. I kept increasing the

FIGURE 4.6 Heavy Debt and Light Equity

Earnings before interest and income tax (EBIT)	$1,800,000	÷	Assets less operating liabilities	$10,000,000	=	18.0%	Return on assets (ROA)
Interest expense	($600,000)	÷	Debt	$8,000,000	=	7.5%	Interest rate
Income tax expense @ 40% of taxable income	($480,000)		Government				
Net income	$720,000	÷	Owners' equity	$2,000,000	=	36.0%	Return on equity (ROE)

FIGURE 4.7 Financial Leverage Gain for Heavy Debt Scenario

$1,800,000 EBIT X 80% Debt percent of total capital = $1,440,000 Debt share of EBIT

($600,000) Interest

$840,000 Financial leverage gain

$1,800,000 EBIT X 20% Equity percent of total capital = $360,000 Equity share of EBIT

$1,200,000 Earnings for equity before income tax

amount of debt (and decreasing the amount of equity capital the same amount) in the worksheet until ROE is exactly 15.0 percent.

Figure 4.8 shows that the business would have to increase its debt to $7,440,000 and reduce its equity capital to $2,560,00 in order to achieve its 15.0 percent ROE for the coming year. Such a major shift from equity to debt probably would be difficult, if not impossible in the short run. Also, taking on more debt would drive up the interest rate demanded by lenders. Furthermore, it may be a very risky policy to follow. A heavy debt load during business downturns can be a heavy albatross around the neck of the business. If the business

FIGURE 4.8 Solving for the Debt and Equity Mix

Earnings before interest and income tax (EBIT)	$1,200,000	÷	Assets less operating liabilities	$10,000,000	= 12.0% Return on assets (ROA)
Interest expense	($558,000)	÷	Debt	$7,440,000	= 7.5% Interest rate
Income tax expense @ 40% of taxable income	($256,800)		Government		
Net income	$385,200	÷	Owners' equity	$2,560,000	= 15.0% Return on equity (ROE)

misses making an interest payment on its debt or otherwise goes into default on any of the covenants of its debt contract, the lender may end up calling the shots. In any case the capital structure model can be used to explore how much of a shift in the debt and equity mix would be necessary to achieve a certain ROE goal.

Summary

Every business must decide on a blend of debt and equity capital to invest in the assets it needs to make profit. The total capital invested in assets should be no more than necessary. Interest has to be paid on debt capital, and the business should earn at least a satisfactory return on equity capital in order to survive and thrive. The starting point is to earn an adequate return on assets (ROA), that is, an adequate amount of earnings before interest and income tax (EBIT) relative to the total capital invested in assets. Operating liabilities (mainly accounts payable and accrued expenses payable) are deducted from total assets to determine the amount of capital invested in assets.

Using debt enlarges the total capital base of a business and with more capital a business can make more sales and generate more profit. Also using debt for part of the total capital invested in assets offers the opportunity to benefit from financial leverage, as well as the risk of suffering a financial leverage loss if the business does not earn a ROA rate greater than the interest rate on its debt. Managers should measure the financial leverage gain or loss component of earnings for shareowners. The financial leverage gain or loss component of earnings is sensitive to changes in the interest rate and the debt level of the business, as well as the ROA rate earned by the business.

CHAPTER 5

Interpreting Financial Statements

The first four chapters of this book focus on the financial information needed by business managers and the most useful ways of arranging this information for management analysis. Chapter 1 introduces and demonstrates the fundamental model that is extraordinarily important for understanding and analyzing profit behavior. Chapter 2 presents a specially designed format for reporting cash flow from profit to managers so that they do not have to trudge through the statement of cash flows, which is strewn with irrelevant details. Chapter 3 identifies the assets needed in making profit and the operating liabilities generated by the profit-making activities of a business. Chapter 4 analyzes debt and equity sources that provide the capital a business invests in its assets. The chapter presents a capital structure model and explains the analysis of financial leverage gain or loss.

The first quartet of chapters talks directly to business managers. The financial statements prepared by a business are designed to talk to its outside investors and lenders. Therefore, financial statements are put on the back burner in these chapters. I don't mean that financial statements are totally ignored in the chapters. Each of the three primary financial statements of a business is introduced in the chapters—although the statements are discussed only briefly. In contrast, this chapter brings financial statements to the forefront and explains how investors and lenders interpret the financial statements of a business.

Welcome to the Real World of Financial Statements

Financial statements are the main and often the only source of information to the lenders and the outside investors in a business regarding its profit performance and financial condition. In addition to reading through the financial statements they use certain *ratios* calculated from the figures in the financial statements to evaluate the profit performance and the financial position of the business. These key ratios are important to managers as well. However, financial statement ratios do not take the place of the financial models and analysis techniques explained in the first four chapters.

A separate financial statement is prepared for each of the three primary financial imperatives of every business:

1. Make *profit*—reported in the *income statement*.
2. Generate *cash flows*—reported in the *statement of cash flows*.
3. Control the *financial condition* of the business—reported in the *statement of financial condition*, or *balance sheet*.

First Some Observations and Cautions

This chapter focuses on the financial statements included in *external* financial reports to investors. These circulate outside the business; once released by a business, its financial statements can end up in the hands of almost anyone, even its competitors. The amounts reported in external financial statements are at a *summary level*; the detailed information used by managers is not disclosed in external financial statements. External financial statements disclose a good deal of information to its investors and lenders that they need to know, but no more. There are definite limits on what information is divulged in external financial statements. For instance a business does not present a list of its major customers or stockholders in its external financial statements.

External financial statements are *general purpose* in nature and *comprehensive* of the entire business. The amounts reported for some assets—in particular inventories and fixed assets—may be fairly old costs, going back several years. Assets are not marked up to current market values. The current replacement values of assets are not reported in external financial statements.

Profit accounting depends on many good-faith *estimates*. A business has to

- Predict the useful lives of its fixed assets for recording annual depreciation expense.
- Estimate how much of its accounts receivable may not be collectible, which is charged off to bad debts expense.
- Estimate how much to write down its inventories and charge to expense for products that cannot be sold or will have to be sold at prices below cost.

For products already sold, a business has to

- Forecast the future costs of warranty and guarantee work, which is charged to expense in the period of recording the sales.

Finally, a business has to

- Predict several key variables that determine the cost of its employees' retirement plan. The amount of retirement benefit cost that is recorded to expense in the current year depends heavily on these estimates.

In short the net income amount in an income statement should be taken with a grain of salt. This bottom-line profit number could have been considerably higher or lower. Much depends on the estimates made by the business in recording its sales and expenses—as well as which particular accounting methods are selected (see Chapter 13).

I don't like to say it, but in many cases the managers of a business manipulate its external financial statements to one degree or another. Managers influence or actually dictate which estimates are used in recording expenses (just mentioned). Managers also decide on the timing of recording sales revenue and certain expenses. Managers massage sales revenue and expenses numbers in order to achieve preestablished targets for net income and to smooth the year-to-year fluctuations of net income. It is common practice to touch up the financial statements, which Chapter 14 explores. Managers should be careful, however. It's one thing to iron out the wrinkles and fluff up the pillows in the financial statements. Yet if managers go too far they can cross the line and commit financial fraud, for which they are legally liable.

Financial statements of public corporations are required to have annual audits by an independent CPA firm; many private companies opt to have annual CPA audits. However, CPA auditors don't necessarily catch all errors and fraud. With or without audits there's a risk that the financial statements are in error, or that the business has deliberately prepared false and misleading financial statements. During the past decade an alarming number of public corporations had to go back and restate their profit reports based on the later discovery of fraud and grossly misleading accounting. This is most disturbing. Investors and lenders depend on the reliability of the information in financial statements. They do not have an alternative source of this information—only the financial statements.

Premises and Principles of Financial Statements

The shareowners of a business are entitled to receive on a regular basis financial statements and other financial information about the business. Financial statements are the main means of communication by which the management of a business renders an accounting, or a summing-up of their stewardship of the business entrusted to them by the investors in the business. The quarterly and annual financial reports of a business to its owners contain other information. However, the main purpose of a financial report is to submit financial statements to shareowners.

Generally accepted accounting principles (GAAP) and financial reporting standards have been extensively developed over the past half-century. These guidelines rest on one key premise—the separation of the management of a business from the outside investors in the business. In the formulation of GAAP it is assumed that financial statements are for those who have supplied the ownership capital to a business but who are not directly involved in managing the business. Financial statements are prepared for the absentee owners of a business, in other words. Generally accepted accounting principles and financial reporting standards do not ignore the need for information by the lenders to a business. But the shareowners of the business are the main constituency for whom financial statements are prepared.

Federal law governs the communication of financial information by businesses whose capital stock shares are traded on public markets. The federal securities laws are enforced mainly by the **Securities and Exchange Commission (SEC)**, which was established in 1934. Also the New York Stock Exchange, Nasdaq, and other securities markets enforce many rules and regulations regarding the release and communication of financial information by companies whose securities are traded on their markets. For instance, a business cannot selectively leak information to some stockholders or lenders and not to others, nor can a business tip off some of them before informing the others later. The laws and requirements of financial reporting are designed to ensure that all stockholders and lenders have equal access to a company's financial information and financial statements.

A business's financial statements may not be the first news about its profit performance. Public corporations put out press releases concerning their earnings for the period just ended before the company releases its actual financial statements. Privately owned businesses do not usually send letters to their owners about profit performance in advance of releasing their financial statements—although a privately owned business could do this.

Financial Statements Example

The financial statements for the business example in earlier chapters are presented as follows:

- Figure 5.1—Income Statement for Year Ended December 31, 2002
- Figure 5.2—Statements of Financial Condition for Years Ended December 31, 2002 and 2001

FIGURE 5.1 Income Statement for Year Ended December 31, 2002

Sales Revenue	$39,661,250
Cost of Goods Sold Expense	$24,960,750
Gross Margin	$14,700,500
Selling & Administrative Expenses	$11,466,135
Earnings before Interest and Income Tax	$3,234,365
Interest Expense	$795,000
Earnings before Income Tax	$2,439,365
Income Tax Expense	$853,778
Net Income	$1,585,587
Earnings Per Share*	$3.75

*Privately owned business corporations do not have to report earnings per share; publicly owned corporations are required to disclose this key ratio in their income statements.

FIGURE 5.2 Statements of Financial Condition for Years Ended December 31, 2002 and 2001

	2002	2001
Assets		
Cash	$2,345,675	$2,098,538
Accounts Receivable	$3,813,582	$3,467,332
Inventories	$5,760,173	$4,661,423
Prepaid Expenses	$822,899	$770,024
Total Current Assets	$12,742,329	$10,997,317
Property, Plant, & Equipment	$20,857,500	$18,804,030
Accumulated Depreciation	($6,785,250)	($6,884,100)
Cost Less Accumulated Depreciation	$14,072,250	$11,919,930
Total Assets	$26,814,579	$22,917,247
Liabilities & Owners' Equity		
Accounts Payable	$2,537,232	$2,180,682
Accrued Expenses Payable	$1,280,214	$1,136,369
Income Tax Payable	$76,500	$35,150
Short-term Debt	$2,250,000	$1,765,000
Total Current Liabilities	$6,143,946	$5,217,201
Long-term Debt	$7,500,000	$5,850,000
Total Liabilities	$13,643,946	$11,067,201
Capital Stock (422,823 and 420,208 shares)	$4,587,500	$4,402,500
Retained Earnings	$8,583,133	$7,447,546
Total Owners' Equity	$13,170,633	$11,850,046
Total Liabilities and Owners' Equity	$26,814,579	$22,917,247

- Figure 5.3—Statement of Cash Flows for Year Ended December 31, 2002
- Figure 5.4—Statement of Changes in Stockholders' Equity for Year Ended December 31, 2002

The income statement ranks first in terms of readability and intuitive understandability. Most people understand that profit equals revenue less expenses, although the technical jargon in income statements is a barrier to many readers. The balance sheet (or statement of financial condition) ranks second. Assets and liabilities are

FIGURE 5.3 Statement of Cash Flows for Year Ended December 31, 2002

Cash Flows from Operating Activities

Net Income	$1,585,587
Changes in Operating Assets and Liabilities	
Accounts Receivable	($346,250)
Inventories	($1,098,750)
Prepaid Expenses	($52,875)
Depreciation Expense	$768,450
Accounts Payable	$356,550
Accrued Expenses Payable	$143,845
Income Tax Payable	($58,650)
Cash Flow from Operating Activities	$1,297,907

Cash Flows from Investing Activities

Investment in Property, Plant, & Equipment	($3,186,250)
Proceeds from Disposals of Property, Plant, & Equipment	$265,480
Cash Used in Investing Activities	($2,920,770)

Cash Flows from Financing Activities

Net Increase in Short-term Debt	$485,000
Increase in Long-term Debt	$1,650,000
Issuance of Capital Stock Shares	$185,000
Cash Dividends to Stockholders	($450,000)
Cash from Financing Activities	$1,870,000
Cash Increase during Year	$247,137
Cash Balance at Beginning of Year	$2,098,538
Cash Balance at End of Year	$2,345,675

FIGURE 5.4 Statement of Changes in Stockholders' Equity for Year Ended December 31, 2002

	Capital Stock	Retained Earnings
Beginning Balances (420,208 shares)	$4,402,500	$7,447,546
Net Income for Year		$1,585,587
Shares Issued During Year (2,615 shares)	$ 185,000	
Dividends Paid During Year		($450,000)
Ending Balances (422,823 shares)	$4,587,500	$8,583,133

familiar to most people—although the values reported in this financial statement are not immediately obvious to many readers.
The statement of cash flows is presented in a very technical format that makes the statement very difficult to read, even for sophisticated investors.

The footnotes that accompany the company's financial statements
are not presented. Footnotes often run several pages. Footnotes, although difficult and time consuming to read through, contain very
important information. Stock analysts and investment managers
scour the footnotes in financial reports, digging for important information about the business. The footnotes are not needed for explaining financial statement ratios. (For a discussion of footnotes
see Chapter 16 in my book *How To Read a Financial Report*, 5th ed.
John Wiley & Sons 1999.)

Publicly owned businesses present their financial statements in a
comparative format for the most recent three years (as required by
SEC rules). The three-year comparative format makes it easier to
follow trends, of course. Many privately owned businesses present
their financial statements for two or three years although practice is
not uniform in this respect.

The company's income statement (Figure 5.1) and statement of
cash flows (Figure 5.3) are presented for the most recent year only.
The statement of financial condition (Figure 5.2) is presented at the
close of its two most recent two years. Financial statement ratios
are calculated for each year. The ratios are calculated the same way
for all years for which financial statements are presented. As a general rule only a few ratios are presented in most financial reports.
Thus, investors and lenders have to calculate ratios or look in financial information sources that report the financial statement ratios for
businesses.

The business in this example is a corporation that is owned by a
relatively small number of persons who invested the capital to start
the business some years ago. The business has more than $39 mil-
lion annual sales (see Figure 5.1). Many publicly owned business
corporations are much larger than this, and most privately owned
businesses are smaller. Size is not the point, however. The techniques of financial analysis and the ratios discussed in the chapter
are appropriate for any size business.

Limits of Chapter

The chapter does not pretend to cover the broad field of *securities
analysis*, that is, the analysis of stocks and debt securities issued by
public corporations that are traded in public market places. This

broad field includes the analysis of the competitive advantages and disadvantages of a business, domestic and international economic developments affecting a business, business combination possibilities, political developments, court decisions, technological advances, demographics, investor psychology, and much more. The key ratios explained in the chapter are the basic building blocks used in securities analysis.

The chapter does not discuss *trend analysis*, which involves comparing a company's latest financial statements with its previous years' statements to identify important year-to-year changes. For example, investors and lenders are very much interested in the sales growth or decline of a business, and the resulting impact on profit performance, cash flows, and financial condition. The chapter has a more modest objective—to explain the basic ratios used in financial statement analysis. Only a handful of ratios are discussed in the chapter but they are extremely important and widely used.

Before Doing Ratios

Upon opening a company's financial report, one of the first things most investors do is to give the financial statements a once-over; they quickly scan the financial statements. What do they look for? They look first at the bottom line in the income statement, to see if the business made a profit or suffered a loss for the year. As one sports celebrity put it when explaining how he keeps tabs on his various business investments, he looks first to see if the bottom line has "parentheses around it." Unfortunately, there may be not just one but two net incomes reported in an income statement—before and after extraordinary gains and losses recorded by the business during the year.

Extraordinary Gains and Losses—An Extraordinary Pain in the Neck

Thank goodness the business example does not report any **extraordinary gains or losses** for the year. Extraordinary means one-time, nonrecurring events. For example a business may

- Sell off or abandon a major segment of its operations and record a large loss or gain.
- Record a substantial loss caused by a major restructuring or downsizing of the organization to recognize the cost of terminating employees who will receive severance packages or early retirement bonuses.

- Lose a major lawsuit and have to pay a huge fine or damage award.
- Write off most of its inventories due to a sudden fall off in demand for its products.

The list goes on and on. These nonordinary, unusual gains and losses are reported separately from the ongoing, continuing operations of a company.

Extraordinary gains and losses are very frustrating in analyzing profit performance. Making matters worse is that many businesses record huge amounts of extraordinary losses in one fell swoop, in order to clear the decks of these costs and losses in future years. This is called taking a **big bath**. In public the investment community wrings their hands and lambastes this practice, which you read in many articles and editorials in the financial press. However, I think that investors would admit in private that they prefer that a business take a big bath in one year and thereby escape losses and expenses in future years. The thinking is that by taking a big bath a business starts over with a clean slate by putting all the bad news behind it, and thereby wipes the slate clean so that future years escape these charges.

Understanding Cash Flows

Cash flow gets a lot of ink in the financial press and in reports on stocks published by brokers and investment advisers. Cash flow from profit (operating activities) is considered a key figure for a business. Some journalists and financial commentators imply that cash flow is a superior measure of profit to the net income amount determined by generally accepted accounting principles. I think what they really mean is that you should not equate net income with cash flow from profit during the year—but they get carried away with their hyperbole about cash flow.

The business realized $1,297,907 cash flow from profit (operating activities) for the year just ended (see Figure 5.3). There are several key demands on this cash flow—capital expenditures and cash dividends in particular. The business spent $3,186,250 on capital expenditures during the year (see Figure 5.3). It received $265,480 proceeds from disposals of fixed assets it no longer needs. Its financing activities provided $1,870,00 during the year net of $450,000 cash dividends to stockholders. Taken together the three sources of cash—from profit, from disposals of old fixed assets, and from financing activities—were a little more than the company's capital expenditures during the year. So the company's cash balance increased $247,137 during the year.

Reading the cash flow statement in this manner provides a useful synopsis of where the business got its money during the year and what it did with the money. The statement of cash flows has been around for 15 years, yet investors and creditors have yet to develop any benchmark ratios for cash flows. You could divide cash flow from operating activities by net income to determine cash flow as a percent of net income: ($1,297,907 cash flow from operating activities ÷ $1,585,587 net income = 81.9%). A ratio below 100.0 percent reveals that the business's negative cash flow factors, such as increases in its accounts receivable and inventories during the year, were more than its positive cash flow factors such as depreciation. When a business is experiencing considerable growth year to year, it's not unusual to see its ratio of cash flow to net income fall below 100.0 percent. In nongrowth situations, however, the ratio should not normally be less than 100.0 percent. If it were, I certainly would take a hard look at which negative cash flow factors caused the dip in cash flow from profit.

Statement of Changes in Stockholders' Equity

Figure 5.4 introduces the Statement of Changes in Stockholders' Equity. This is a supporting schedule that summarizes changes in a business's capital stock and retained earnings accounts. From this statement you see that the business issued additional capital stock shares during the year. The business did not buy any of its stock shares during the year nor did it retire any shares during the year. So the balance in its capital stock account increased by the proceeds from issuance of the stock shares. Net income for the year increased retained earnings and cash dividends paid to stockholders decreased the account.

When a business has a complex capitalization structure that includes two or more classes of stock and when a business buys some of its own capital stock shares during the year, the statement of changes in stockholders' equity is much more extensive (and more complicated) than shown in Figure 5.4. Also, technical losses and gains from foreign currency translations and other very technical gains and losses are recorded directly in the retained earnings account and are not disclosed in the income statement. Investors have to read this statement to find out about these special gains and losses.

Profit Ratios

Owners take the risk of whether their business can earn a profit and sustain its profit performance over the years. How much would you be willing to pay for a business that reports a loss year after year? The value of the owners' investment depends first and foremost on the profit performance of the business. Making sales and controlling expenses is how a business makes profit, of course. The profit residual from sales revenue is measured by a **return on sales ratio**, which equals a particular measure of profit divided by sales revenue for the period. An income statement reports several profit lines, beginning with *gross margin* down to bottom-line *net income*.

Figure 5.5 shows four **profit ratios** for the business example; each ratio equals the profit on that line divided by sales revenue. These return on sales profit ratios are *not* required to be disclosed in the income statement. Generally speaking businesses do not report profit ratios with their income statements, although many companies comment on one or more of their profit ratios elsewhere in their financial reports.

The company's net income return on sales ratio is 4.0 percent: ($1,585,587 net income ÷ $39,661,250 sales revenue = 4.0%). From each $100.00 of its sales revenue the business earned $4.00 net income—and had expenses of $96.00. The net income profit ratio varies quite markedly from one industry to another. Some businesses do well with only a 1 percent or 2 percent return on sales; others need more than 10 percent to justify the large amount of capital invested in their assets.

A popular misconception of many people is that most businesses rip off the public because they keep 20, 30, or more percent of their sales revenue as bottom-line profit. In fact very few businesses earn more than a 10 percent bottom-line profit on sales. If you don't be-

FIGURE 5.5 Return on Sales Profit Ratios

Income Statement		Profit Ratios
Sales Revenue	$39,661,250	
Cost of Goods Sold Expense	$24,960,750	
Gross Margin	$14,700,500	37.1%
Selling & Administrative Expenses	$11,466,135	
Earnings before Interest and Income Tax	$3,234,365	8.2%
Interest Expense	$795,000	
Earnings before Income Tax	$2,439,365	6.2%
Income Tax Expense	$853,778	
Net Income	$1,585,587	4.0%

lieve me, scan a sample of 50 or 100 earnings reports in the *Wall Street Journal* or the *New York Times*. The 4.0 percent net income profit ratio in the example is not untypical, although 4.0 percent is a little low compared with most other businesses.

Serious investors watch all the profit ratios shown in Figure 5.5. The first ratio—the gross margin return on sales ratio—is the starting point for the other profit ratios. Gross margin (also called gross profit) equals sales revenue minus only cost of goods sold expense. The company's gross margin equals 37.1 percent of sales revenue (see Figure 5.5). If its gross margin ratio is too low, a business typically cannot compensate for all the deficiency in gross margin by cutting other operating expenses, so its bottom-line suffers. An inadequate gross margin cascades down to the bottom line, in other words. Therefore, investors keep a close watch for any slippage in a company's gross margin profit ratio.

Investors and stock analysts keep a close eye on year-to-year trends in profit ratios—to test whether a business is able to maintain its profit margins over time. Slippage in profit ratios is viewed with some alarm. A business's profit ratios are compared with its main competitors' profit ratios, which is a way to test the comparative marketing strength of the business. Higher than average profit ratios often are evidence that a business has developed very strong brand names for their products, or has nurtured other competitive advantages.

A Quick Analysis of Financial Leverage Gain

Chapter 4 demonstrates that the amount of financial leverage gain for the year can be a significant part of earnings for shareowners. Nevertheless, in actual practice financial leverage gets short shrift in financial statement analysis—which is surprising to me. I recommend doing a quick analysis of financial leverage for the year. Financial leverage gain derives from a business earning a greater return on capital invested in its assets than the interest on its debt sources of capital. Figure 5.6 presents the calculation of the business's financial leverage gain for the year (following the same format as Figure 4.3 in Chapter 4).

First, the business's total amount of operating liabilities (the sum of its accounts payable, accrued expenses payable, and income tax payable) is deducted from its total assets to arrive at $22,920,633 capital invested in its assets. Short-term plus long-term debt supplied $9,750,000, or 43 percent of its total capital and owners' equity supplied the other 57 percent. By dividing EBIT in these proportions

FIGURE 5.6 Financial Leverage Gain

				Debt percent of total			Debt share
$3,234,365	EBIT	X	43%	capital	=	$1,375,837	of EBIT
						($795,000)	Interest
						$580,837	Financial leverage gain
				Equity percent of total			Equity share of
$3,234,365	EBIT	X	57%	capital	=	$1,858,528	EBIT
						$2,439,365	Earnings for equity before income tax

$1,375,837 is attributed to debt capital (see Figure 5.6). The business paid $795,000 interest on its debt capital. Therefore, the business made a $580,837 financial leverage gain before income tax (as shown in Figure 5.6). Its financial leverage gain for the year equals 24 percent of its pretax earnings for stockholders. This percent should be compared with previous years to see if the business benefited more or less from financial leverage gain.

Book Value Per Share

Suppose I tell you that the market price of a stock is $60.00 per share and ask you whether this value is too high or too low, or just about right. You could compare the $60.00 market price with the stockholders' equity per share reported in its most recent balance sheet—which is called the **book value per share**. The book value per share in the business example (see Figure 5.2) equals $31.19: ($13,188,483 total owners' equity ÷ 422,823 capital stock shares = $31.19). Book value per share has a respectable history in securities analysis. The classic book *Security Analysis* by Graham and Dodd puts a fair amount of weight on the book value behind a share of stock.

Just the other day I read an article in the Business Section of the *New York Times* that was very critical of a business. Among several cogent points discussed in the article was the fact that the current market price of its stock was 29 percent below its book value. Generally speaking the market value of stocks trade higher than their book values. The reason for the comment in the article is that when a stock trades below its book value, the investors trading in the stock are of the opinion that the stock is not worth even its book value. But the assets of the business back up book value.

To illustrate this point, suppose the business in the example were to liquidate all of its assets at the amounts reported in its balance sheet, then pay off all its liabilities, and finally distribute the money left over to its stockholders. Each share of stock would receive cash equal to the book value per share, or $31.19 per share. So book value is a theoretical liquidation value per share. From this point of view the market value of the shares should not fall below $31.19. But the profit prospects of the business may be very dim; the stockholders may not see much chance of improving profit performance in the near future. They may think that the business could not sell off its assets at their book values, and that no one would pay book value for the business as a whole.

Of course most businesses do not plan to liquidate their assets and go out of business in the foreseeable future. They plan to continue as a going concern and make profit, at least for as far ahead as they can see. Therefore, the dominant factor in determining the market value of capital stock shares is the *earnings potential* of the business, not the book value of its ownership shares. The best place to start in assessing the earnings potential of a business is its most recent earnings performance.

Suppose I owned 10,000 capital stock shares of the business in the example and you were interested in buying my shares. What price would you offer for my shares? You've studied the financial statements of the business and you predict that the business will probably improve its profit performance in the future. So you might be willing to pay $40, $50, or higher per share for my stock shares, which is based on your assessment of the future earnings potential of the business. Private corporations have no ready market value information for their capital stock shares. So you're on your own regarding what price to pay for my stock shares.

Stockholders in public corporations have market value information at their fingertips, which is reported in the *Wall Street Journal*, the *New York Times*, *Barron's*, *Investor's Business Daily*, and many other sources of financial market information. They know the prices at which buyers and sellers are trading stocks. The main factor driving the market price of a stock is its **earnings per share (EPS)**.

Earnings Per Share

The income statement presented in Figure 5.1 includes earnings per share (EPS), which is $3.75 for the year just ended. Privately owned businesses, whose capital stock shares are not traded in public markets, do not have to report their earnings per share, and most don't. I include it in Figure 5.1 because publicly owned businesses whose capital stock shares are traded in a public market place (such as the New York Stock Exchange or Nasdaq) are required to report EPS.

Earnings per share is calculated as follows for the business (see Figures 5.1 and 5.2 for data):

$$\frac{\$1,585,587 \text{ net income available for stockholders}}{422,823 \text{ total number of outstanding capital stock shares}} = \$3.75 \text{ Basic EPS}$$

To be more accurate the *weighted average* number of shares outstanding during the year should be used to calculate EPS—which takes into account that some shares may have been issued and outstanding only part of the year. Also a business may have reduced the number of its outstanding shares during part of the year. I use the ending number of shares to make it easier to follow the computation of EPS.

The numerator (top number) in the EPS ratio is *net income available for common stockholders*, which equals bottom-line net income minus dividends paid to preferred stockholders of the business. Many business corporations issue preferred stock shares that require a fixed amount of dividends to be paid each year. The total of annual dividends to the preferred stockholders is deducted from net income to determine net income available for the common stockholders. The business in the example has issued only one class of capital stock shares. It has not issued any preferred stock so all of its net income is available for its common stock shares.

Basic and Diluted EPS

Please notice the word *basic* in the above EPS calculation. Basic means that the *actual number* of common stock shares in the hands of stockholders is used as the denominator (bottom number) for calculating EPS. If a business were to issue more shares, the denominator would become larger and EPS would decrease. The larger number of shares would dilute EPS. In fact many business corporations have entered into contracts that oblige them to issue additional stock shares in the future. These shares have not yet been issued, but the business is legally committed to issue more shares in the future. In other words there is the potential that the number of capital stock shares will be inflated and net income will have to be divided over a larger number of stock shares.

Many public businesses award their high-level managers *stock options* that give them the right to buy stock shares at fixed prices. These fixed purchase prices generally are set equal to the market price at the time of granting the stock options. The idea is to give the managers an incentive to improve the profit performance of the business that should drive up the market price of its stock shares. When (and if) the market value of the stock shares rises, the managers exercise their rights and buy stock shares at the lower prices fixed in their option contracts. Managers can make millions of dollars by exercising their stock options. There is a wealth transfer from the nonmanagement stockholders to some of the management stockholders because the market price per share is lower than it would have been if shares had not been issued to the managers.

The calculation of **basic EPS** does *not* recognize the additional shares that may be issued when management stock options are exercised in the future. Also some businesses issue convertible bonds and convertible preferred stock that at the option of the security holders can be traded in for common stock shares based on predetermined exchange rates. Conversions of senior securities into shares of common stock also cause dilution of EPS.

To alert investors to the potential effects of management stock options and convertible securities, a second EPS is calculated by public corporations, which is called the **diluted EPS**. This lower EPS takes into account the effects on EPS that would be caused by the issue of additional common stock shares under terms of management stock option plans and convertible securities (plus any other commitments a business has entered into that requires it to issue additional stock shares in the future). Both basic EPS and diluted EPS (if applicable) are reported in the income statements of publicly owned business corporations. The diluted EPS is a more conservative figure on which to base market value.

Market Value Ratios

The capital stock shares of more than 10,000 business corporations are traded on public markets—the New York Stock Exchange, Nasdaq, and other stock exchanges. The day-to-day market price changes of these shares receive a great deal of attention, to say the least. More than any other factor the market value of capital stock shares depends on the earnings per share performance of a business—its past performance and its future profit potential. It's difficult to prove whether basic EPS or diluted EPS is the driver of market value. In many cases the two are very close and the gap is not significant. In some cases, however, the spread between the two EPS figures is fairly large.

In addition to earnings per share (EPS) investors in stock shares of publicly owned companies closely follow two other ratios: (1) the *dividend yield ratio*; and (2) the **price/earnings (P/E) ratio**. The dividend yield and P/E ratios are reported in the stock trading tables published in the *Wall Street Journal*, which demonstrates how important are these two market value ratios for stock shares.

Dividend Yield Ratio

The dividend yield ratio equals the amount of cash dividends per share during the most recent, or trailing 12 months divided by the current market price of a stock share. The dividend yield ratio is the measure of cash income from a share of stock based on its current market price. The annual return on an investment in stock shares includes both the cash dividends received during the period and the gain or loss in market value of the stock shares over the period. The calculation of the historical rate of return for a stock investment over two or more years and for a stock index such as the Dow Jones 30 Industrial or the Standard & Poor's 500 assumes that cash dividends have been reinvested in additional shares of stock. Of course individual investors may not reinvest their dividends. They may spend their dividend income or put the cash flow into other investments.

Price/Earnings Ratio

The market price of stock shares of a public business is divided by its most recent annual EPS to determine the price/earnings ratio:

$$\frac{\text{Current market price of stock share}}{\text{Earnings per share (either Basic or Diluted EPS)}} = \text{Price/Earnings Ratio, or P/E}$$

Suppose a company's stock shares are trading at $60.00 per share and its EPS for the most recent year (called the trailing 12 months) is $3.00. Thus, its P/E ratio is 20. By the way the *Wall Street Journal* uses diluted EPS to report P/E ratios in its stock trading tables. Like the other ratios discussed in the chapter the P/E ratio is compared with industry-wide and market-wide averages to judge whether it's too high or too low. I remember when a P/E ratio of 8 was typical. Today P/E ratios of 20 or higher are common.

The stock shares of a privately owned business are not actively traded and the market value of its shares is difficult to ascertain. When shares do change hands occasionally, the price is usually kept private between the seller and buyer. Nevertheless, stockholders in these businesses are interested in what their shares are worth. To estimate the value of their stock shares a P/E multiple can be used. In the example the company's EPS is $3.75 for the most recent year (see Figure 5.1). Suppose you own some of the capital stock shares, and someone offers to buy your shares. You could establish an offer price at, say, 12 times basic EPS. This gives $45 per share. The potential buyer may not be willing to pay this price, of course. Or he or she might be willing to pay 15 or even 18 times EPS.

Debt-Paying Ability Ratios

If a business cannot pay its liabilities on time, bad things can happen. **Solvency** refers to the ability of a business to pay its liabilities when they come due. Maintaining solvency (debt-paying ability) is essential for every business. If a business defaults on its debt obligations, it becomes vulnerable to legal proceedings by its lenders that could stop the company in its tracks, or at least could seriously interfere with its normal operations.

Therefore, investors and lenders are very much interested in the general solvency and debt-paying ability of a business. Bankers and other lenders when deciding whether to make and renew loans to a business direct their attention to certain solvency ratios. These ratios provide a useful profile of the business for assessing its creditworthiness and for judging the ability of the business to pay its loans and interest on time.

Short-term Solvency Test: The Current Ratio

The **current ratio** is used to test the short-term liability-paying ability of a business. The current ratio is calculated by dividing total current assets by total current liabilities. From the data in the company's balance sheet (Figure 5.2) its current ratio is computed as follows:

$$\frac{\$12,742,329 \text{ current assets}}{\$6,126,096 \text{ current liabilities}} = 2.08 \text{ current ratio}$$

The current ratio is hardly ever expressed as a percent (which would be 208 percent in this case). The current ratio is stated as 2.08 to 1.00 for this company, or more simply just as 2.08. The general expectation is that the current ratio for a business should be 2 to 1 or higher.

Most businesses find that their creditors expect them to maintain this minimum current ratio. In other words short-term creditors generally prefer that a business limit its current liabilities to one-half or less of its current assets.

Why do short-term creditors put this limit on a business? The main reason is to provide a safety cushion of protection for payment of its short-term liabilities. A current ratio of 2 to 1 means there is $2.00 of cash and assets that should be converted into cash during the near future that will be available to pay each $1.00 of current liabilities, which come due in roughly the same time period. Each $1.00 of short-term liabilities is backed up with $2.00 of cash on hand plus near-term cash inflows. The extra dollar of current assets provides a margin of safety.

In summary short-term sources of credit generally demand that a company's current assets be double its current liabilities. After all, creditors are not owners—they don't share in the profit success of the business. The income on their loans is limited to the interest they charge. As a creditor they quite properly minimize their loan risks; they are not compensated to take on much risk.

Acid Test Ratio, or Quick Ratio

Inventory is many weeks away from conversion into cash. Products usually are held two, three, or four months before being sold. If sales are made on credit, which is normal when one business sells to another business, there's a second waiting period before accounts receivables are collected. In short, inventory is not nearly as liquid as accounts receivable; it takes a lot longer to convert inventory into cash. Furthermore, there's no guarantee that all the products in inventory will be sold, or can be sold above cost.

A more severe test of the short-term liability-paying ability of a business is the **acid test ratio**, which excludes inventory (and prepaid expenses also). Only cash, marketable securities investments (if the business has any), and accounts receivable are counted as sources to pay the current liabilities of the business. This ratio is also called the **quick ratio** because only cash and assets quickly convertible into cash are included in the amount available for paying current liabilities.

In the example the company's acid test ratio is calculated as follows (the business has no investments in marketable securities):

$$\frac{\$2,345,675 \text{ cash} + \$3,813,582 \text{ accounts receivable}}{\$6,126,096 \text{ total current liabilities}} = 1.01 \text{ acid test ratio}$$

The general expectation is that a company's acid test ratio should be 1 to 1 or better, although you find many more exceptions to this rule compared with the 2 to 1 current ratio standard.

Debt to Equity Ratio

Some debt is good, but too much is dangerous. The **debt to equity ratio** is an indicator whether a company is using debt prudently, or may be overburdened with debt that could cause problems. For the example the company's debt to equity ratio is calculated as follows (see Figure 5.2 for data):

$$\frac{\$13{,}626{,}096 \text{ total liabilities}}{\$13{,}188{,}483 \text{ total stockholders' equity}} = 1.03 \text{ debt to equity ratio}$$

This ratio reveals that the company is using $1.03 of liabilities for each $1.00 of stockholders' equity. Notice that *all* liabilities (noninterest as well as interest-bearing, and both short-term and long-term) are included in this ratio.

Most industrial businesses stay below a 1 to 1 debt to equity ratio. They don't want to take on too much debt, or they cannot convince lenders to put-up more than one-half of their assets. On the other hand some businesses are much more aggressive and operate with large ratios of debt to equity. Public utilities and financial institutions have much higher debt to equity ratios than 1 to 1.

Times Interest Earned

To pay interest on its debt, a business needs to earn a sufficient amount of earnings before interest and income tax (often abbreviated EBIT). To test the ability to pay interest the **times interest earned** ratio is calculated. Annual earnings before interest and income tax is divided by interest expense as follows for the example (see Figure 5.1 for data):

$$\frac{\$3{,}234{,}365 \text{ earnings before interest and income tax}}{\$795{,}000 \text{ interest expense}} = 4.07 \text{ times interest earned}$$

There is no standard guideline for this particular ratio—although obviously the ratio should be higher than 1 to 1. In this example the company's earnings before interest and income tax is more than four times its annual interest expense, which is comforting from the lender's point of view. Lenders would be very much alarmed if a business barely covered its annual interest expense. The company's management should be equally alarmed, of course.

Three Asset Turnover Ratios

A business has to keep its assets busy, both to remain solvent and to be efficient in making profit. Inactive assets are like a dead weight around the neck of the business. Slow moving assets can cause serious trouble. Investors and lenders use certain *turnover ratios* as indicators of how well a business is using its assets and to test whether some assets are sluggish and might pose a serious problem.

Accounts Receivable Turnover Ratio

Accounts receivable should be collected on time and not be allowed to accumulate beyond the normal credit term offered to customers. To get a sense of how well the business is controlling its accounts receivable the **accounts receivable turnover ratio** is calculated as follows for the business example (see Figures 5.1 and 5.2 for data):

$$\frac{\$39,661,250 \text{ annual sales revenue}}{\$3,813,582 \text{ accounts receivable}} = 10.4 \text{ times}$$

The accounts receivable turnover ratio is one of the ratios published by business financial information services such as Dun & Bradstreet, Standard & Poor's, and Moody's. In this example the business turns its customers' receivables a little more than 10 times a year, which indicates that it waits about one-tenth of a year on average to collect its receivables from credit sales. This appears reasonable, assuming that the business extends one-month credit to its customers. (A turnover of 12 would be even better.)

Inventory Turnover Ratio

In the business example the company sells products. Virtually every company that sells products carries an inventory, or stockpile of products for a period of time before the products are sold and delivered to customers. The holding period depends on the nature of the business. Supermarkets have short holding periods; retail furniture stores have fairly long inventory holding periods. Products should not be held in inventory longer than necessary. Holding inventory is subject to several risks and requires several costs. Products may become obsolete, or may be stolen, or may be damaged, or even misplaced. Products have to be stored, usually have to be insured, and may have to be guarded. And, the capital invested in inventory has a cost, of course.

To get a feel for how long the business holds its inventory before sale investors and lenders calculate the **inventory turnover ratio** examine what follows (see Figures 5.1 and 5.2 for data):

$$\frac{\$24{,}960{,}750 \text{ cost of goods sold expense}}{\$5{,}760{,}173 \text{ inventories}} = 4.3 \text{ times}$$

The inventory turnover ratio is another of the ratios published by business information service organizations. The company's 4:3 inventory turnover ratio indicates that it hold products about one-fourth of a year before selling them. The inventory turnover ratio is compared with the averages for the industry and with previous years of the business.

Asset Turnover Ratio

The *asset turnover ratio* is a test of how well a business is using its assets overall. This ratio is computed by dividing annual sales revenue by total assets (see Figures 5.1 and 5.2 for data):

$$\frac{\$39{,}661{,}250 \text{ annual sales revenue}}{\$26{,}814{,}579 \text{ total assets}} = 1.5 \text{ times}$$

This ratio reveals that the business made $1.50 sales for every $1.00 of total assets. Or put the reverse way, the business needed $1.00 of assets to make $1.50 of sales during the year. The ratio tells us that business is relatively asset heavy. The asset turnover ratio is compared with the averages for the industry and with previous years of the business.

Final Comments

Individual investors, investment managers, stock analysts, lenders, and credit rating services commonly use the financial statement and market value ratios explained in the chapter. Business managers use the ratios to keep watch on how their business is doing and whether there might be some trouble spots that need attention. Nevertheless, the ratios are not a panacea.

A financial statement ratio is like your body temperature. A normal temperature is good and means that probably nothing serious is wrong, though not necessarily. A very high or low temperature means something probably is wrong, but it takes additional diagnosis to discover the problem. Financial statement ratios are like measures of your vital signs, such as your pulse rate, blood pressure, cholesterol level, body fat, and so on. Financial ratios are the vital signs of a business.

There's no end to the number of ratios that can be calculated from financial statements. The trick is to focus on a reasonable number of ratios that have the most interpretive value. Calculating the ratios takes time. Many investors and lenders do not actually calculate the ratios. They do eyeball tests instead of computing ratios. They visually compare the two numbers in the ratio and do rough arithmetic in their heads—to see if anything appears to be out of whack. For example they observe that current assets are more than twice current liabilities. They do not bother to calculate the exact measure of the current ratio. This is a practical and time-saving technique rather than calculating ratios. Many investors and lenders use the financial statement ratios that are published by information service providers who compile data and information on thousands of businesses.

CHAPTER 6

Improving Profit— Basics

Business managers face constant change. All the factors that determine profit are subject to change caused both by external changes beyond the control of the business and changes initiated by managers themselves. A good many management decisions are triggered by changes. Indeed, managers are characterized as change agents.

The costs of the products sold by the business may increase; the company may raise wages for some or all of its employees, or wage rates might actually decrease due to employee give-backs; the landlord may raise the rent; competitors may drop their sales prices and the business may follow them down. Or managers may decide that they have to raise sales prices to keep up with cost inflation.

All profit factors are subject to change. Management neglect or ineptitude can lead to profit deterioration, sometimes very quickly. Increases in product cost, as well as increases in variable and fixed expenses can do serious damage to profit performance. Managers may not be able to improve certain factors much. Fixed expenses may already be cut to the bone. One vendor may control product costs or, alternative vendors may offer virtually the same prices. Competition may put a fairly tight straitjacket on sales prices. Customers are sensitive to sales price increases.

One basic function of managers is to keep a close watch on all relevant changes, and know how to deal with them. Changes set in motion a new round of profit-making decisions. This chapter concentrates on changes in the key factors that drive profit. These factors are explained in Chapter 1, which introduces the fundamental profit model for understanding and analyzing profit behavior (see Figure 1.1). In this chapter changes are analyzed—singularly, or one at a time. One factor only is changed in each scenario. The effects of a combination of changes in profit factors are analyzed in Chapter 7—in particular trading off one factor against another.

New and Improved Profit Model

Figure 6.1 presents a new and improved management profit model that is more useful for analyzing the effects of changes in the variables that drive profit. The new model takes the factors from the profit model introduced in Chapter 1 and blends them with conventional income statement components. In this format the manager sees the per unit values for each key factor that drives profit as well as the totals of sales revenue and expenses.

I should mention that the management profit model shown in Figure 6.1 contains confidential information that is not released outside the business. For instance the profit model begins with sales volume for the period, but this key profit factor is not disclosed in external income statements. Neither are the per unit values shown in the profit model. Nor are expenses classified between revenue-driven

FIGURE 6.1 Management Profit Report for Year Just Ended

	Per Unit	Totals
Sales Volume	100,000 units	
Sales Revenue	$100.00	$10,000,000
Cost of Goods (Products) Sold	$60.00	$6,000,000
Gross Margin	$40.00	$4,000,000
Unit-Driven Expenses	$5.00	$500,000
Revenue-Driven Expenses	8.5%	$850,000
Contribution Margin	$26.50	$2,650,000
Fixed Operating Expenses		$1,590,000
Profit (Earnings before Other Expenses)		$1,060,000

versus unit-driven in external income statements. You might want to compare the income statement reported externally to investors and creditors of a business with the profit model shown in Figure 6.1. (Figures 1.5 and 5.1 show examples of external income statements.)

The example shown in Figure 6.1 is new; I have not used this example before. The example is for one of the main profit modules of a business. Consider yourself the general manager of this division of the business. You have no authority over or responsibility for the central office overhead costs of the business. The bottom line you're responsible for is the one shown in Figure 6.1—earnings before other expenses (central office expenses, interest, and income taxes). You have broad authority over all the factors affecting the profit performance of your division, although you cannot violate company-wide policies in operating your division.

For the year just ended you earned $1,060,000 profit on $10,000,000 sales revenue, which is 10.6 percent return on sales. This is not bad but keep in mind that company-wide operating expenses are not reflected in your profit and neither are the interest and income tax expenses of the business. In fact you're under pressure from the head office to improve the profit performance of your division for the coming year.

How did you earn $1,060,000 profit for the year? A recap of profit analysis explained in Chapter 1 is this: You sold 100,000 units at an average $26.50 unit margin that generated $2,650,000 contribution margin. Deducting the $1,590,000 fixed operating expenses leaves $1,060,000 earnings before other expenses (your profit). Your break-even point for the year was 60,000 units: ($1,590,000 fixed costs ÷ $26.50 unit margin = 60,000 units breakeven volume). You sold 40,000 units in excess of breakeven, which multiplied times the $26.50 unit margin gives $1,060,000 profit. Are there any questions?

Sales Volume Changes

Business managers, quite naturally, are sales oriented. No sales, no business—as simple as that. As they say in marketing "Nothing happens until you sell it." Many businesses do not make it through their start-up phase because it's very difficult to build up and establish a sales base. Customers have to be won over. Once established, sales volume can never be taken for granted. Sales are vulnerable to competition, shifts in consumer preferences and spending decisions, and general economic conditions.

Thinking more positively, sales volume growth is the most realistic way to increase profit. Sales price increases are met with some degree of customer resistance in most cases as well as competitive response. Indeed, demand may be extremely sensitive to sales prices. Cost containment and expense control are important to be sure, but are more in the nature of defensive tactics and don't constitute a profit growth strategy as such.

Increasing Sales Volume

Suppose that you could increase sales volume 10 percent next year and that all your other profit factors would remain the same as for the year just ended. This is not a totally realistic scenario of course, but it permits focusing on the sales volume variable by itself. Figure 6.2 shows the impacts of increasing sales volume 10 percent next year, holding all other profit factors the same. Before looking at Figure 6.2 you might quickly estimate in your head by what percent profit would increase. I have found that many people, including business managers who ought to know better, think that profit would increase 10 percent, the same percent increase in sales volume. What do you think? Compare your guesstimate with the answer in Figure 6.2. Are you surprised, or what? Profit would increase 25.0 percent, much higher than the 10.0 percent sales volume increase.

An experienced manager would ask: How are you going to increase sales volume? Would your customers buy 10 percent more without any increase in advertising, without any sales price incentives, without product improvements or other inducements? Not too likely, to say the least. Increasing sales volume usually requires some stimulant such as more advertising that would increase your fixed costs. Improving product quality would increase product cost per unit. And so on.

An experienced manager also would ask whether the business has

FIGURE 6.2 Ten Percent Sales Volume Increase Scenario

	For Year Just Ended		New Scenario		Changes	
Sales Volume	100,000	units	110,000	units	10,000	+10.0%
	Per Unit	**Totals**	**Per Unit**	**Totals**	**Totals**	
Sales Revenue	$100.00	$10,000,000	$100.00	$11,000,000	$1,000,000	+10.0%
Cost of Goods Sold	$60.00	$6,000,000	$60.00	$6,600,000	$600,000	+10.0%
Gross Margin	$40.00	$4,000,000	$40.00	$4,400,000	$400,000	+10.0%
Unit-Driven Expenses	$5.00	$500,000	$5.00	$550,000	$50,000	+10.0%
Revenue-Driven Expenses	8.5%	$850,000	8.5%	$935,000	$85,000	+10.0%
Contribution Margin	$26.50	$2,650,000	$26.50	$2,915,000	$265,000	+10.0%
Fixed Operating Expenses		$1,590,000		$1,590,000		
Profit (Earnings before Other Expenses)		$1,060,000		$1,325,000	$265,000	+25.0%

enough *capacity* to handle 10 percent additional sales volume. It's a good idea to run a capacity check whenever you're looking at sales volume increases. Fixed operating expenses may have to be increased to support additional sales volume. However, assume that your division has enough slack, or untapped capacity to take on 10 percent more sales volume without having to increase any fixed operating expenses. This means that your production facilities could crank out 10 percent more output without increasing fixed manufacturing costs, and that your sales and administrative staff could handle 10 percent more sales volume without hiring additional employees (and without increasing their salaries).

In the 10 percent sales volume increase scenario (with no changes in other profit factors) profit increases $265,000—see Figure 6.2. This increase is calculated as follows:

PROFIT INCREASE CALCULATION

$26.50 unit margin

× 10,000 additional units sold

= $265,000 contribution margin increase

− 0 no change in fixed operating expenses

= $265,000 profit increase

Contribution margin (profit before fixed operating expenses) is 10 percent higher by 10 percent sales volume increase—see Figure 6.2. Fixed operating expenses do not increase at the higher sales volume in this scenario. As mentioned above, the assumption is that your division has unused or idle manufacturing capacity and slack in your sales force to handle an additional 10 percent volume increase without having to increase any fixed operating expenses. In actual fact one or more of the company's fixed operating expenses might have to be increased to support a higher sales volume. You might have to rent more retail floor space, or hire more salaried employees, or purchase additional equipment on which depreciation is recorded. (All these are examples of fixed expenses.)

Figure 6.2 reveals that profit is 25 percent higher for a 10 percent sales volume increase. Hold it. How can a ten percent sales volume increase generate a 25 percent profit increase? How can a 10 percent sales volume increase have a two and a half times effect on profit? The $265,000 contribution margin increase flows entirely to profit because fixed operating expenses do not increase in this scenario. The $265,000 increase is a 10 percent gain in contribution margin but equals a 25 percent gain in profit—see Figure 6.2 again. The percent swing in profit is 2.5 times the swing in sales volume: (25.0% gain in profit ÷ 10.0% gain in sales volume = 2.5 times).

Profit Leverage Effect from Fixed Costs That Stay Fixed

As just explained, profit increases 25 percent even though sales volume increases only 10 percent—assuming that fixed costs do not increase. Last year you sold 40,000 units in excess of breakeven. Your breakeven sales level was 60,000 units (determined above), and your actual sales volume was 100,000 units. Each unit sold in excess of the breakeven volume generates $26.50 additional contribution margin. Once over the breakeven hurdle the contribution margin from each additional unit sold can be viewed as pure profit because the first 60,000 units of sales cover fixed costs. Your sales for the year just ended can be divided into two piles—a pile of 60,000 units that covered fixed operating expenses, and a second pile of 40,000 units that provided contribution margin.

Dividing the additional 10,000 units sold by the 40,000 units in excess of breakeven equals a 25.0 percent increase to the profit pile. Therefore profit increases 25 percent, assuming that fixed costs don't increase with the increase in sales volume. When fixed costs stay put there is a *leverage effect* on profit. Profit swivels up a greater percent than the percent increase sales volume. For instance if you sell five percent, or 5,000 more units next year, your profit would increase 12.5 percent: (5,000 units increase ÷ 40,000 units over breakeven volume = 12.5%). In short, there is a 2.5 times leverage effect on profit as long as your fixed operating expenses are not increased to support a higher sales volume level.

The fact that fixed costs do not increase with an increase in sales volume reflects that you have not been fully using your production and/or sales capacity provided by the fixed operating expenses of your division. The main reason fixed costs don't increase, in other words, is that a business has slack, or idle capacity from the level of fixed costs it has committed to. When capacity is reached, and sooner or later it will be with continued sales volume growth, fixed costs will have to be increased to provide more capacity. If your division had already been selling at its maximum capacity, your fixed costs would have to be increased to provide the support for the higher sales level.

Sales Volume Decrease

Suppose that things don't look good for next year; you forecast that your division will sell 5 to 10 percent less units next year, and perhaps even worse. You would be very much concerned of course, and probe into the reasons for the decrease. More competition? Are people switching to substitute products? Are hard times forcing customers to spend less? Is the location deteriorating? Has customer service slipped? Perhaps you should look into total quality management (TQM) techniques.

Sales volume declines are one of the most serious problems confronting any business manager. Unless the decline is quickly reversed, managers have to make extremely wrenching decisions regarding how to downsize the business. These decisions may result in laying off employees, selling off fixed assets, shutting down plants, and so on. The late economist Kenneth Boulding has called downsizing "the management of decline," which hits the nail on the head I think. It's a very unpleasant task to say the very least.

The profit impact of a sales volume decrease depends heavily on whether the business can reduce its fixed operating expenses in the short run to adjust down to the lower sales level. Assume not. Assume that your fixed operating expenses will remain the same next year. If your sales volume drops, say, 10 percent next year the effects would be a negative mirror image of Figure 6.2. Instead of increases and positive percent changes there would be equal amounts of decreases and negative percent signs. In short, your profit would plunge 25 percent, or 2.5 times the 10 percent sales volume decrease. This is due to the profit leverage effect when fixed costs remain constant.

Recall from the discussion above that for the year just ended your 100,000 units sales volume was 40,000 units in excess of breakeven. These 40,000 units provided your profit for the year. Giving up 10,000 of these units (if sales volume next year drops 10 percent) means giving up 25 percent of your profit pile. You can use the 2.5 leverage multiplier to quickly estimate how much profit damage will be done at a lower sales level next year. For each 1 percent of sales volume decrease your profit will drop 2.5 times, or 2.5 percent.

Suppose you forecast sales volume will decrease 4 percent during the coming year. Profit should drop 10 percent (2.5 times the sales volume drop) assuming all other profit factors remain constant next year. Figure 6.3 presents the results for the 4 percent sales volume decrease. As you see, profit does indeed fall exactly 10.0 percent, equal to 2.5 times the 4.0 percent sales volume decrease.

Suppose you forecast that sales will decrease 10 percent next year, and you predict that you will be able to reduce fixed costs next year by 10 percent. (This might be wishful thinking on your part.) Figure 6.4 shows the outcome for this scenario. Your contribution margin would drop $265,000 (see Figure 6.4). But your fixed operat-

FIGURE 6.3 Four Percent Sales Volume Decrease Scenario

	For Year Just Ended		New Scenario		Changes	
Sales Volume	100,000 units		96,000 units		-4,000	-4.0%
	Per Unit	**Totals**	**Per Unit**	**Totals**	**Totals**	
Sales Revenue	$100.00	$10,000,000	$100.00	$9,600,000	($400,000)	-4.0%
Cost of Goods Sold	$60.00	$6,000,000	$60.00	$5,760,000	($240,000)	-4.0%
Gross Margin	$40.00	$4,000,000	$40.00	$3,840,000	($160,000)	-4.0%
Unit-Driven Expenses	$5.00	$500,000	$5.00	$480,000	($20,000)	-4.0%
Revenue-Driven Expenses	8.5%	$850,000	8.5%	$816,000	($34,000)	-4.0%
Contribution Margin	$26.50	$2,650,000	$26.50	$2,544,000	($106,000)	-4.0%
Fixed Operating Expenses		$1,590,000		$1,590,000		
Profit (Earnings before Other Expenses)		$1,060,000		$954,000	($106,000)	-10.0%

FIGURE 6.4 Ten Percent Sales Volume Decrease with Ten Percent Fixed Costs Decrease Scenario

	For Year Just Ended		New Scenario		Changes	
Sales Volume	100,000 units		90,000 units		-10,000	-10.0%
	Per Unit	**Totals**	**Per Unit**	**Totals**	**Totals**	
Sales Revenue	$100.00	$10,000,000	$100.00	$9,000,000	($1,000,000)	-10.0%
Cost of Goods Sold	$60.00	$6,000,000	$60.00	$5,400,000	($600,000)	-10.0%
Gross Margin	$40.00	$4,000,000	$40.00	$3,600,000	($400,000)	-10.0%
Unit-Driven Expenses	$5.00	$500,000	$5.00	$450,000	($50,000)	-10.0%
Revenue-Driven Expenses	8.5%	$850,000	8.5%	$765,000	($85,000)	-10.0%
Contribution Margin	$26.50	$2,650,000	$26.50	$2,385,000	($265,000)	-10.0%
Fixed Operating Expenses		$1,590,000		$1,431,000	($159,000)	
Profit (Earnings before Other Expenses)		$1,060,000		$954,000	($106,000)	-10.0%

ing expenses decrease would offset $159,000 of the contribution margin decrease—the net effect would be only a $106,000 profit decrease. In other words, your profit would have gone down only 10 percent—if you can reduce your fixed costs 10 percent to match the 10 percent drop in sales volume.

Sales Price Changes

First, I have a question for you. Suppose you could have one or the other but not both: Would you prefer a 10 percent sales *volume* increase or a 10 percent *sales price* increase? There is a huge profit difference between the two. Everything else being equal, you should always opt for the sales price increase. Seldom is everything else equal. But in a theoretical situation in which you could have one or the other, a higher sales price is always preferable to a higher sales volume. Marketing managers would quickly argue that higher sales volume would increase market share and in the long run a bigger market share leads to more control over sales prices.

Setting sales prices is one of the most perplexing decisions facing business managers. Competition normally dictates the basic range of sales prices. But usually there is some room for deviation from your competitors' prices because of product differentiation, brand loyalty, location advantages, and quality of service—to cite only some of the many reasons that permit higher sales prices than the competition's.

Fixed operating expenses generally are insensitive to sales price increases. In contrast, sales volume increases could require increases in fixed operating expenses, especially when sales volume is already pushing on the limits of the company's capacity. Very few fixed expenses are directly affected by raising sales prices, even if the company were operating near full capacity. Advertising (a fixed cost once spent) might be stepped up to persuade customers that the hike in sales prices is necessary or beneficial. Other than this, it's hard to find many fixed operating expenses that are tied directly to sales price increases.

Increasing Sales Price

Suppose that next year you could sell the same volume at five percent higher sales prices across the board on all products. Figure 6.5 presents this scenario for your division. Before you look at Figure 6.5 please make a ballpark estimate of the percent increase in profit you would expect from a five percent increase in sales prices. Profit increases over 43 percent. Would this be realistic? Well, only to the

FIGURE 6.5 Five Percent Sales Price Increase Scenario

	For Year Just Ended		New Scenario		Changes	
Sales Volume	100,000 units		100,000 units			
	Per Unit	**Totals**	**Per Unit**	**Totals**	**Totals**	
Sales Revenue	$100.00	$10,000,000	$105.00	$10,500,000	$500,000	+5.0%
Cost of Goods Sold	$60.00	$6,000,000	$60.00	$6,000,000		
Gross Margin	$40.00	$4,000,000	$45.00	$4,500,000	$500,000	+12.5%
Unit-Driven Expenses	$5.00	$500,000	$5.00	$500,000		
Revenue-Driven Expenses	8.5%	$850,000	8.5%	$892,500	$42,500	+5.0%
Contribution Margin	$26.50	$2,650,000	$31.08	$3,107,500	$457,500	+17.3%
Fixed Operating Expenses		$1,590,000		$1,590,000		
Profit (Earnings before Other Expenses)		$1,060,000		$1,517,500	$457,500	+43.2%

extent that a five percent sales price increase would be realistic. In this situation only one variable operating expense increases—the one driven by sales revenue.

Cost of goods sold expense does not increase because the number of units sold remains the same in the higher sales price scenario. In the 10 percent sales volume increase scenario (see Figure 6.2) the sales revenue increase is offset substantially by the increase in cost of goods sold expense. In contrast of the $500,000 sales revenue increment $457,500 carries down to profit in the sales price increase scenario (see Figure 6.5). Revenue-driven expenses offset a small part of the sales revenue increase. These expenses vary directly with changes in the dollar amounts of sales (not with the quantity of products sold). As sales revenue (dollars) increases, these expenses increase directly in proportion. In the example revenue-driven expenses are 8.5 percent of sales revenue, so these expenses increase $42,500 (see Figure 6.5).

The large majority of businesses have one or more revenue-driven expenses. For example most retailers accept national credit cards, such as VISA, MasterCard, Discover, American Express, Diners Club, and so on. The credit card charge slips are deposited daily with a local participating bank. The bank discounts the total amount and credits the net balance in the business' checking account. Discount rates vary between 2 percent to 4 percent (sometimes lower or higher). In short, the business nets only 98¢ to 96¢ from the dollar on its credit card sales. The credit card discount expense comes right off the top of the sales dollar. The business avoids the expenses of extending and administering credit directly to its customers. So the discount may be a bargain.

Sales commissions are another common example of a revenue dependent expense. As you probably know many retailers and other businesses pay their sales staff on a commission basis, which usually is a certain percent of the total sales amount such as 5 or 10 percent. The salespersons may receive a base salary, which would be the fixed floor of the expense; only the commission over and above the fixed base would be variable. (This requires the separation of the fixed part from the variable part in the management profit model.)

In selling to other businesses a company usually extends short-term credit, which is called *trade credit*. No matter how carefully customers are screened before they are extended credit, a few never pay their accounts owed to the business. Eventually, after making repeated collection efforts, the business ends up having to write off all or part of these receivables' balances as uncollectible. These losses are called *bad debts* and are a normal expense of doing business on credit. This expense depends on the sales amount, not sales volume (number of units sold).

Another example of an expense that varies with sales revenue is one you might not think of—rent. Companies often sign lease agreements that call for rental amounts based on gross sales. There is a base amount, or fixed minimum monthly rent. In addition there is a variable amount equal to a percent of total sales revenue. This is common for retailers renting space in shopping centers. There are several other examples of expenses that vary with total sales revenue, such as franchise fees based on gross sales.

To sum up, sales revenue increases five percent but this is offset by a five percent increase in the revenue-driven expenses, yielding a net $457,500 increase in contribution margin as shown in Figure 6.5. Your division's fixed operating expenses do not change at the higher sales price level. So the five percent sales price hike results in a rather hefty 43.2 percent gain in profit. A 43 percent profit increase from only a five percent sales price increase can also be viewed as a type of leverage—*sales price leverage*.

The reason for such a large percent increase in profit is the huge jump in the unit margin—which increases from $26.50 to $31.08, an increase of 17.3 percent. This is the key change. You bump the average sales price $5.00. Revenue-driven expenses are 8.5 percent of sales revenue. So 42.5¢ comes off the top leaving a $4.575 net sales price gain per unit. The 100,000 units sold times the $4.575 gain in unit profit margin equals $457,500, the increase in total profit contribution margin.

A five percent increase in sales prices with no increase in the product costs and no increases in the other expenses may not be entirely realistic. Other costs are held constant to illustrate the powerful impact of a sales price increase, and to contrast it with an increase in sales volume. A five percent sales volume increase would increase profit 2.5 times, or 12.5 percent (see discussion above on the leverage effect). As shown in Figure 6.5 a 5 percent sales price increase yields a 43.2 percent gain in profit!

The reason for the superiority of a sales price increase is brought out in the following side-by-side computations:

COMPARISON OF 5% SALES PRICE INCREASE AND 10% SALES VOLUME INCREASE

$26.50 unit margin × +10,000 units increase = $265,000 contribution margin increase

+$4.575 unit margin increase × 100,000 units = $457,500 contribution margin increase

Selling 10,000 more units at $26.50 profit per unit is not nearly as good as selling 100,000 units at $4.575 higher margin per unit.

Sales Price Decreases

What goes up can go down. What if you were to reduce sales prices and all other profit factors remained the same? Managers hardly need to be reminded of the bad effects of decreasing sales prices, although they may not realize just how damaging sales price reductions can be on the bottom line. It takes a very large sales volume increase to offset sales price decreases, which I demonstrate in Chapter 7. At this point I'll simply mention that an equal percent sales volume resulting from a sales price decrease does not even come close to making up for the contribution margin loss from decreasing sales prices.

The purpose here is to analyze the damage done by a sales price decrease, assuming sales volume remains the same. Instead of showing a 10 percent sales price decrease—which would be the reverse mirror image of the 10 percent sales price increase scenario analyzed earlier—I focus on how devastating even a minor sales price decrease would be. Suppose your product line has come under competitive pressure and you are thinking of lowering your sales prices by, say, three percent. You plan to offer special rebates and more attractive quantity discounts as the means to lower sales prices. List prices will not be reduced but the net effect is to reduce the actual sales prices of the products you sell by an average of three percent. A three percent sales price cut may not seem too bad on the surface.

Figure 6.6 shows that even a seemingly small three percent sales price reduction would be a minor disaster. You would give up $300,000 off the top (from sales revenue) and only one operating expense would decrease. Contribution margin would decrease $274,500, which reduces profit the same amount. Your division's profit would drop almost 26 percent!

FIGURE 6.6 Three Percent Sales Price Decrease Scenario

	For Year Just Ended		New Scenario		Changes	
Sales Volume	100,000 units		100,000 units			
	Per Unit	Totals	Per Unit	Totals	Totals	
Sales Revenue	$100.00	$10,000,000	$97.00	$9,700,000	($300,000)	-3.0%
Cost of Goods Sold	$60.00	$6,000,000	$60.00	$6,000,000		
Gross Margin	$40.00	$4,000,000	$37.00	$3,700,000	($300,000)	-7.5%
Unit-Driven Expenses	$5.00	$500,000	$5.00	$500,000		
Revenue-Driven Expenses	8.5%	$850,000	8.5%	$824,500	($25,500)	-3.0%
Contribution Margin	$26.50	$2,650,000	$23.76	$2,375,500	($274,500)	-10.4%
Fixed Operating Expenses		$1,590,000		$1,590,000		
Profit (Earnings before Other Expenses)		$1,060,000		$785,500	($274,500)	-25.9%

In summary managers should carefully analyze the profit impact of decreasing sales prices before moving ahead. Sales price reductions have a many times effect on profit because the percent decrease in unit margin often is two or three times the percent decrease in sales price. The result is that the decrease in contribution margin takes away a large chunk from profit.

Expense Changes

Sales volume changes and sales price changes are the two that have the biggest impact on profit in most cases. Product cost ranks as the next most critical profit factor for most businesses (except service businesses that do not sell products). A retailer needs smart, tough-nosed, sharp-pencil, aggressive purchasing tactics to control its product costs. On the other hand it can be carried to an extreme. A good friend was a purchasing agent when I lived in California some years ago. George was a real tiger. He would even return new calendars sent by vendors at the end of the year with a note saying "Don't send me this calendar; give me a lower price." This may be overkill although George eventually became general manager of the business.

Even with close monitoring and relentless control the variable and fixed operating expenses of a business can spin out of control. For one thing salaries, rent, insurance, utility bills, audit and legal fees—virtually all operating expenses—are subject to inflation.

Two Types of Cost Increases

General price level inflation throughout the economy pushes up the expenses of a business like a rising tide lifts all boats. The defining characteristic of inflation is that the real, or actual quality and quantity (or size) of an economic good doesn't change but its price increases. Inflation-driven cost increases are quite distinct from deliberate cost increases a business makes to improve its sales volume or, as strange as it might sound, in order to improve its profit margins by increasing sales prices more than the increases in costs. These *strategic cost changes* should be distinguished from general inflation cost changes.

Consider the cost of a product that a business manufactures or purchases. An inflation-caused cost increase means that the product remains the same but now costs more per unit. A strategic cost increase would improve the quality or size of the product; the product itself is changed. Inflation is external to a business—cost increases are driven by outside forces over which the business has little or no control. Strategic cost increases are internal to a business. They are the result of deliberate decisions by a business to change its products or operating expenses as part of an overall plan to improve sales volume or sales prices, or both.

To illustrate cost inflation consider the case in which your division's sales prices and sales volume remain the same next year but your product costs and all operating expenses increase five percent due to general cost inflation. Figure 6.7 presents the outcome for this cost inflation scenario. The five percent increases in product cost and operating expenses cause profit to plunge $447,000, or 42.2 percent. You could ill afford to let product cost and operating expenses get out of control by five percent. You might be able to take action to mitigate the cost inflation. More than likely you will have to raise sales prices to offset the cost inflation.

Inflation Pass-Through Pricing

One basic function of business managers, though seldom discussed, is raising sales prices in order to pass along to customers the increases in product costs and operating expenses of the business that are caused by inflation. Managers must get customers to pay higher prices to cover the higher costs of the business, which is not an easy task to say the least. The main purpose is not to improve profit performance as such but rather simply to increase sales prices to pay for cost increases.

The costs of the large majority of products (with some notable exceptions) tend to rise over time. Customers generally accept higher sales prices if they perceive that the company is operating in an inflationary environment. In their minds everything is going up. A particular

FIGURE 6.7 Five Percent Cost Inflation

	For Year Just Ended		New Scenario		Changes	
Sales Volume	100,000	units	100,000	units		
	Per Unit	**Totals**	**Per Unit**	**Totals**	**Totals**	
Sales Revenue	$100.00	$10,000,000	$100.00	$10,000,000		
Cost of Goods Sold	$60.00	$6,000,000	$63.00	$6,300,000	$300,000	+5.0%
Gross Margin	$40.00	$4,000,000	$37.00	$3,700,000	($300,000)	−7.5%
Unit-Driven Expenses	$5.00	$500,000	$5.25	$525,000	$25,000	+5.0%
Revenue-Driven Expenses	8.5%	$850,000	8.925%	$892,500	$42,500	+5.0%
Contribution Margin	$26.50	$2,650,000	$22.83	$2,282,500	($367,500)	−13.9%
Fixed Operating Expenses		$1,590,000		$1,669,500	$79,500	+5.0%
Profit (Earnings before Other Expenses)		$1,060,000		$613,000	($447,000)	−42.2%

product does not cost more relative to price increases of other products they purchase, and hopefully their wages or other incomes are going up at about the same rate as inflation. (This is not true for people on fixed incomes, of course.)

Higher sales prices may not adversely affect sales volume in a market with an inflation mentality. Assuming competitors also face general cost inflation, a company's sales volume may not suffer from passing along product cost increases in higher sales prices—the competition is doing the same thing. On the other hand if customers' incomes are not rising in proportion with sales price increases, demand will likely fall off at higher sales prices.

Suppose that due to inflation pressures the average cost of the products your division sells increases $3.66 next year, from $60.00 to $63.66 per unit. This is an increase of 6.1 percent. An overall inflation rate of 6.1 percent certainly would worry the Federal Reserve. I can't predict what action the Fed might take; I'm more interested in what action you should take. You cannot simply raise your average sales price $3.66. In the example your revenue-driven expenses are 8.5 percent of sales revenue. So the required sales price increase is determined as follows:

CALCULATION OF SALES PRICE INCREASE TO COMPENSATE FOR PRODUCT COST INFLATION

$$\frac{\$3.66 \text{ product cost increase}}{(1 - .085)} = \$4.00 \text{ sales price increase}$$

Dividing by $(1 - .085)$, or .915, recognizes that only 91.5¢ from each sales revenue dollar is available for the product cost increase. Increasing the average sales price exactly $4.00 keeps the unit margin exactly the same:

UNIT MARGIN BEFORE AND AFTER SALES PRICE INCREASE FOR PRODUCT COST INCREASE

	Before	*After*
Sales price	$100.00	$104.00
Product cost	60.00	63.66
Gross margin	$ 40.00	$ 40.34
Unit-driven expenses	5.00	5.00
Revenue-driven expenses at 8.5%	8.50	8.84
Unit margin	$ 26.50	$ 26.50

Figure 6.8 shows that profit remains the same if you raise your average sales prices by $4.00 to cover the product cost inflation. In this

FIGURE 6.8 Cost Inflation Pass-Through Pricing

	For Year Just Ended		New Scenario		Changes	
Sales Volume	100,000 units		100,000 units			
	Per Unit	**Totals**	**Per Unit**	**Totals**	**Totals**	
Sales Revenue	$100.00	$10,000,000	$104.00	$10,400,000	$400,000	+4.0%
Cost of Goods Sold	$60.00	$6,000,000	$63.66	$6,366,000	$366,000	+6.1%
Gross Margin	$40.00	$4,000,000	$40.34	$4,034,000	$34,000	+0.9%
Unit-Driven Expenses	$5.00	$500,000	$5.00	$500,000		
Revenue-Driven Expenses	8.5%	$850,000	8.5%	$884,000	$34,000	+4.0%
Contribution Margin	$26.50	$2,650,000	$26.50	$2,650,000	$0	
Fixed Operating Expenses		$1,590,000		$1,590,000		
Profit (Earnings before Other Expenses)		$1,060,000		$1,060,000	$0	

scenario unit-driven expenses and fixed operating expenses are held constant—and sales volume is held constant also. Of course inflation may cause your other costs to increase and the higher sales price needed to cover all the cost increases could dampen demand and cause sales volume to suffer.

As mentioned earlier a business may deliberately increase its product costs and other operating expenses in order to stimulate demand for its products and increase sales volume. Or a business may intentionally increase its operating expenses as part of a larger strategy to raise sales prices more than the cost increases and thereby improve the unit margins on the products. The analysis for these types of decisions, which are referred to as trade-offs, are analyzed in Chapter 7.

Summary

The chapter presents a more comprehensive profit model that managers can use to analyze and compare changes in the critical factors that determine profit. Change is always in the air. Costs do not remain stable very long. Sales volume often increases or decreases even when other profit factors don't change. Resetting sales prices in response to cost increases should be based on careful analysis. Managers need a sure-handed analytical grip on the factors that drive profit.

The chapter compares an increase in sales volume with an equal percent increase in sales price. A sales price increase is much better than a sales volume increase of equal percent. You get much more profit bang for the buck from a five percent sales price increase than a five percent sales volume increase, for example. When sales prices cannot be increased, increasing sales volume usually is the best means for improving profit. Even a relatively small percent sales volume increase causes a much larger percent increase in profit from the leverage effect when fixed operating expenses do not increase at the higher sales volume.

Managers should keep their attention riveted on unit margin— sales price less product cost and variable expenses. Profit performance is extremely sensitive to changes in unit margin. Cost increases cause unit margin to deteriorate—and rather quickly if not dealt with immediately. Depending on higher sales volume to offset cost increases is not very realistic; sales volume would have to increase too much. Cost increases generally have to be recovered through higher sales prices. The comprehensive profit model provides an invaluable analytical frame of reference, to help managers in reaching decisions regarding how to deal with changes.

CHAPTER 7

Improving Profit— Continued

Chapter 6 explains the analysis of changes in profit factors singularly, or one factor at a time. All other factors are held constant in order to isolate the effects of a change in just one profit factor. The single-change analysis explained in Chapter 6 lays the foundation for this chapter, which delves into multifactor change analysis. In most cases two or more profit factors change from period to period. Many decisions being considered by managers would change two or more profit factors. Managers must grapple with analyzing the joint effects of multiple changes.

The chapter first explains the comparative analysis of profit performance from one period to the next, which is no walk in the park, I should tell you. Next, the chapter explains the analysis of *trade-off decisions*. A classic trade-off decision is reducing sales prices to increase sales volume. The reverse trade-off is increasing sales prices with the expectation that sales volume will decrease, but hoping to make more profit with higher unit margins. The chapter also examines other multifactor changes such as implementing a quality improvement plan that would increase product costs and variable operating expenses in order to stimulate demand for the company's products.

Comparative Analysis of Profit

The example from Chapter 6 is continued in this chapter. Recall that you are the general manager of one of the major divisions of a business. You have broad authority over and responsibility for the profit performance of the division. You have just received your management profit report for the year just ended and the previous year—see Figure 7.1. You have received monthly and quarterly interim reports from the Accounting Department during the year, so the final numbers in the management profit report do not surprise you.

Management Profit Report

The **management profit report** shown in Figure 7.1 is designed to be a useful management analysis tool. It is much more than just a historical summary of sales revenue and expenses. Therefore the report includes *per unit values* and *sales volume* for each year, as well as total dollar amounts for sales revenue and expenses. The two columns on the right deserve special attention. The second column from the right reports the change in sales volume, the changes in per unit values, and the change in profit (both the dollar amount of profit change and the percent change).

The column on the right edge of the report is not commonly presented in internal management profit reports. Nevertheless, I strongly recommend that this information be included unless it is not feasible to do so. The information is especially useful for the comparative analysis of profit from period to period. The purpose is to provide

FIGURE 7.1 Management Profit Report

	Previous Year		Year Just Ended		Changes	Profit Impact
Sales Volume	92,500	units	100,000	units	7,500	$197,672
	Per Unit	Totals	Per Unit	Totals		
Sales Revenue	$97.50	$9,018,750	$100.00	$10,000,000	$2.50	$250,000
Cost of Goods Sold	$58.25	$5,388,125	$60.00	$6,000,000	$1.75	($175,000)
Gross Margin	$39.25	$3,630,625	$40.00	$4,000,000		
Unit-Driven Expenses	$4.85	$448,625	$5.00	$500,000	$0.15	($15,000)
Revenue-Driven Expenses	8.25%	$744,047	8.50%	$850,000	$0.46	($45,625)
Contribution Margin	$26.36	$2,437,953	$26.50	$2,650,000		
Fixed Operating Expenses		$1,486,500		$1,590,000	$103,500	($103,500)
Profit (Earnings before Other Expenses)		$951,453		$1,060,000	$108,547 11.4%	$108,547

ready-made information in order to save managers the time and effort of doing these calculations themselves.

The right column shows the impact that the change in each factor had on the total change in profit, which is $108,547 in the example (see Figure 7.1). To begin, sales volume increased 7,500 units. The sales volume increase multiplied by the previous year's $26.36 unit margin would have, by itself, increased profit $197,672. In other words, if all other factors had remained the same, profit would have increased almost $200,000 because of the increase in sales volume. But other factors also changed and the impacts of these other changes have to be brought into the analysis, of course.

The average sales price increased from $97.50 last year to $100.00 this year (the year just ended), an increase of $2.50 per unit. This one change generated $250,000 additional profit based on the 100,000 units sales volume this year. The average product cost increased $1.75 per unit; when multiplied by 100,000 units sales volume this one change caused profit to *decrease* $175,000. (All these numbers are found in Figure 7.1, which you should refer to.) *Unit-driven expenses* increased 15¢ per unit over last year. This 15¢ increase multiplied by 100,000 units sales volume for the most recent year gives the $15,000 negative change in profit. The increase in revenue-driven operating expenses caused profit to decrease $45,625, and fixed operating expenses increased by a whopping $103,500. The total of these individual changes equals the $108,547 overall profit increase.

You are reasonably pleased with the profit performance of your division. Profit increased 11.4 percent over last year. The Executive Committee of the company conducts an annual review of operations and profit performance of every division. They receive a copy of each division's management profit report. Each divisional manager presents a briefing to the Executive Committee. You will have a few minutes to review the performance of your division and answer questions. The CEO and other members of the Executive Committee are experienced managers. They expect you to deliver an insightful analysis of your division's profit performance in comparison with the previous year.

Open-Ended Nature of Comparative Profit Analysis

You must succinctly explain to the Executive Committee the profit performance of your division—in particular how you improved profit over last year. They do not want long-winded explanations that wander all over the place. They have read your division's profit report and they can do their own analysis, of course. But they want to hear your thinking regarding the main reasons for your division's profit improvement. They don't want to delve into too many details. They expect you to concentrate on the big picture. This poses a dilemma. When it comes to the comparative analysis of profit from one period to the next there are many ways to skin a cat. There is no one standard way, or one generally accepted method for explaining a profit increase from one period to the next.

The internal management profit report presented in Figure 7.1 is designed to be a good road map for analyzing profit behavior. Every profit factor changed from the previous year and every change caused a change in profit. Singling out just one or two changes as the most important depends on how you look at things. The biggest change was caused by the sales price increase, which increased profit $250,000. But the sales price increase should be coupled with the increase in product cost. You experienced increases in your product costs and you decided to pass-through the increases to your customers by raising sales prices. The net effect of these two interconnected changes was a $75,000 increase in profit: ($250,000 sales price effect – $175,000 product cost effect = $75,000 net profit increase). Furthermore, most of this net increase in profit was offset by profit decreases caused by increases in your unit-driven and revenue-driven operating expenses (see Figure 7.1).

If I were general manager my opening comments to the Executive Committee would emphasize the sales volume increase. This increase contributed almost $200,000 to your profit increase. Your unit margin increased slightly, from $26.36 to $26.50 because the sales price increase was slightly more than the increases in product cost and variable expenses. The biggest reason your profit increased was from selling 7,500 more units. Unfortunately, the gain from selling more units was substantially offset by the increase in your fixed operating expenses. Undoubtedly, the Executive Committee will expect you to go into some detail regarding your fixed operating expenses.

Fixed Operating Expenses

Why do fixed operating expenses increase? General inflationary pressures may drive up these costs. For instance, utility bills, real estate taxes, and insurance premiums drift relentlessly upward and seem hardly ever to go down. You don't find very many **fixed expenses** that follow a steady downward trend line. Can you think of many? There may be a few but certainly not many.

When fixed operating expenses increase due to general inflationary trends, there is no change in a company's warehouse and retail space or the appearance (attractiveness) of the retail space, or in the number of employees, and so on. As far as customers can tell, there have been no changes that would benefit them. A business has to increase its sales prices to pass-through the increase in its fixed expenses, which is explained in Chapter 6.

On the other hand fixed operating expenses may be deliberately increased (over and above any inflation-driven increases) to expand *capacity*. A business may rent a larger space or hire more employees on fixed salaries to provide for a larger sales capacity. A manufacturer may expand its plant, facilities, and workforce to provide greater production capacity. Over time a business has to keep its capacity (and thus its fixed operating expenses) in alignment with its sales volume. In any one year a business may have a certain amount of idle, or unused capacity. But the business has to plan carefully to keep its capacity consistent with sales volume. Instead of expanding capacity, fixed expenses may be increased by a business to improve demand for its products and to improve the customer traffic of its present location. For example a business could invest in better furnishings and equipment.

Looking Ahead

You now turn to the question of how to improve profit performance in the coming year. The head office requires that you submit

Are Accounting Methods Consistent?

The comparative analysis of profit performance between periods makes one critical assumption—that accounting methods are consistent period to period. Furthermore, it is assumed that managers have not deliberately massaged the numbers in order to meet their profit objectives for the period. One technique for manipulating fixed operating expenses recorded in a period is called deferred maintenance.

Buildings, machines, equipment, and land improvements need routine repairs and maintenance. The scheduling of these expenditures is at the discretion of managers. Most of these expenditures do not have to follow a fixed timetable. To minimize the amount of expenses recorded in a period, a manager could intentionally delay, or defer repair and maintenance work. Deferred maintenance is an illusory cost saving method because the repair and maintenance work has to be done later. There are several other tricks of the trade for manipulating the timing of expenses, which Chapter 14 explores.

a budget plan for the coming year, which is based on your forecasts for the coming year and changes you are planning to make during the coming year. The budgeting process is explained in Chapter 9.

Before putting the final touches on your budget, you have to make final decisions regarding certain profit strategy changes that you're seriously considering making during the coming year. One is a proposal to reduce sales prices in order to expand sales volume. As you might suspect this proposal comes from the sales manager of your division. This strategy shift might be a good way to improve profit. Then again, making these changes may actually decrease profit. You don't know for sure until you analyze how the changes would impact profit performance.

Cutting Sales Prices to Pump-up Sales Volume

The sales manager of your division has put forth a proposal to decrease sales prices five percent. He predicts that this sales price reduction would increase sales volume 10 percent. On the surface this two-for-one trade-off appears to be a good move. Giving up 5 percent of your sales price for 10 percent gain in sales volume appears to be a good trade-off. Before cranking the numbers to determine what would happen to profit, you should think about several non-quantitative aspects of making such a fundamental change in your profit model.

Your competition may follow you down in price, and your sales volume may not increase. On the other hand your competitors may not follow you down on sales prices. Your products are differentiated from your competitors' products. And your products have stronger brand names. For several years there have been sales price spreads between your products and those offered by the competition. In your opinion a five percent price cut probably would not trigger price reductions by your competitors. Even if the competition followed you down in sale prices the total, market-wide demand for all products may increase at the lower sales prices.

One reason for seriously considering the proposal is that your division is not selling up to its capacity. This is not unusual; many businesses have some slack, or unused capacity that is provided by their fixed operating expenses. Assume that your fixed operating expenses provide enough space and personnel to handle a sizable increase in sales volume. For the year just ended your division sold 100,000 units (see Figure 7.1), but you could have sold 120,000 units given the level of your fixed operating expenses.

Therefore, the sales manager's proposal to increase sales volume is attractive. Fixed costs would be spread over a larger number of units, which is called *economies of scale*. Fixed cost per unit sold would decrease, which is also referred to as *leveraging* fixed costs. In a recent article discussing the large sales volume decrease of a company compared with the previous year, I noticed that the reporter used the term "deleveraging" fixed costs. The company's fixed costs had to be spread over fewer units sold, with the result that the company's average fixed cost per unit sold increased.

Your customers may not respond to the sales price reductions as much as your sales manager predicts. Or sales volume may increase more than 10 percent. In any case you would closely monitor the reaction of customers. One serious risk is that if a sales volume doesn't materialize, you may not be able to reverse directions. You may not be able to roll back the sales price decreases. Customers may see only the reversals and perceive that you are raising prices. All in all you and the sales manager are of the opinion that lower prices would induce customers to buy more.

Analyzing the Proposal

The management profit report presented in Figure 7.1 provides an excellent analytical framework for the comparison of profit from period to period—and for preparing a profit budget for the coming period. This tool of analysis could be used to do a simulation, or dress rehearsal of the proposal to cut sales prices and increase sales volume. However, this would be like using a sledgehammer to pound a nail.

Instead of using the full-blown profit report presented in Figure 7.1, a narrowly focused analytical method is more efficient, one that focuses just on the factors that would change by the decision. This limited analysis technique sometimes is called a "back of an envelope" method because all the calculations could quite literally fit in the space on the back of an envelope. The idea is not to develop a complete profit report for the proposal, but rather to zero in as quickly as possible on the profit impact of the proposal.

To recap the proposal: Drop sales prices 5 percent in exchange for a 10 percent sales volume increase, and assume that fixed operating expenses would not increase at the higher sales volume. Since fixed costs don't change, contribution margin becomes the focus. Recall that contribution margin equals sales volume times unit margin (contribution margin per unit sold).

Figure 7.2 compares the present state of affairs, that is, for the year just ended, against the proposed state of affairs in which sales

FIGURE 7.2 Five Percent Lower Sales Price and Ten Percent Higher Sales Volume

	Unit Margin		Sales Volume		Contribution Margin
Present	$26.500	x	100,000 units	=	$2,650,000
Proposed	$21.925	x	110,000 units	=	$2,411,750
Change	($4.575)		10,000 units		($238,250)
% Change	−17.3%		10.0%		−9.0%

prices are 5 percent lower and sales volume is 10 percent higher. The average sales price for the year just ended was $100.00. A five percent decrease would decrease the average sales price $5.00. Unit margin would not decrease by the entire $5.00 because revenue-driven expenses are 8.5 percent of sales price and would therefore decrease $0.425. The net decrease in unit margin would be $4.575: ($5.00 sales price decrease − $0.425 revenue-driven expenses decrease = $4.575 decrease in unit margin).

It might seem on the surface that a 10 percent sales volume gain is enough in exchange for a 5 percent sales price reduction. But sales price is the wrong place to look. The key change to keep your eye on is not sales price but the unit margin. It drops 17.3 percent (see Figure 7.2). This large percent decrease in unit margin is the killer in this trade-off proposal. Sales volume does not increase enough to overcome the drop in unit margin.

As shown in Figure 7.2 contribution margin would decrease $238,250, or 9.0 percent. A 10 percent gain in sales volume is not nearly enough to overcome the plunge in unit margin. Sales volume would have to increase to 120,867 units just to maintain contribution margin at the same level, which is shown in Figure 7.3. Of course, you may not be able to increase sales volume 20,867 units, which is more than a 20 percent increase. Furthermore, even if you could sell this many units, the higher sales volume may push your capacity to the limit, and you might have to increase fixed operating expenses.

In summary the sales price reduction proposal should be DOA (dead on arrival). The 5 percent sales price reduction needs much more than a 10 percent sales volume increase, and thus would not be a good decision. Yet you frequently see advertisements of sales price reductions of 10 percent or more. What's going on? First of all many sales price reductions are discounts from list prices, which no one takes seriously as the final price, such as sticker prices on new cars.

FIGURE 7.3 Sales Volume Needed to Keep Contribution Margin the Same with Five Percent Lower Sales Prices

	Unit Margin		Sales Volume		Contribution Margin
Present	$26.500	x	100,000 units	=	$2,650,000
Proposed	$21.925	x	120,867 units	=	$2,650,000
Change	($4.575)		20,867 units		no change
% Change	−17.3%		20.9%		no change

List prices are only the point of departure for getting to the real price. Everyone wants a discount. I'm sure you've heard "I can get it for you wholesale."

The example uses the real price, that is, the actual sales revenue per unit actually received by the business net of any discounts, rebates, allowances, or whatever device is used to reach the actual sales price. Could any business cut its (real) sales price 5 percent and increase profit if sales volume increased 10 percent? No; unless its unit margin is extraordinarily high, such that unit margin would be reduced less than 10 percent.

In the analysis of the sales price reduction proposal just discussed, fixed operating expenses are pushed to the side and not included in the computations. Fixed operating expenses are treated as an *irrelevant cost* in the decision analysis, because it is assumed that fixed costs would be the same no matter which decision is taken. If, on the other hand, the increase in sales volume required increasing fixed costs to provide more capacity for the higher sales level, then the increase in fixed costs is relevant and definitely should be included in the analysis.

Short-Term Sales Promotions

The sales reduction proposal presented above is for a general, across-the-board sales price reduction over the entire year. In contrast many sales price reductions are limited to a relatively few items and are short lived, just for a day or weekend. Having a sale may bring in customers who buy other items not on sale. Unit margin is sacrificed on selected items to make additional sales of other products at normal unit margins.

Some retailers always have some products on sale, virtually every

Relevant, Irrelevant, and Sunk Costs

For decision-making analysis a *relevant cost* is a cost that is different between the alternatives being considered. An *irrelevant* cost is a cost that is the same for all the alternatives being considered. In the lower sales price/higher sales volume scenario it is implicitly assumed that product cost, unit-driven expenses, and revenue-driven expenses are *relevant* to the decision. These costs would be different between alternative A (do not change sales prices) and alternative B (decrease sales prices to increase sales volume).

Sometimes a business ends up holding with certain products in inventory that have reached the end of their life cycles. Or demand for some products plunges suddenly and a business cannot sell the products in the normal channels of distribution. A business has to get rid of such products at the best price it can get. In these cases product cost is called a sunk cost. A sunk cost is like water over the dam, or like spilt milk. The cost is irrelevant in setting a sales price for the products. The business should simply get the best price it can or get rid of the products for whatever salvage value it can get for the products.

day of the year. In these cases the normal unit margin is hard to pin down, since almost every product takes its turn at being on sale. Every product may have two unit margins—one when not on sale and one when on sale. The average unit margin for the year depends on how often the item goes on sale weighted by the sales volume at each price.

The analysis method shown in Figure 7.2 can be applied to short-term, limited sales price reductions. The manager should calculate, or at least estimate how much additional sales volume would be needed on the sale items just to remain even with the profit that would have been earned at normal sales prices. Complicating the picture are the sales of other products (not on sale) that would not have been made without the increase in sales traffic from shoppers for the items on sale. Obviously, the additional sales made at their normal unit margins are an important factor to consider, although these incremental sales may be difficult to estimate with any confidence.

Sacrificing Sales Volume For Higher Sales Prices

Suppose an idea has been floating around in the back of your head. Why not *increase* sales prices in order to improve unit margin? Sure, sales volume probably would fall off. But you think the sales volume decrease would be limited. Furthermore, at the lower sales volume you would be able to downsize your fixed operating expenses. Your sales manager doesn't think along these lines. Sales managers generally are opposed to giving up sales volume, especially a loss of market share that would be hard to recapture later. Any decision that deliberately decreases sales volume should be considered very carefully. For the moment put aside these warnings.

To carry on the analysis assume that if you raise sales prices 10 percent, then sales volume would fall off, say, 20 percent. Would contribution margin decrease, or would it increase in fact? (Fixed expenses are considered later; these costs certainly would not have to be increased at the lower sales level.) Figure 7.4 shows the result of this scenario. Contribution margin would increase $202,000, or 7.6 percent—before savings in fixed operating expenses are considered. Note that unit margin would increase 34.5 percent, which is more than enough to offset the 20 percent sales volume decrease.

It is instructive to prepare the management profit report for this scenario, which is presented in Figure 7.5. You would increase profit $800,000 by selling 80,000 units at a $10.00 higher sales price. The revenue-driven expenses increase $.085 per unit sold (8.5 percent of the $10.00 sales price increase). Based on 80,000 units sold this increase causes a $68,000 profit decrease. Selling 20,000 fewer units at the previous $26.50 unit margin decreases profit $530,000.

The $800,000 gain in profit from the sales price increase overcomes these two negative impacts and overall profit would increase $202,000. Moreover, at the lower sales level you probably would be able to decrease your fixed operating expenses. By the way this change to a higher sales price and lower sales volume would have a very favorable impact on operating cash flow, which is explained in Chapter 8.

The knee-jerk reaction of most business managers to this analysis

FIGURE 7.4 Ten Percent Higher Sales Price and Twenty Percent Lower Sales Volume

	Unit Margin		Sales Volume		Contribution Margin
Present	$26.500	x	100,000 units	=	$2,650,000
Proposed	$35.650	x	80,000 units	=	$2,852,000
Change	$9.150		−20,000 units		$202,000
% Change	34.5%		−20.0%		7.6%

FIGURE 7.5 Management Profit Report for Ten Percent Higher Sales Prices and Twenty Percent Lower Sales Volume Scenario

	Year Just Ended		Proposal		Changes	Profit Impact
Sales Volume	100,000 units		80,000 units		(20,000)	($530,000)
	Per Unit	**Totals**	**Per Unit**	**Totals**		
Sales Revenue	$100.00	$10,000,000	$110.00	$8,800,000	$10.00	$800,000
Cost of Goods Sold	$60.00	$6,000,000	$60.00	$4,800,000		
Gross Margin	$40.00	$4,000,000	$50.00	$4,000,000		
Unit-Driven Expenses	$5.00	$500,000	$5.00	$400,000		
Revenue-Driven Expenses	8.50%	$850,000	8.50%	$748,000	$0.85	($68,000)
Contribution Margin	$26.50	$2,650,000	$35.65	$2,852,000		
Fixed Operating Expenses		$1,590,000		$1,590,000		
Profit (Earnings before Other Expenses)		$1,060,000		$1,262,000	$202,000 19.1%	$202,000

would be to decide *against* the proposal—even though the numbers show a nice gain in profit. By and large you'll find that successful companies have built their success on getting and keeping a base of loyal and satisfied customers that make repeat purchases. Few businesses are willing to give up market share. When a business has a significant market share it is a major player and dominant force in the marketplace, which provides very important competitive advantages.

The profit increase shown in Figure 7.5 is based on the prediction that sales volume would drop 20 percent. Sales volume might fall 25 percent or more. Profit can be calculated for any particular sales volume decrease. You can determine the sales volume that would keep contribution margin the same. This keep-even sales volume is computed as follows:

$$\frac{\$2,650,000 \text{ contribution margin}}{\$35.65 \text{ unit margin}} = 74,334 \text{ units sales volume}$$

Sales may not drop off this much, at least in the short run. And, as mentioned before, fixed operating expenses could probably be reduced at the lower sales level.

Generally speaking it is difficult to predict how sales demand would respond to a sales price increase. A 10 percent sales price increase for most products is a bug chunk of change. If new auto prices jumped 10 percent, for example, I believe that sales demand would fall off significantly. On the other hand, increasing sales prices may actually stimulate demand for some products. The higher prices might enhance the prestige or premium image of the company's products and attract more of an upscale clientele who are quite willing to pay higher prices.

Given their druthers I think that the large majority of business managers would rather keep their market share and not give up any sales volume, even though profit could theoretically be increased in the short run with a higher sales price/lower sales volume combination. Protecting sales volume and market share is deeply ingrained in the thinking of most business managers, and for good reason.

In closing I should also mention that some businesses carve out a relatively small market niche and build their profit performance on low sales volume at premium prices. The analysis above demonstrates the profit logic of the niche strategy, which is built on high unit margins that make up for smaller sales volume.

Quality Improvement Plan

Inflation is one thing; quite another is when a business makes changes that increase the costs of its products. The quality of the products is improved to make them more attractive to customers. Making product improvements is a common marketing strategy, designed to give customers a better product at the same sales price in order to stimulate demand and increase sales volume. At the same sales price customers would buy more—perhaps a lot more.

Also, a business may increase its variable operating expenses to improve the quality of the service to customers. For example, faster delivery methods such as overnight Federal Express or UPS could be used, even though this would cost more than traditional truck and rail delivery methods. These changes would increase unit-driven operating expenses. A business may increase the percentage of sales commissions to improve the personal time and effort the sales staff spends with each customer.

Suppose you have developed a broad-based quality improvement plan for your division. After careful and detailed analysis of many factors you have budgeted the following cost changes for the coming year using the year just ended as the point of departure:

- Product cost will be increased from $60.00 to $64.50 per unit.
- Unit-driven operating expenses will be increased from $5.00 to $5.30 per unit.
- Revenue-driven operating expenses will be increased from 8.5 percent to 10.0 percent of sales revenue (higher sales commissions for better service to customers).

Tentatively, and I should say very tentatively, you have decided not to increase sales prices. You predict that demand should increase 15 percent to 20 percent for the improved products and service. It goes without saying that demand would increase only if customers are made aware of and become convinced of the improvements. Is this a wise trade-off decision? Would profit increase for this scenario of higher costs and higher sales volume?

To start the analysis notice that your unit margin would drop rather precipitously:

DROP IN UNIT MARGIN

Present unit margin	$26.50
Product cost increase	($ 4.50)
Unit-driven expense increase	($ .30)
Revenue-driven expense increase	($ 1.50)
Proposed unit margin	$20.20

At the lower $20.20 unit margin you would have to sell 131,188 units just to earn the same contribution margin as before, which is computed as follows:

$$\frac{\$2,650,000 \text{ contribution margin}}{\$20.20 \text{ unit margin}} = 131,188 \text{ units sales volume}$$

Would demand for the improved products cause sales volume to increase more than 30,000 units, or more than 30 percent? And, if sales volume did increase 30 percent would you have to expand capacity and increase fixed operating expenses? These questions suggest that you probably should plan on increasing sales prices.

You would need to bump your average sales price $7.00 per unit in order to keep contribution margin the same:

	Present	*Proposed*
Sales price	$100.00	$107.00
Product cost	($ 60.00)	($ 64.50)
Unit-driven expenses	($ 5.00)	($ 5.30)
Revenue-driven expenses	($ 8.50)	($ 10.70)
Unit margin	$ 26.50	$ 26.50

Sales price increases should be considered very carefully of course. Customer reaction is never easy to predict. An optimistic scenario is that sales prices could be raised even more than $7.00 and even at the higher price level sales volume would increase because of the improvements in product quality and service. Assume that you take the quality upgrade program as an opportune time for improving both average unit margin and sales volume. This might work.

To raise sales prices for quality improvements a business needs a carefully orchestrated advertising and marketing promotion program—one that makes customers aware of the changes and that convinces them that they are getting more value added than the increase in sales prices. Probably you would have to increase your fixed costs, in particular your advertising and other marketing promotion outlays. So assume you budget $100,000 increase in these costs to communicate and promote your quality upgrade plan.

To carry through on this scenario assume you raise sales prices $8.50 on average and you sell five percent additional sales volume. The outcome of this scenario is shown in Figure 7.6. Profit would increase more than 16 percent. Whether you could pull this off is the question, of course.

Decreasing Costs: Productivity Gains, or Otherwise?

Suppose you lower your product costs and variable operating expenses. On the one hand such cost savings may be true efficiency and productivity gains. Sharper bargaining may reduce purchase costs. Wasteful expenses could be eliminated. Labor productivity gains would reduce unit product costs of manufacturers.

FIGURE 7.6 Quality Improvement Plan

	Year Just Ended		Proposal		Changes	Profit Impact
Sales Volume	100,000 units		105,000 units		5,000	$132,500
	Per Unit	Totals	Per Unit	Totals		
Sales Revenue	$100.00	$10,000,000	$108.50	$11,392,500	$8.50	$892,500
Cost of Goods Sold	$60.00	$6,000,000	$64.50	$6,772,500	$4.50	($472,500)
Gross Margin	$40.00	$4,000,000	$44.00	$4,620,000		
Unit-Driven Expenses	$5.00	$500,000	$5.30	$556,500	$0.30	($31,500)
Revenue-Driven Expenses	8.50%	$850,000	10.00%	$1,139,250	$2.35	($246,750)
Contribution Margin	$26.50	$2,650,000	$27.85	$2,924,250		
Fixed Operating Expenses		$1,590,000		$1,690,000	$100,000	($100,000)
Profit (Earnings before Other Expenses)		$1,060,000		$1,234,250	$174,250	$174,250
					16.4%	

If a business can lower its costs and still deliver the same product and identical quality of service, then sales volume should not be affected. Customers should see no differences in products or service. The cost savings would improve unit margin and profit would increase accordingly. Suppose you could lower unit product costs an average $2.40 per unit because of true efficiency and productivity gains that do not cause any degradation of the products you sell.

In this scenario the $2.40 per unit reduction in product cost would increase unit margin from $26.50 to $28.90. At the higher unit margin your contribution margin would increase $240,000, equal to the $2.40 unit margin increase times the 100,000 units sales volume. The contribution margin increase would carry down to profit, assuming your fixed operating expenses do not change. So your profit would increase $240,000 or by about 23 percent. Paying attention to cost efficiencies has it rewards.

The key test for cost reductions is whether products remain the same and whether the quality of service to customers remains the same. Maybe so, maybe not. Product cost decreases may cause quality degradations, or may result from reducing sizes (such as smaller candy bars or fewer ounces in breakfast cereal boxes). Reducing variable operating expenses may adversely affect the quality of service to customers—for instance, spreading fewer sales personnel over the same number of customers.

Total quality management (TQM) has gotten a lot of press, indicated by the fact that it has been reduced to an acronym. Managers have always known that product quality and quality of service to customers are absolutely critical, though sometimes they lose sight of this in the pursuit of short-term profits. Cost savings may cause degradation in the quality of products or service to customers. Therefore, it should be no surprise that sales volume may decrease because of cost reduction techniques. Unit margins would improve, but a sales volume decrease may offset the profit gain from the higher unit margins.

Summary

Managers need a sure analytical grip on each profit factor. They should be able to pinpoint the reasons why profit increased or decreased compared with the previous period. The chapter presents a management profit report that focuses on the critical factors that drive profit each period and that highlights the profit increase or decrease effect caused by changes in each factor. The management profit report explained in the chapter also serves as an excellent platform for preparing the profit plan and budget for the coming year.

To control profit performance managers must keep their attention riveted on unit margins, sales volume, and fixed operating expenses. Profit is sensitive to relatively small changes in unit margins, sales volume, and fixed operating expenses. Seemingly small slippages in any of these key profit factors can have a devastating impact on profit.

When deciding whether to decrease sales prices to increase sales, volume managers should not rely solely on their intuitive feel for what the outcome would be. They should crank the numbers and determine whether the trade-off could actually put a big dent in profit. The chapter presents an analysis tool that can be used to quickly calculate the profit impact of this and a wide range of other trade-off decisions. The analysis tool is compact. The calculations can be done in the space on the back of an envelope.

CHAPTER 8

Profit Changes and Cash Flow

Suppose that you increased profit $265,000 over the previous year. Do you expect this should also increase cash flow $265,000? Intuitively it seems that cash flow should increase as much as profit. But as a matter of fact the actual change in cash flow can be significantly different from the change in profit. The two amounts are hardly ever equal. In some cases an increase in profit can cause a decrease in cash flow. Or a decrease in profit can cause an increase in cash flow. The cash flow effect from a change in profit depends on which factors cause profit to change—sales volume, sales prices, costs, or a combination of these factors.

Changes in profit factors are not created equal regarding their cash flow consequences. Some changes are much better for cash flow than others. Suppose you could increase profit the same amount by either increasing sales volume or, alternatively, by increasing sales prices. Which of these two alternatives should you prefer from the cash flow point of view? One is definitely better.

Approach of Chapter

This chapter follows the philosophy espoused in Chapter 2—which is that managers should understand the fundamentals of cash flow but should let their accountants do the detailed analysis that is required to develop cash flow information. This approach is exemplified in the cash flow report for managers explained in Chapter 2 (see Figure 2.2).

It's my firm opinion that managers should take a hands-off approach and not get involved in the detailed analysis of cash flow from profit. Managers should know the basic reasons for differences between cash inflow and sales revenue, and between cash outflow and expenses. But they should let their accountants do the grungy work of determining the cash flow differences. I'll be your accountant in this chapter; you can rely on me to do the dirty work.

Getting Started

This chapter is a companion to Chapters 6 and 7. Those two chapters investigate the increase or decrease in profit caused by changes in one or more of the factors that drive profit. This chapter shifts attention to the cash flow effects of profit changes. Cash flow from profit may be affected by other developments during the period as well. Suppose a business implements a new inventory control system that substantially reduces its inventory levels without hurting sales. This has a favorable impact on cash flow from profit. Or suppose a business extends the credit period offered to customers and its accounts receivable increases. This slowdown in collecting sales has an unfavorable impact on cash flow from profit.

This chapter focuses on the *changes* in cash flow caused by *changes* in the factors that drive profit. Here's one example: In Chapter 6 the change in profit resulting from a 10 percent sales volume increase is determined. Profit increases $265,000 in this scenario (see Figure 6.2). This chapter analyzes the cash flow result from the sales volume increase. As it turns out, cash flow increases only $86,000—quite a bit less than the profit increase to say the least. The scenarios presented in Chapters 6 and 7 are put through the cash flow sieve in this chapter.

The business example used in Chapters 6 and 7 is carried forward into this chapter. You ought to be familiar with this example by now. You are the general manager of one of the major divisions of a business. You are responsible for the profit performance of the division and for keeping the division's assets and operating liabilities under control. Your management profit report for the most recent two years is presented in Figure 7.1. This profit report focuses on the key factors that drive sales revenue and expenses and highlights the changes in these factors period to period that cause profit to increase or decrease. The profit report does not deal with cash flows. You need a second report for them.

Cash Flow Management Report

The general manager of each division of the business receives a cash flow report for his or her division. These divisional reports do not include cash flows from the investing and financing activities of the business. These important decisions are made at headquarters; the general managers of the divisions do not have authority or responsibility for these cash flows. They do have responsibility for operating cash flow (cash flow from profit) of their divisions, however.

Your cash flow report for the most recent two years is presented in Figure 8.1. This report follows the design of the internal cash flow report that is introduced in Chapter 2 (see Figure 2.2). Please keep in mind that this is an *internal management report*. This report differs from the statement of cash flows that is reported outside the business to its shareowners and lenders.

The external statement of cash flows is prepared in accordance with generally accepted accounting principles (GAAP). These standards have been developed over the years for financial reporting to investors and lenders. Internal accounting reports to managers are not governed by the rules for external financial reporting. Internal accounting reports are tailor made to fit the scope of responsibility of each manager and focus on key factors for management planning and control.

In cash flow report (Figure 8.1) note that depreciation expense is

FIGURE 8.1 Cash Flow from Profit

	Previous Year	Cash Flow Differences	Year Just Ended	Cash Flow Differences
Sales Revenue	$9,018,750	($78,356)	$10,000,000	($92,464)
Cost of Goods Sold	$5,388,125	($127,854)	$6,000,000	($138,849)
Gross Margin	$3,630,625		$4,000,000	
Unit-Driven Expenses	$448,625	$6,285	$500,000	$7,113
Revenue-Driven Expenses	$744,047	$12,588	$850,000	$14,670
Contribution Margin	$2,437,953		$2,650,000	
Fixed Operating Expenses	$1,161,500	$9,845	$1,240,000	$10,869
Depreciation Expense	$325,000	$325,000	$350,000	$350,000
Profit (Earnings Before Other Expenses)	$951,453		$1,060,000	
Net Cash Flow Difference	$147,508	$147,508	$151,341	$151,341
Cash Flow from Profit	$1,098,961		$1,211,341	

separated from other fixed operating expenses. Depreciation is a unique expense from the cash flow point of view. (In Chapter 7 depreciation is lumped in with other costs and only one total is given for fixed operating expenses.) As shown in Figure 8.1 your division's cash flow from profit is higher than profit in both years. The total of cash flow from depreciation plus the other positive cash flow differences is more than the sum of the two negative cash flow differences. However, in both years a good chunk of your depreciation cash flow was used for the increases in accounts receivable and inventories during the year.

Capsule Review of Cash Flow from Profit

Chapter 2 explains that the changes during the period in the assets and operating liabilities that are connected with sales revenue and expenses either decrease or increase cash flow from profit for the period. A brief refresher on cash flow from profit follows.

- **Point of reference:** The point of reference for determining cash flow from profit is the profit measure for the period. The idea is to adjust, or to convert the profit measure into the net amount of cash flow from sales and expenses during the period that are recorded according to the accrual basis of accounting. Cash flow from profit, basically, is the amount of profit that would have been recorded if the *cash basis* of accounting had been used instead of the accrual basis of accounting. Please keep in mind that to measure profit the accrual basis is required by generally accepted accounting principles (GAAP).

- **Accounts receivable:** The balance in the accounts receivable asset account is the amount of sales made on credit that has not yet been collected from customers. An increase in accounts receivable reduces cash flow from profit because the total of cash collections from customers during the period is less than the amount recorded in sales revenue. A decrease in accounts receivable benefits cash flow because the total of cash collections from customers is more than the sales revenue amount. To sum up: *When accounts receivable go up, cash flow goes down. And when accounts receivable goes down, cash flow goes up.*

- **Inventories:** Inventories are products held for sale. An increase in inventories reduces cash flow from profit because the total of cash payments for the purchase or manufacture of products during the period is more than the amount recorded in cost of goods sold expense. A decrease in inventories helps cash flow from profit because the total of cash outlays for the purchase or manufacture of products during the period is less than the cost of goods sold expense. To sum up: *When inventories go up, cash flow goes down. And when inventories go down, cash flow goes up.*

- **Depreciation expense:** Part of the total cost of a company's long-lived assets is carved off as it were and recorded as depreciation expense for the period. There is no cash outlay in recording depreciation expense. Rather, cash outlay occurred sometime in the past when the long-lived assets being depreciated were purchased or constructed. From the cash flow point of view depreciation is not an expense. So the amount of depreciation expense is added back to profit to put the profit measure on a cash flow basis.

  The total amount of cash collections from sales during the period includes an embedded amount that reimburses the business for the depreciation expense of using its fixed assets during the period. Each year a business converts part of the original cost of its fixed assets into cash. The depreciation add-back to profit is to recognize the conversion of a fraction of the cost invested in fixed assets into cash.

- **Accounts payable from inventory purchases:** Accounts payable are short-term liabilities of a business arising from two different sources. One source is when a business purchases on credit the products it sells or the materials it uses in manufacturing the products it sells. Accounts payable from inventory purchases generally are paid a month or so later, whereas typically products are held in inventory for two or three months before being sold. In the cash flow report (Figure 8.1) the increase in accounts payable for inventory purchases is netted against the increase in inventories. The cash flow difference reported for the cost of goods sold is the net effect of the increase in inventories minus the increase in accounts payable for inventory purchases.

- **Accounts payable for unpaid expenses, accrued expenses payable, and prepaid expenses:** In recording expenses a business uses the *prepaid expenses* asset account and two operating liability accounts—*accounts payable* and *accrued expenses payable*. The ending balance in the prepaid expenses account is the amount of costs that already have been paid, but have not yet been charged to expense. In contrast a certain amount of a business's total expenses for the period are unpaid at the end of the period. These unpaid expenses are recorded in accounts payable and accrued expenses payable. Increases or decreases in these three accounts during the period have effects on cash flow from profit for the period. Compared with changes in accounts receivable and inventories, however, the changes in these three accounts usually are relatively minor.

In your latest cash flow report (Figure 8.1) note that the cash flow differences for sales revenue and cost of goods sold expense are the two largest items, other than the depreciation cash flow. Your sales increased over last year and accounts receivable increased accordingly. The increase in accounts receivable causes the negative cash flow difference reported in Figure 8.1 for sales revenue. To support the higher sales volume you increased your inventories and this increase (less the offsetting increase in accounts payable for inventory purchases) causes the negative cash flow effect reported for cost of goods sold expense. The cash flow differences for operating expenses are relatively minor and are not discussed much in this chapter.

Cash Flow Effects of Profit Changes

Chapter 2 explains cash flow from profit, which is also called operating cash flow. In the formal statement of cash flows (see Figure 2.3 for an example) this key figure is called cash flow from operating activities. Cash flows from investing activities and financing activities are not discussed in this chapter. Therefore, the shorter expression *cash flow* is used frequently in this chapter as shorthand for cash flow from profit.

As mentioned earlier, a business may tighten or loosen its investments in accounts receivable and inventories, independent of changes (if any) in the factors that propel profit. An increase or decrease of accounts receivable and inventories, for whatever reason, causes a reverse effect on cash flow. This chapter focuses on changes in cash flow driven by changes in profit factors that are analyzed throughout Chapters 6 and 7. The examples from those two chapters are revisited in this chapter in order to determine the cash flow effect for each scenario. The changes in sales revenue, cost of goods sold, and operating expenses—as the case may be for each scenario—provide the launch pad for determining the change in cash flow.

Sales Volume Increase

The first profit change scenario examined in Chapter 6 is a 10 percent sales volume increase, while holding other profit factors constant.

You may want to review Figure 6.2, which presents the profit impact of this change. Profit increases $265,000 in this scenario. Cash flow does not fare as well. Figure 8.2 presents a typical cash flow outcome for the 10 percent sales volume increase.

Cash flow increases only $86,000, which is a relatively small cash flow payoff from the profit increase. The cash flow outcome may appear at odds with the increase in profit. The twofold explanation is that the increase in sales revenue causes accounts receivable to increase, and the larger sales volume causes inventories to increase. Both these changes have relatively large negative impacts on cash flow from profit.

The cash flow differences in the right column in Figure 8.2 are based on reasonable assumptions. Sales revenue increases 10 percent in this scenario. Therefore, accounts receivable would increase 10 percent give or take a little. At the end of the most recent year your accounts receivable had a balance of about $961,000. At the higher sales revenue level accounts receivable would increase about 10 percent, which is the $96,000 negative cash flow difference for the sales revenue increase (see Figure 8.2).

The 10 percent higher sales volume causes cost of goods sold to increase 10 percent. To support the higher sales volume you would increase inventories 10 percent (give or take a little). At the end of the most recent year inventories has a cost balance of $1,500,000. At the same date the balance of accounts payable for inventory purchases stood at $460,000. In other words not all the amount of inventories at year-end had been paid for—only $1,040,000 had been paid for (the $1,500,000 cost of inventories less the $460,000 of accounts

FIGURE 8.2 Cash Flow Change: 10 Percent Sales Volume Increase

	Year Just Ended	New Scenario	Increase (Decrease)	Cash Flow Difference
Sales Revenue	$10,000,000	$11,000,000	$1,000,000	($96,000)
Cost of Goods Sold	$6,000,000	$6,600,000	$600,000	($104,000)
Gross Margin	$4,000,000	$4,400,000	$400,000	
Unit-Driven Expenses	$500,000	$550,000	$50,000	$8,000
Revenue-Driven Expenses	$850,000	$935,000	$85,000	$13,000
Contribution Margin	$2,650,000	$2,915,000	$265,000	
Fixed Operating Expenses	$1,240,000	$1,240,000		
Depreciation Expense	$350,000	$350,000		
Profit	$1,060,000	$1,325,000	$265,000	
Net Cash Flow Difference			($179,000)	($179,000)
Cash Flow Increase (Decrease)			$86,000	

payable for inventory purchases). Inventories would increase about 10 percent, or $150,000, and accounts payable for inventory purchases would increase about 10 percent, or $46,000. The net difference of these two changes is $104,000, which is the negative cash flow difference for the cost goods sold increase in Figure 8.2.

The increases in accounts receivable and inventories cause relatively large cash flow differences. The cash flow differences caused by the increases in operating expenses are not nearly as significant, although the net effect of these increases is positive. I won't bother going into detail regarding these minor cash flow differences.

The end result is that cash flow for the period increases only $86,000 compared with the $265,000 profit increase. Increasing sales volume helps profit but does not improve cash flow nearly as much. The increment in profit is much more than the increment in your cash balance. When sales volume increases, you have to increase your investments in accounts receivable and inventories, which are drains on cash flow.

Sales Volume Decrease

Chapter 6 examines the profit change caused by a four percent decrease in sales volume—see Figure 6.3 for reference. Profit decreases $106,000 in this scenario. However, cash flow decreases only $34,000 as shown in Figure 8.3.

At the lower sales volume level sales revenue and cost of goods sold expense decrease. These two decreases should cause four percent decreases in accounts receivable and inventories. These asset decreases have positive cash flow effects, as shown in Figure 8.3.

FIGURE 8.3 Cash Flow Change: 4 Percent Sales Volume Decrease

	Year Just Ended	New Scenario	Increase (Decrease)	Cash Flow Difference
Sales Revenue	$10,000,000	$9,600,000	($400,000)	$38,000
Cost of Goods Sold	$6,000,000	$5,760,000	($240,000)	$42,000
Gross Margin	$4,000,000	$3,840,000	($160,000)	
Unit-Driven Expenses	$500,000	$480,000	($20,000)	($3,000)
Revenue-Driven Expenses	$850,000	$816,000	($34,000)	($5,000)
Contribution Margin	$2,650,000	$2,544,000	($106,000)	
Fixed Operating Expenses	$1,240,000	$1,240,000		
Depreciation Expense	$350,000	$350,000		
Profit	$1,060,000	$954,000	($106,000)	
Net Cash Flow Difference			$72,000	$72,000
Cash Flow Increase (Decrease)			($34,000)	

The downsizing of accounts receivable and inventories represent the partial liquidations of the two assets into cash. The decline in operating expenses at the lower sales volume causes minor negative cash flow effects.

Although profit suffers from the sales volume decrease, cash flow from profit does not suffer as much, which is some degree of consolation. If, on the other hand, you don't downsize your accounts receivable and inventories at the lower sales level, then cash flow would suffer as much as profit.

Higher Sales Prices

The gain in profit from increasing sales prices five percent is presented in Figure 6.5. Profit increases a whopping $457,500, or 43 percent. Does cash flow increase as much? A 10 percent sales volume increase doesn't do all that well for cash flow. Profit increases $265,000 but cash flow increases only $86,000. Things are quite different for a five percent hike in sales prices. Figure 8.4 shows that cash flow increases $416,000, which is not far behind the profit increase.

The increase in sales revenue causes accounts receivable to increase about $48,000, which is a drag against cash flow. The higher operating expenses have a relatively small positive effect. Overall cash flow increases $416,000 from the sales price increase (see Figure 8.4). Compare this with the rather puny $86,000 cash flow increase from a 10 percent increase in sales volume. In the higher sales prices scenario sales volume does not increase. So inventories do not increase. You avoid the negative cash flow effect of increasing inventories, which makes a big difference.

FIGURE 8.4 Cash Flow Change: 5 Percent Sales Price Increase

	Year Just Ended	New Scenario	Increase (Decrease)	Cash Flow Difference
Sales Revenue	$10,000,000	$10,500,000	$500,000	($48,000)
Cost of Goods Sold	$6,000,000	$6,000,000		
Gross Margin	$4,000,000	$4,500,000	$500,000	
Unit-Driven Expenses	$500,000	$500,000		
Revenue-Driven Expenses	$850,000	$892,500	$42,500	$6,500
Contribution Margin	$2,650,000	$3,107,500	$457,500	
Fixed Operating Expenses	$1,240,000	$1,240,000		
Depreciation Expense	$350,000	$350,000		
Profit	$1,060,000	$1,517,500	$457,500	
Net Cash Flow Difference			($41,500)	($41,500)
Cash Flow Increase (Decrease)			$416,000	

If you had your choice of increasing profit by raising sales prices or by raising sales volume, you should opt for higher sales prices every time from the cash flow point of view. Of course, you may not be able to raise sales prices without hurting sales volume, which always is a consideration. But if you had your choice, go for the sales price increase.

Lower Sales Price

Like it or not you may have to lower sales prices to stay competitive or just to stay in business. Figure 6.6 shows the result of decreasing sales prices three percent, which may not seem like much but has devastating effects on profit. Profit decreases $274,500 because even a small decrease in sales prices causes a significant reduction in your unit margin. In the higher sales price scenario, just examined, the cash flow increase is almost as much as the profit increase. When heading south (lower prices) instead of north (higher prices), cash flow suffers almost as much as profit. Figure 8.5 shows the bad news about cash flow caused by decreasing sales prices just three percent.

In this three percent lower sales prices scenario sales revenue decreases $300,000, which causes a $29,000 decrease in accounts receivable. This decrease benefits cash flow (see Figure 8.5). Overall, however, the decrease in cash flow from profit is close behind the decrease in profit. Decreasing sales prices wreaks havoc on both profit and cash flow.

FIGURE 8.5 Cash Flow Change: 3 Percent Sales Price Decrease

	Year Just Ended	New Scenario	Increase (Decrease)	Cash Flow Difference
Sales Revenue	$10,000,000	$9,700,000	($300,000)	$29,000
Cost of Goods Sold	$6,000,000	$6,000,000		
Gross Margin	$4,000,000	$3,700,000	($300,000)	
Unit-Driven Expenses	$500,000	$500,000		
Revenue-Driven Expenses	$850,000	$824,500	($25,500)	($4,000)
Contribution Margin	$2,650,000	$2,375,500	($274,500)	
Fixed Operating Expenses	$1,240,000	$1,240,000		
Depreciation Expense	$350,000	$350,000		
Profit	$1,060,000	$785,500	($274,500)	
Net Cash Flow Difference			$25,000	$25,000
Cash Flow Increase (Decrease)			($249,500)	

Cost Inflation Changes

Inflation is a fact of life as most people know. Product costs and the costs of operating a business are subject to persistent inflation pressures. A business could do nothing and simply absorb the higher costs without increasing sales prices. Of course this course of action is not recommended; profit would suffer more than you might suspect. Figure 6.7 presents the consequences of doing nothing to deal with five percent cost inflation. Profit decreases $447,000, which is a 42.2 percent plunge. Surely this is unacceptable.

The question here is whether cash flow would suffer as bad as the drop in profit. The answer, unfortunately, is yes. Figure 8.6 reveals that cash flow decreases $476,500, which actually is a little more than the drop in profit. The higher costs mean more money is tied up in inventories. The increase in inventories causes a negative cash flow effect, as shown in Figure 8.6. Even though you make less profit, you have to increase the amount invested in inventories because of the higher costs. This is not a happy state of affairs to say the least.

Business managers cannot stand by idle and do nothing about inflation-driven cost increases. Chapter 6 discusses that one of the functions of business managers is to pass through inflationary cost increases by raising sales prices to customers.

Cost Inflation Pass-Through Pricing

Chapter 6 includes a scenario in which product cost inflation is passed through to customers by raising sales prices just enough to

FIGURE 8.6 Cash Flow Change: 5 Percent Cost Inflation

	Year Just Ended	New Scenario	Increase (Decrease)	Cash Flow Difference
Sales Revenue	$10,000,000	$10,000,000		
Cost of Goods Sold	$6,000,000	$6,300,000	$300,000	($52,000)
Gross Margin	$4,000,000	$3,700,000	($300,000)	
Unit-Driven Expenses	$500,000	$525,000	$25,000	$4,000
Revenue-Driven Expenses	$850,000	$892,500	$42,500	$6,500
Contribution Margin	$2,650,000	$2,282,500	($367,500)	
Fixed Operating Expenses	$1,240,000	$1,319,500	$79,500	$12,000
Depreciation Expense	$350,000	$350,000		
Profit	$1,060,000	$613,000	($447,000)	
Net Cash Flow Difference			($29,500)	($29,500)
Cash Flow Increase (Decrease)			($476,500)	

cover the higher costs—see Figure 6.8 for reference. Profit does not change. So cash flow from profit would not change, right? Wrong.

Figure 8.7 shows that even though profit does not change, cash flow *decreases* $96,000 because the increases in sales revenue and cost of goods sold expense cause increases in accounts receivable and inventories. Profit would hold constant but your cash flow decreases in this scenario. This poses a real dilemma. You could argue that sales prices should be increased enough to prevent a negative cash flow effect.

Sacrificing Sales Volume for Higher Unit Margin

Chapter 7 discusses a trade-off proposal to raise sales prices and thereby to increase unit margin, even though sales volume would suffer. Depending on how far sales volume drops, this strategy could increase profit. Figure 7.5 looks at a scenario in which sales prices are bumped 10 percent and sales volume drops off 20 percent. Profit increases $202,000, or 19.1 percent. What about cash flow in this scenario?

In this scenario cash flow would increase almost $500,000, or more than twice the profit increase! Figure 8.8 gives the details. Accounts receivable and inventories would decrease at the lower sales volume level, and these decreases would cause relatively large increases in cash flow from profit. In essence you would liquidate part of your investments in accounts receivable and inventories. Your cash balance would increase substantially from converting some of these assets into cash.

FIGURE 8.7 Cash Flow Change: Cost Inflation Pass-Through Pricing

	Year Just Ended	New Scenario	Increase (Decrease)	Cash Flow Difference
Sales Revenue	$10,000,000	$10,400,000	$400,000	($38,000)
Cost of Goods Sold	$6,000,000	$6,366,000	$366,000	($63,000)
Gross Margin	$4,000,000	$4,034,000	$34,000	
Unit-Driven Expenses	$500,000	$500,000		
Revenue-Driven Expenses	$850,000	$884,000	$34,000	$5,000
Contribution Margin	$2,650,000	$2,650,000		
Fixed Operating Expenses	$1,240,000	$1,240,000		
Depreciation Expense	$350,000	$350,000		
Profit	$1,060,000	$1,060,000		
Net Cash Flow Difference			($96,000)	($96,000)
Cash Flow Increase (Decrease)			($96,000)	

FIGURE 8.8 Cash Flow Change: Higher Sales Prices and Lower Sales Volume

	Year Just Ended	New Scenario	Increase (Decrease)	Cash Flow Difference
Sales Revenue	$10,000,000	$8,800,000	($1,200,000)	$115,000
Cost of Goods Sold	$6,000,000	$4,800,000	($1,200,000)	$208,000
Gross Margin	$4,000,000	$4,000,000		
Unit-Driven Expenses	$500,000	$400,000	($100,000)	($15,000)
Revenue-Driven Expenses	$850,000	$748,000	($102,000)	($16,000)
Contribution Margin	$2,650,000	$2,852,000	$202,000	
Fixed Operating Expenses	$1,240,000	$1,240,000		
Depreciation Expense	$350,000	$350,000		
Profit	$1,060,000	$1,262,000	$202,000	
Net Cash Flow Difference			$292,000	$292,000
Cash Flow Increase (Decrease)			$494,000	

Quality Improvement Plan

A quality improvement plan and its impact on profit are analyzed in Chapter 7. In the scenario for this plan you increase sales prices slightly more than the cost increases caused by the quality upgrades in the products you sell and the quality of services to customers. Figure 7.6 shows that profit increases $174,250 in this scenario. Unfortunately, cash flow would *decrease* about $25,000—see Figure 8.9. At the higher levels of sales prices and costs accounts receivable and inventories would increase rather substantially. The increases in

FIGURE 8.9 Cash Flow Change: Quality Improvement Plan

	Year Just Ended	New Scenario	Increase (Decrease)	Cash Flow Difference
Sales Revenue	$10,000,000	$11,392,500	$1,392,500	($134,000)
Cost of Goods Sold	$6,000,000	$6,772,500	$772,500	($134,000)
Gross Margin	$4,000,000	$4,620,000	$620,000	
Unit-Driven Expenses	$500,000	$556,500	$56,500	$9,000
Revenue-Driven Expenses	$850,000	$1,139,250	$289,250	$45,000
Contribution Margin	$2,650,000	$2,924,250	$274,250	
Fixed Operating Expenses	$1,240,000	$1,340,000	$100,000	$15,000
Depreciation Expense	$350,000	$350,000		
Profit	$1,060,000	$1,234,250	$174,250	
Net Cash Flow Difference			($199,000)	($199,000)
Cash Flow Increase (Decrease)			($24,750)	

these assets would have correspondingly large negative impacts on cash flow.

In this quality upgrade scenario your cash balance would decrease about $25,000 (see Figure 8.9). In the long run, however, this may prove to be a good investment.

Summary

Business managers should not expect that an increase in profit will increase cash flow the same amount. In many cases a dollar of profit increase does not translate into a dollar of cash flow increase. The chapter returns to the change-in-profit examples that are analyzed in the previous two chapters. For each example the increase or decrease in cash flow caused by the change in profit is examined.

The most favorable change—both for profit and cash flow—is an increase in sales prices, without decreases in sales volume or increases in expenses. The increase in cash flow from increasing sales prices matches the profit increase almost dollar for dollar. Increasing sales volume does not generate nearly as much cash flow as the increase in profit. In the case of a 10 percent sales volume increase, cash flow increases only about one-third of the amount of profit increase. In the example of a five percent sales price increase, cash flow increases about 90 percent of the profit increase.

Increases in accounts receivable and inventories are the main culprits regarding why cash flow lags behind an increase in profit. In formulating profit improvement strategies, managers should pay particular attention to how these two assets would be affected. Changes in expenses cause changes in prepaid expenses (an asset) as well as accounts payable and accrued expenses payable. The changes in these three accounts also affect cash flow from profit. In most cases the changes in accounts receivable and inventories are the dominant reasons for the gap between a change in profit and the corresponding change in cash flow.

CHAPTER 9

Basic Budgeting Methods

For planning and control purposes large business organizations employ comprehensive budgeting systems. Many mid-sized and smaller businesses do not. They may not have the infrastructure needed to implement a budgeting system. Or they may not be willing to take the time to develop detailed forecasts and to assemble all the data into intricate budget schedules and reports. Many businesses are of the opinion that the costs outweigh the benefits of budgeting. Yet, all businesses—from very large to very small—should plan ahead and prepare for the future.

This chapter explains basic budgeting methods. Virtually any size business can benefit from this planning technique. These budgeting methods are illustrated at a very aggregate level of information. Wide brush strokes are painted on the budget canvass instead of fine details. These methods of budgeting can be done quickly, and provide very useful profit and cash flow benchmarks for the coming year.

The budgeting techniques explained in this chapter build on the profit and cash flow models developed in earlier chapters. The profit model is an excellent platform for constructing a summit-level profit budget for the coming period. The cash flow budget pivots off the profit budget. It provides a look ahead at the estimated cash flow from profit for the coming period. This chapter illustrates how the profit and cash flow improvement strategies analyzed in the preceding three chapters are wrapped together into an integrated financial plan for the coming period.

Budgeting Profit

I take it as a given that business managers should (must?) look ahead and plan for the future. They should predict how general economic changes would affect their business, and they should prepare for how they will deal with the changes. Of course, no one has a crystal ball. Predictions may turn out to be seriously wrong. Nevertheless, I take it as an article of faith that some planning is better than none. Business managers cannot simply assume that next year will be an exact replica of the year just ended. Rather, the year just ended is like the train that has just arrived at the station; managers have to prepare for the next leg of the journey.

Management Profit Report for the Year Just Ended

The business case introduced in the review exercise at the end Chapter 1 serves as the point of departure for this chapter. Its income statement for the year just ended is presented in Chapter 1 and it is repeated here in Figure 9.1. (The underlying data for the income statement are given in the review exercise at the end of Chapter 1.) For the year just ended the business garnered sales of about $40.0 million and turned a profit of about $1.6 million, which is 4.0 percent profit on sales. Not a stellar year for profit performance, but not a bad

FIGURE 9.1 External Income Statement of Business for Year Just Ended

Sales Revenue	$39,661,250
Cost of Goods Sold Expense	$24,960,750
Gross Margin	$14,700,500
Selling & Administrative Expenses	$11,466,135
Earnings before Interest and Income Tax	$3,234,365
Interest Expense	$795,000
Earnings before Income Tax	$2,439,365
Income Tax Expense	$853,778
Net Income	$1,585,587

year, either. The business complies with generally accepted accounting principles (GAAP) for recording its sales and expenses and for presenting its financial statements in its external financial reports.

Figure 9.1 is a standard issue income statement, which is typical of what you find in the external financial reports by businesses to their outside shareowners and lenders. The business may have a CPA firm audit its financial statements. The CPA auditor would give a clean opinion on this income statement. By the way, the business is a privately owned corporation whose capital stock shares are not traded in a public market. So it does not have to include earnings per share (EPS) in its external income statement.

For management purposes the external income statement has a serious impediment. The disclosure of operating expenses (Selling & Administrative Expenses in Figure 9.1) is not adequate for management analysis. Managers need a better look at their operating expenses. For internal reporting to managers *variable* operating expenses should be separated from *fixed* operating expenses. And variable operating expenses should be divided into two classes: those costs driven by *sales volume* (how many units of product are sold), and those costs driven by *sales revenue* (how many dollars are billed to customers).

Figure 9.2 presents the business's internal management profit report for the year just ended. In this report the two variable operating expenses (unit-driven and revenue-driven) are separated from fixed operating expenses. Contribution margin, which equals sales revenue minus cost of goods sold and variable operating expenses, is reported in the management profit report—but not in the external income statement. Depreciation expense is separated from other fixed operating expenses in the internal report. It is a unique expense from the cash flow point of view. The company's cash flow budget is developed later in the chapter.

Bottom-line net income is the same in the internal management profit report and the external income statement; it is $1,585,587 in both. A popular myth is that many businesses keep two sets of books. The business does not use different methods for recording sales revenue and expenses for internal versus external profit accounting. On the other hand, a business may take advantage of certain accounting options in the federal income tax law (some call them loopholes) that cause timing differences between the amounts of earnings before income tax reported in its annual income statements and the amounts of taxable income in its annual income tax returns. There are no such differences in this example. The company's income tax rate is 35 percent of its earnings before income tax.

FIGURE 9.2 Internal Management Profit Report of
Business for Year Just Ended

Sales Revenue	$39,661,250
Cost of Goods Sold	$24,960,750
Gross Margin	$14,700,500
Unit-Driven Expenses	$2,677,875
Revenue-Driven Expenses	$3,049,010
Contribution Margin	$8,973,615
Fixed Operating Expenses	$4,970,800
Depreciation Expense	$768,450
Earnings before Interest and Income Tax (EBIT)	$3,234,365
Interest Expense	$795,000
Earnings before Income Tax	$2,439,365
Income Tax	$853,778
Net Income	$1,585,587

Aggregation Problems in Accounting Reports

The typical business sells hundreds or more different products. Each distinct product has distinct costs. Furthermore, the typical business has hundreds or more of different operating expenses, to say nothing about the large number of individual accounts payable, accounts receivable, products held in inventory, and other assets. This multitude of data causes serious reporting problems. Managers can be overcome with a flood of details that obscure important points and trends.

The trick is to report aggregate information without losing sight of important differences and details. This is a major challenge in internal reporting to managers—not only in accounting reports to managers, but also for most of the reports they receive such as reports on employee performance, sales backlogs, customer complaints, and so on. Generally speaking the way most businesses deal with this problem is to report to managers two or more levels of information. At the highest level the information is very aggregated; underneath this top layer two or more supporting layers provide more detailed information than the layer above it. The layers are dovetailed.

The logic and layout of the management profit report (Figure 9.2) is explained in earlier chapters. This chapter uses this report for the year just ended to build the profit budget for the coming year. The premise is that you have to know where you have been (the year just ended) to get where you are going (the coming year)—the most recent chapter in your profit history is the stepping stone to the future.

Preparing the Profit Budget

The word *budgeting* puts off many people. When they hear the word, they think of a financial straitjacket that goes into painstaking detail regarding expenditures, down to how much can be spent on paper clips next year. Full-fledged budgets can be very detailed, that's for sure. This chapter takes the opposite approach to budgeting. The profit budget is based on wide-scope forecasts of changes that managers predict for the coming year. Instead of predicting changes for each and every product sold by the business and for each and every expense, managers make broad-based forecasts of *average* changes they see on the horizon. These broad-based forecasts are used to prepare the overall profit budget for the coming year, and from this profit budget the budget for cash flow from profit is prepared.

Figure 9.3 presents the profit budget of the business for the coming year. The right column in the profit budget summarizes the forecasts on which budgeted sales revenue and expenses are based. These sales and cost of goods sold forecasts are *general averages* across all products. The business plans to increase its sales prices

FIGURE 9.3 Profit Budget for Next Year

	Year Just Ended	Budget Next Year	Broad Forecasts for Profit Factors
Sales Revenue	$39,661,250	$42,685,420	Sales prices +2.5%; Sales volume +5.0%
Cost of Goods Sold	$24,960,750	$26,995,051	Product cost +3.0%; Sales volume +5.0%
Gross Margin	$14,700,500	$15,690,369	+6.7%
Unit-Driven Expenses	$2,677,875	$2,924,240	Cost increase +4.0%; Sales volume +5.0%
Revenue-Driven Expenses	$3,049,010	$3,281,497	Same commission percents on sales revenue
Contribution Margin	$8,973,615	$9,484,633	+5.7%
Fixed Operating Expenses	$4,970,800	$5,328,750	+7.2% general cost increases; additional capacity
Depreciation Expense	$768,450	$813,200	New fixed assets increase depreciation
Earnings before Interest and Income Tax (EBIT)	$3,234,365	$3,342,683	+3.3%
Interest Expense	$795,000	$825,000	Additional debt; slightly lower interest rates
Earnings before Income Tax	$2,439,365	$2,517,683	+3.2%
Income Tax	$853,778	$881,189	Same income tax rate (35%)
Net Income	$1,585,587	$1,636,494	+3.2%

2.5 percent on average, and predicts that sales volume will increase 5.0 percent on average. (Increasing both sales prices and sales volume may be a tall order.) Managers forecast that product costs will increase 3.0 percent on average across all products, which is a little more than the 2.5 percent average sales price increase.

The $42,685,420 budgeted sales revenue amount is explained in two steps, as follows. If only sales prices increased 2.5 percent and sales volume did not change, then sales revenue next year would be $40,652,781: ($39,661,250 sales revenue for the period just ended × 102.5%). However, the business predicts that it will sell 5.0 percent more units at the higher sales prices. So, its sales revenue for the coming year is budgeted at $42,685,420: ($40,652,781 sales revenue at the higher sales prices × by 105.0%).

In like manner the budgeted amount for cost of goods sold is computed. If only product costs increased 3.0 percent and sales volume did not change, then cost of goods sold next year would be $25,709,573: ($24,960,750 cost of goods sold for the period just ended × 103.0%). However, the business predicts that it will sell 5.0 percent more units during the coming year. So, its cost of goods sold for the coming year is budgeted at $26,995,051: ($24,960,750 cost of goods sold at the higher product costs × 105.0%). Unit-driven operating expenses are calculated in the same manner.

The average percent of revenue-driven operating expenses is forecast to remain the same during the coming year—at about 7.7 percent of sales revenue—because the sales commission percents will not be changed next year. This average percent is applied to the budgeted amount of sales revenue for the coming year. Budgeting fixed operating expenses requires forecasting general increases for these costs (examples include insurance premiums, utility costs, employee salaries, property taxes, etc.). Also, managers have to estimate the cost of enlarging the capacity of the business (hiring new employees, etc.).

Depreciation expense is based on the depreciation schedules for the company's fixed assets, including new fixed assets that will be purchased or constructed during the coming year. The interest expense forecast is based on two elements—that interest rates will decrease slightly and that the business will increase its debt load somewhat. The chief financial officer of the business does not see any change in its basic income tax rate in the coming year.

A Word about Budget Forecasts

It goes without saying that the actual changes next year almost surely will turn out different from the forecasts for sales prices, sales volume, and costs. Sales prices probably will not increase *exactly* 2.5 percent on average during the coming year, and sales volume probably will not increase *exactly* 5.0 percent on average. Likewise, expenses probably will not increase exactly by the percentages used to forecast the expenses for the coming year. Therefore, actual net income for the coming year will almost certainly deviate from the budgeted amount shown in Figure 9.3. Prediction errors are an inescapable feature of budgeting.

Every budget is based on forecasts, estimates, and predictions. These numbers can turn out to be wrong—almost assuredly so! This is an inherent characteristic of budgeting. If you want precision, you'll have to do it with hindsight, not foresight. Budgets are based on the most reasonable and realistic forecasts you can make, knowing in the back of your mind that the actual numbers will turn out different. Every one of the forecasts, estimates, and predictions can be challenged. To move ahead, however, the budgeting process has to make projections for the future, and pull together a profit budget. The point of the exercise is to produce a preview of the most likely scenario for the coming year.

Managers know that changes will take place during the coming year. It's better to calculate in advance how the changes will affect sales revenue and expenses in order to get an advance look at profit for the coming year. (As a matter of fact publicly owned businesses face intense pressure to provide stock analysts accurate earnings forecasts for the coming period.) Moreover, the profit budget is needed for budgeting cash flow from profit for the coming year. The estimate of cash flow from profit for the coming year is essential for planning the investing and financing decisions of the business during the coming year—capital expenditures, cash dividends, borrowings and payments on short-term and long-term debt, and the issue or retirement of capital stock shares.

How Does the Profit Budget Look?

The profit budget for the coming year has been prepared—see Figure 9.3. The overriding question facing managers is whether the forecast profit performance is acceptable. If not, then managers have to go back to the drawing board and decide how to improve one or more of the profit factors during the coming year.

One thing in the profit budget (Figure 9.3) that I don't like is the slippage in profit margins starting with gross margin and going down to net income. Gross margin increases 6.7 percent; contribution margin increases 5.7 percent; EBIT increases only 3.3 percent; and net income increases only 3.2 percent. These profit improvement measures deteriorate as you go down the profit lines, which is not good news.

Also I noticed that the budgeted bottom-line profit *ratio* for the coming year is 3.8 percent of sales revenue: ($1,636,494 net income ÷ by $42,685,420 sales revenue = 3.8%). This compares with the 4.0 percent profit ratio for the year just ended. Chapter 5 explains that this profit ratio is one of several key ratios used by investors and lenders in interpreting the financial statements of a business. Its shareowners would take notice of the profit ratio slippage compared with the preceding year. The board of directors would also notice this fall-off in the profit ratio, and may ask the CEO to explain how this slippage will be reversed in the future.

In the profit budget (Figure 9.3) note that fixed operating expenses are forecast to outstrip the contribution margin increase. Contribution margin is budgeted to increase 5.7 percent, but fixed operating expenses are scheduled to increase 7.2 percent. Managers probably should take a hard and close look at the major cost items in this expense category. The explanation in the profit budget mentions that additional capacity will be added (more employees, more equipment and machinery, more building space, etc.). The CEO and other high-level managers might want to reconsider whether the additional capacity is really needed as soon as scheduled. Perhaps the capacity expansion could be delayed and brought online sometime later.

Budgeting Cash Flow from Profit

From the profit budget (Figure 9.3) the cash flow from profit budget for the coming year is prepared. (I don't like to harp on terminology, but you should recall that cash flow from profit also is called *operating cash flow*, and *cash flow from operating activities*.) Cash flow from profit is an extremely important figure for planning a business's other sources and uses of cash during the coming period. In fact it's hard to imagine planning cash flows without this critical number to start with. Cash flow from profit is the cash mainspring of a business. It's the main spigot of cash—unless the business is hemorrhaging cash because of persistent losses.

Chapter 8 explains that changes in sales revenue and expenses from period to period cause corresponding increases in accounts receivable, inventories, prepaid expenses, accounts payable, and accrued expenses payable. The increases in these assets and operating liabilities have effects on cash flow from profit for the period. As a general rule increases in these assets and operating liabilities have a net *negative* effect on cash flow from profit—not always, but generally so. This is why simply adding back depreciation to net income does not render a good measure of cash flow from profit. During a time of growth the negative cash flow effects caused by increases in accounts receivable and inventories can substantially offset the cash flow from depreciation.

A business may be planning major policy changes in its inventory holding periods or in the credit terms offered to customers. These key changes should be factored into a cash flow budget for the coming year, of course. In the example the business does not plan to change the credit terms offered to customers or its average inventory-holding period. Therefore, the only changes in accounts receivable and inventories should be those driven by the increases in sales revenue and cost of goods sold during the coming year that will be caused by increases in sales prices, sales volume, and product costs.

The budget for cash flow from profit for the coming year is presented in Figure 9.4. Sales revenue is budgeted to increase about $3.0 million next year (see Figure 9.3), which is an increase of about 7.6 percent over last year. This should cause an increase in the company's accounts receivable of about the same percent, which equals $290,786 in the example. Remember that the balance in a business's accounts receivable asset account represents its uncollected sales revenue, or cash that has not yet been received from customers (but should be in the near future). Because of the anticipated increase in accounts receivable, cash collections from customers will be $290,786 less than the budgeted sales revenue for the coming year.

Because of higher product costs and higher sales volume the company's inventories are budgeted to increase during the coming year, as well as its accounts payable for inventory purchases. Cost of goods sold is budgeted to increase about $2.0 million next year (see Figure 9.3), which is an increase of about 8.2 percent over last year. This should cause an increase in the company's inventories and its accounts payable for inventory purchases of about the same percent. The amount of increase in inventories less the amount of increase in accounts payable for inventory purchases is projected to be $312,969 for the coming year. The business will make cash payments $312,969 more than the budgeted cost of goods sold expense for the coming year. Thus, the additional $312,969 cash outlay is shown as a negative difference in the cash flow budget. Cash outflow for inventories will be $312,969 higher than the cost of goods sold expense budgeted for next year, as shown in Figure 9.4.

The accounts payable and accrued expenses payable liability accounts should increase in close proportion with the increases in the operating expenses budgeted for the coming year. The increases in these operating liabilities mean that cash payments for operating expenses will be less than the amounts budgeted for the expenses during the coming year. Thus, these liability increases are shown as positive cash flow differences in the cash flow budget (Figure 9.4). The cash outlays for the expenses will be slightly less than the amounts budgeted for the coming year. The business will record $813,200 depreciation expense in the coming year. As explained in Chapter 2 depreciation is a cash recovery of part of the original cost invested in its fixed assets by a business in previous years. Depreciation is a positive cash flow difference, of course; it's the largest cash flow difference in the cash flow budget.

As Figure 9.4 shows cash flow from profit is budgeted at $1,920,085 for the coming year. In summary, the depreciation cash flow is offset in large part by the negative cash flow effects of the increases in accounts receivable and inventories. But the business should realize $1,920,085 cash flow from profit for the coming year according to budget.

There are several demands on the cash flow from profit during the coming year, such as for capital expenditures (purchases and construction of new buildings, machinery, and equipment) and *cash dividends* to shareowners from profit. The business also may prefer to reduce its *debt load* and pay down part of its short-term and long-

FIGURE 9.4 Cash Flow from Profit Budget for Coming Year

	Profit Budget	Cash Flows Budget	Differences
Sales Revenue	$42,685,420	$42,394,635	($290,786)
Cost of Goods Sold	($26,995,051)	($27,308,020)	($312,969)
Gross Margin	$15,690,369		
Unit-Driven Expenses	($2,924,240)	($2,902,920)	$21,320
Revenue-Driven Expenses	($3,281,497)	($3,261,378)	$20,119
Contribution Margin	$9,484,633		
Fixed Operating Expenses	($5,328,750)	($5,297,774)	$30,976
Depreciation Expense	($813,200)		$813,200
Earnings Before Interest and Income Tax (EBIT)	$3,342,683		
Interest Expense	($825,000)	($823,269)	$1,731
Earnings before Income Tax	$2,517,683		
Income Tax	($881,189)	($881,189)	
Net Income	$1,636,494	$1,920,085	$283,591

term notes payable. The business may need to build up its *working cash balance* to support the higher level of sales activity. The shareowners may be pressuring the business to increase cash dividends. The budgeted $1.9 million of cash flow from profit is not enough to meet all the demands for cash during the coming year, which is discussed next.

Budgeting Investing and Financing Activities

To complete the budget for the coming year several major financial questions have to be addressed. These questions are answered at the highest levels of management. Some of the decisions need approval by the board of directors of the business. These key questions concern the *investing* and *financing* activities of the business during the coming year. A convenient, ready-made checklist for these issues is provided by the format of the statement of cash flows. Recall that this is one of the primary financial statements prepared by a business that is included in its external financial reports to its shareowners and lenders.

Checklist for Investing and Financing Decisions

Figure 9.5 presents the budget checklist for the major investing and financing questions facing the business for the coming period, which includes the actual amounts for the year just ended for comparison. The amounts of cash flow from profit (cash flow from operating activities) for each year are taken from Figure 9.4. These pieces yet to be filled in the budget puzzle are indicated with the $??? notations in Figure 9.5.

During the year just ended the business spent $3,186,250 on *capital expenditures*, which comprise the costs of purchase or construction of new fixed assets (property, plant, and equipment). Many of these acquisitions replaced old fixed assets that were junked or sold for their salvage value. From disposals of old fixed assets the business realized $265,480 proceeds. (See Figure 9.5.) The remainder of the total cost of capital expenditures was to expand the capacity of the business (additional building space, more tools and machinery, more delivery trucks, bigger computers and telecommunications equipment, etc.). The business is planning its capital expenditures for the coming year. Some of its fixed assets need to be replaced, and the business intends to expand its capacity during the coming year. These expenditures are major outlays and require substantial lead-time. Generally speaking the board of directors approves the capital expenditures budget for the coming year.

FIGURE 9.5 Checklist of Investing and Financing Issues for Coming Year

	Cash Flows for Year Just Ended	Cash Flows for Coming Year
Cash Flows from Operating Activities (see Figure 9.4)	$1,297,907	$1,920,085
Cash Flows from Investing Activities		
Investment in Property, Plant, & Equipment	($3,186,250)	$???
Disposals of Property, Plant, & Equipment	$265,480	$???
Cash Used in Investing Activities	($2,920,770)	
Cash Flows from Financing Activities		
Net increase in Short-term Debt	$485,000	$???
Increase in Long-term Debt	$1,650,000	$???
Issuance of Capital Stock Shares	$185,000	$???
Cash Dividends to Stockholders	($450,000)	$???
Cash from Financing Activities	$1,870,000	
Cash Increase during Year	$247,137	$???
Cash Balance at Beginning of Year	$2,098,538	$2,345,675
Cash Balance at End of Year	$2,345,675	$???

Free Cash Flow

As explained above, profit should provide $1.9 million cash during the coming year (see Figure 9.4). Financial analysts and other financial professionals, though very few accountants, refer to cash flow from profit as free cash flow. I should immediately warn you that cash flow terminology has not settled down and has not become standardized. Recall that cash flow from profit is also called operating cash flow, and cash flow from operating activities. The term free cash flow usually refers to cash flow from profit, although I have seen it used otherwise (for example to mean net income plus depreciation). The idea of free cash flow is that a business is free, or unbound regarding what it can do with its cash flow from profit. Well, please take this statement with a grain of salt.

A business usually has many competing demands on its operating cash flow (free cash flow). One demand is to pay cash dividends. All things being equal the shareowners of a business want the maximum amount of cash dividends to be distributed to them. But of course all things usually are not equal. Last year the board of directors approved $450,000 cash dividends to shareowners. For the coming year the board would like to increase cash dividends to $500,000.

This amount would be less than one-third of budgeted net income for the year. By the way, annual cash dividends divided by annual net income is called the **dividend payout ratio**.

Capital for Capital Expenditures

Suppose that the business in the example sees the need to spend about $4.5 million on capital expenditures during the coming year. Major pieces of equipment will have to be replaced and the business is planning a substantial expansion of its manufacturing capacity. If the business pays $500,000 cash dividends during the coming year its remaining free cash flow would be $1.4 million: ($1.9 million cash flow from profit – $.5 million cash dividends = $1.4 million). This amount would be available for capital expenditures and for other demands on cash.

One demand on cash is cash itself—that is, the need for an adequate day-to-day working cash balance. Roughly speaking this is the average amount a business has on deposit in its checking accounts, from which it cuts checks to pay bills, payroll, dividends, capital expenditures, operating expenses, and so on. There is no standard guideline or general rule regarding how much working cash balance is needed by a business. The business is budgeting approximately $42.7 million sales for the coming year and $41.1 total expenses (sales revenue – net income for the coming year). This translates to about $790,000 cash disbursements per week on average.

At the start of the coming year the business has more than $2.3 million cash (see Figure 9.5), which is enough for about three weeks of expenses at the clip of $790,000 per week. The chief financial officer (CFO) thinks this is enough. Other businesses keep more than three weeks of cash on hand, but many businesses out of choice or necessity get by with only two weeks or one week of working cash balance. Most businesses from time to time experience unexpected delays in collecting their accounts receivable, or they don't sell inventory as quickly as they planned, or they have unplanned expense outlays. To be prudent a business should maintain an adequate cash balance to cover gaps of cash inflow and to meet unusual demands for cash outflow. In the example, the business may prefer that its cash balance be increased $100,000 or $200,000. But as it is mentioned above, the business is planning $4.5 million of capital expenditures for the coming year.

A business the size of the one in the example ($42 million annual sales) would employ a CFO. One of his or her functions is to prepare a plan of action concerning how to raise the capital needed for the investments planned for the coming year. The cash flow from profit budget (Figure 9.4) indicates that about $1.9 million cash will be available. If cash dividends of $.5 million are paid, only $1.4 million is available for other uses. To fund capital expenditures of $4.5 million, the business clearly will have to go to lenders or its shareowners, or both. The business will have to raise more than $3.0 million capital. Its lenders may or may not be willing to loan an additional $3.0 million to the business. Its shareowners may or may not be willing to put more capital into the business.

In any case having a profit budget and a cash flow from profit budget for the coming year provides essential information for planning the investing and financing decisions of the business. Without this information a business would be at a serious disadvantage in making its decisions and for persuading lenders and shareowners to provide the additional capital needed to grow the business.

Summary

Budgeting can be done at a very detailed level—for the sales and costs of every different product the business sells, for every operating expense, for every asset, for every liability, and so on. Larger businesses use detailed budgeting for planning and control purposes. They have the infrastructure to implement a comprehensive budgeting system. They are of the opinion that the benefits are worthwhile compared with the costs of budgeting.

On the other hand, many mid-sized and smaller businesses decide against this type of budgeting, or they simply don't have the time to assemble a detailed and comprehensive budget for the coming year. Nevertheless, they should develop a profit plan for the coming year and estimate cash flow from profit for the coming year. Changes are bound to happen during the coming year. Managers should, indeed must, forecast the major changes ahead that will affect the profit factors of their business.

The chapter explains a summary-level approach for budgeting profit and cash flow from profit, which any size business can use to its advantage. Forecasts are made at a very aggregate level and use general averages for the key factors that drive the profit performance of a business. Using these forecasts the amounts for sales revenue and expenses are calculated and the profit budget is assembled for the coming period. The profit budget provides the platform for developing the cash flow from budget for the coming year. The management cash flow model and report explained in earlier chapters provide the framework for preparing the operating cash flow budget for the coming year.

Cash flow from profit is an extraordinarily important piece of information. Managers absolutely need a good estimate for this source of cash as the starting point for planning their investing and financing activities during the coming year. The availability of cash flow from profit heavily influences decisions regarding cash dividends to shareowners, capital expenditures, and raising money from debt and owners' equity sources. These key financial decisions require a fair amount of lead-time. Preparing a profit budget with its companion cash flow budget provides the information for planning the financial future of the business.

CHAPTER 10

Determining Investment Returns

This chapter explains how the cost of capital is factored into the analysis of business investments in order to determine the future returns needed from an investment. An investment has to pay its way. The future returns from an investment should recover the capital put into the investment *and* provide for the cost of capital each period along the way. The future returns should do at least this much. If not the investment will turn out to be a poor decision; the capital should have been invested elsewhere.

The analysis in the chapter is math free. No mathematical equations or formulas are involved. I use a computer spreadsheet model to illustrate the analysis and to do the calculations. The main example in the chapter provides a general-purpose template that can be easily copied by anyone familiar with a spreadsheet program. However, you don't have to know anything about using spreadsheets to follow the analysis.

A Business as an On-Going Investment Project

Chapter 3 explains that a business needs a portfolio of assets to carry on its profit-making operations. For the capital needed to invest in its assets a business raises money from its owners, retains all or part of its annual earnings, and borrows money. The combination of these three sources constitutes the capital structure, or capitalization of a business. Taken together the first two capital sources are called owners' equity, or just equity for short. Borrowed money is referred to as debt. Interest is paid on debt, as you know. Its shareowners expect a business to earn an annual return on their equity at least equal to, and preferably higher than what they could earn on alternative investment opportunities for their capital.

Cost of Capital

A business's earnings before interest and income tax (EBIT) for a period needs to be sufficient to do three things: (1) pay interest on its debt; (2) pay income tax; and (3) leave residual net income that satisfies the shareowners of the business. Based on the total amount of capital invested in its assets and its capital structure a business determines its EBIT goal for the year. For instance a business may establish an annual EBIT goal equal to 20 percent of the total capital invested in its assets. This rate is referred to as its **cost of capital**.

The annual cost of capital rate of most businesses is in the range of 15 percent to 25 percent, although there is no hard and fast standard that applies to all businesses. The cost of capital rate depends heavily on the target rate for net income on its owners' equity that is adopted by a business. The interest rate on a business's debt is definite, and its income tax rate is fairly definite. On the other hand the rate of net income that a business sets as the goal to earn on its owners' equity is not definite. A business may adopt a rather modest, or a more aggressive benchmark for earnings on its equity capital.

Of course, a business may fall short of its cost of capital goal. Its actual EBIT for the year may be enough to pay its interest and income tax, but its residual net income may be less than what the business should earn on its owners' equity for the year. For that matter a business may suffer an *operating loss* and not even cover its interest obligation for the year. One reason for reporting financial statements to outside shareowners and lenders is to provide them information so they can determine how the business is performing as an investor, or user of capital.

A company's cost of capital depends on its capital structure. Assume the following facts for a business:

CAPITAL STRUCTURE AND COST OF CAPITAL FACTORS

35% debt and 65% equity mix of capital sources
8.0% annual interest rate on debt
40% income tax rate (combined federal and state)
18.0% annual ROE objective

These assumptions are realistic for a broad range of businesses, but not for every business of course. Some businesses use less than 35 percent debt capital and some more. Over time interest rates fluctuate for all businesses. Furthermore, one could argue that an 18.0 percent ROE objective is too ambitious. The 40 percent combined federal and state income tax rate is based on the present rate for the federal taxable income brackets for mid-sized businesses plus a typical state income tax rate. In any case, the cost of capital factors can be easily adapted to fit the circumstances of a particular business once an investment spreadsheet model has been prepared.

Suppose the business with this capital structure has $10.0 million capital invested in its assets. What amount of annual earnings before interest and income tax (EBIT) should the business make? This question strikes at the core idea of the cost of capital—the minimum amount of operating profit that is needed to pay interest on its debt, pay its income tax, and produce residual net income that achieves the ROE goal of the business.

Figure 10.1 shows the answer to this question. Given its debt to equity ratio the company's $10.0 million capital comes from $3.5 million debt and $6.5 million equity—see the condensed balance sheet in Figure 10.1. The annual interest cost of its debt is $280,000: ($3.5 million debt × 8.0% interest rate = $280,000 interest). The business needs to make $280,000 operating profit to pay this amount of interest. Interest is deductible for income tax, as you probably know. This means that a business needs to make operating profit equal to its interest, but no more than this amount to pay its interest. In other

FIGURE 10.1 Operating Profit (EBIT) That Should Be Realized Based on Capital Structure of Business

Condensed Balance Sheet		Condensed Income Statement	
Assets Less Operating Liabilities	$10,000,000	Earnings before Interest and Income Tax (EBIT)	$2,230,000
		Interest	($280,000)
Sources of Capital		Taxable Income	$1,950,000
Debt	$3,500,000	Income Tax	($780,000)
Equity	$6,500,000	Net Income	$1,170,000
Total	$10,000,000		

words, the $280,000 of operating profit is offset with an equal amount of interest deduction, so the business's taxable income is zero on this layer of operating profit.

The cost of equity capital is a much different matter. On its $6.5 million equity capital the business needs to earn $1,170,000 net income: ($6.5 million equity × 18.0% ROE = $1,170,000 net income). To earn $1,170,000 net income *after income tax* the business needs to earn $1,950,000 operating earnings before income tax: ($1,170,000 net income goal ÷ .6 = $1,950,000). The ".6" is the after-tax keep; for every $1.00 of taxable income the company keeps only 60¢ because the income tax rate is 40 percent, or 40¢ on the dollar. On $1,950,000 earnings after interest and before income tax the income tax is $780,000 at the 40 percent income tax rate, which leaves $1,170,000 net income after tax.

This is a key difference between net income on equity compared with interest on debt. From each $1.00 of operating profit (earnings before interest and income tax, or EBIT) a business can pay $1.00 of interest to its debt sources of capital. But from each $1.00 of operating profit a business earns only 60¢ net income for its equity owners after deducting the 40¢ income tax on the dollar. Put another way, on a before-tax basis a business needs to earn just $1.00 of operating profit to cover $1.00 of interest expense. But it needs to earn $1.67 (rounded) to end up with $1.00 net income because income tax takes out 67¢.

In summary, based on its capital structure the business should aim to earn at least $2,230,000 operating profit, or EBIT for the year. If it falls short of this benchmark, its residual net income for the year will fall below its 18.0 percent annual ROE goal. If it does better, its ROE will be more than 18.0 percent, which should help increase the value of the equity shares of the business.

Short-term and Long-term Asset Investments

Looking down the asset side of a business's balance sheet, you find a mix of short-term and long-term asset investments. One major short-term asset investment is inventories. The inventories asset represents the cost of products held for sale. These products will be sold during the coming two or three months, perhaps even sooner. Another important short-term investment is accounts receivable. Accounts receivable will be collected within a month or so. These two short-term investments turn over relatively quickly. The capital invested in inventories and accounts receivable is recovered in a short period of time. The capital is then reinvested in the assets in order to continue in business. The cycle of capital investment, capital recovery, and capital reinvestment is repeated several times during the year.

In contrast a business makes *long-term* investments in many different operating assets—land and buildings, machinery and equipment, furniture, fixtures, tools, computers, vehicles, and so on. A business also may make long-term investments in *intangible* assets—patents and copyrights, customer lists, computer software, established brand names and trademarks developed by other companies, and so on. The capital invested in long-term business operating assets is gradually recovered and converted back into cash over three to five years, or longer for buildings and heavy machinery and equipment.

The annual sales revenue of a business includes a component to recover the cost of using its long-term operating assets. (Of course, sales revenue also has to recover the cost of the goods sold and other operating costs to make a profit for the period.) The cost of using long-term assets is recorded as depreciation expense each year. Chapter 2 explains that depreciation expense is not a cash outlay—in fact, just the opposite.

Depreciation is one of the costs embedded in sales revenue and therefore the cash inflow from sales includes a component that reimburses the business for the use of its fixed assets during the year. A sliver of the cash inflow from the annual sales revenue of a business provides recovery of part of the total capital invested in its long-term operating assets. What to do with this cash inflow is one of the most important decisions facing a business.

To continue as a *going concern* a business has to purchase or construct new long-term operating assets to replace the old ones that have reached the end of their useful economic lives. In deciding whether to make capital investments in long-term operating assets managers should determine whether or not the new assets are really needed of course, and how they will be used in the operations of the business. They should look at how the new assets blend into the present mix of operating assets. Managers should focus primarily on how well all assets work together in achieving the financial goals of the business. These long-term capital investments of a business are just one part, though an important part to be sure, of a business's overall profit strategy and planning.

The Whole Business versus Singular Capital Investments

From the cost of capital viewpoint the key criterion for guiding investment decisions for the replacement and expansion of long-term assets is whether the business will be able to maintain and improve its return on assets (ROA) performance. Suppose a business has been able to earn an annual 20 percent ROA consistently over several years. In other words, its annual EBIT divided by the total capital invested in its assets has hovered around 20 percent for the past several years. And assume that the business does not plan any significant change in its capital structure in the foreseeable future.

Assume that this level of financial performance is judged to be acceptable by both management and the shareowners of the business. Therefore, in making decisions on capital expenditures to carry on and to grow the business, its managers should apply a 20 percent cost of capital test: Will EBIT in future years be sufficient to maintain its 20 percent ROA performance? This is the key question from the cost of capital point of view.

Return on assets is an investment performance measure for the business as a whole. The entire business is the focus of the analysis. Its entire assemblage of assets is treated as one investment portfolio. Its earnings before interest and income tax (EBIT) for the year is divided by this amount of capital to determine the overall ROA performance of the business.

In contrast, specific capital investments can be isolated and analyzed as singular projects, each like a tub standing on its own feet. Each individual asset investment opportunity is analyzed on its own merits. One important criterion is whether the investment passes muster from the cost of capital point of view.

Capital Investment Example

Suppose that a retailer is considering buying new, state-of-the-art electronic cash registers. These registers read bar coded information on the products it sells. The registers would be connected with the company's computers to track information on sales and inventory stock quantities. The main purpose of switching to these cash registers is to avoid marking sales prices on products. Virtually all the products sold by the retailer are already bar coded by the manufacturers of the products. The retailer would avoid the labor cost of marking initial sales prices and sales price changes on its products, which take many hours. The new cash registers would provide better control over sales prices, which is another important advantage. Some of the company's cashiers frequently punch in wrong prices by error; worse, some cashiers intentionally enter lower than marked prices for their friends and relatives coming through their checkout line.

Investing in the new cash registers would generate labor cost savings in the future. The company's future annual cash outlays for wages and fringe benefits would decrease if the new cash registers were used. Avoiding a cash outlay is as good as a cash inflow; both increase the cash balance. The cost of the new cash registers—net of the trade-in allowance on its old cash registers and including the cost of installing the new cash registers—would be $500,000, which would be paid immediately.

The company would tap its general cash reserve to invest in the new cash registers. The retailer would not use direct financing for this investment, such as asking the vendor to lend the company a large part of the purchase price. The retailer would not arrange for a third-party loan, or seek a lease-purchase arrangement to acquire the cash registers. As the old expression says, the business would pay "cash on the barrelhead" for the purchase of the cash registers.

The manager in charge of making the decision decides to adopt a five-year *planning horizon* for this capital investment. In other words the manager limits the recognition of cost savings to five years, even though there may be benefits beyond five years. Labor hour savings and wage rates are difficult to forecast beyond five years and other factors can change as well. At the end of five years the cash registers are assumed to have no residual value, which is very conservative.

The future labor cost savings depend mainly on how many work hours the new cash registers would save. Of course, estimating the annual labor cost savings is no easy matter. Instead of focusing on the precise forecasting of future labor cost savings, the manager takes a different approach. The manager asks: How much would annual labor cost savings have to be to justify the investment?

For example would future labor cost savings of $160,000 per year for five years be enough? The labor cost savings would occur throughout the year. For convenience of analysis however, assume that the cost savings occur at each year-end. The company's cash balance would be this much higher at each year-end due to the labor cost savings.

The retailer's capital structure is that presented in the earlier example. As shown in Figure 10.1 and as explained earlier, the company's before-tax annual cost of capital rate is 22.3 percent: ($2,230,000 required annual EBIT ÷ $10,000,000 total capital invested in assets = 22.3% annual cost of capital rate). However, this cost of capital rate cannot be simply multiplied by the $500,000 cost of the cash registers to determine the future returns needed from the investment. The cost of capital factors must be applied in a different manner.

Furthermore, the future returns from the investment have to recover the $500,000 capital invested in the cash registers. After five years of use the cash registers will be at the end of their useful lives to the business and will have no residual, salvage value. In summary the future returns have to be sufficient to recover the cost of the cash registers and to provide for the cost of capital each year over the life of the investment.

Before moving on to the analysis of this capital investment, I should mention that there would be several incentives to invest in the cash registers. As already referred to earlier the new cash registers would eliminate data entry errors by cashiers, and should also prevent cashiers from deliberately entering low prices for their friends and relatives. Employee fraud is a common and expensive problem, unfortunately. Also the company may anticipate that it will be increasingly difficult to hire qualified employees over the next several years. Also the new cash registers would enable the company to collect marketing data on a real-time basis, which it cannot do at present. In short, there are several good reasons for buying the cash registers. However, the following discussion focuses on the *financial* aspects of the investment decision.

Analyzing the Investment

The first step is to make a ballpark estimate of about how much the future returns would have to be for the investment. The business has to recover the capital invested in the cash registers, which is $500,000 in the example. The business has five years to recover this amount of capital. But, clearly, future returns of just $100,000 per year for five years is not enough. This amount of yearly return would not cover the company's cost of capital each year. So to start the ball rolling an annual return of $160,000 is used in the analysis, which might seem to be adequate to cover the company's cost of capital. But is $160,000 per year actually enough?

First Pass at Analyzing the Investment

Figure 10.2 presents a spreadsheet analysis of the investment in the new cash registers. (In the old days, i.e., before personal computers, this two-dimensional layout was called a worksheet.) This is only a first pass to see whether $160,000 annual returns on the investment would be sufficient. The analysis may seem complex at first glance, but it is quite straightforward. The method begins with the return for each year and makes demands on the cash return.

The demands are four in number: (1) interest on debt capital; (2)

FIGURE 10.2 Analysis of Investment in Cash Registers, Assuming $160,000 Annual Returns

Interest Rate	8.0%				
ROE	18.0%	Cost of Capital Factors			
Income Tax Rate	40.0%	←			
Debt % of Capital	35.0%				
Equity % of Capital	65.0%				

	Year One	Year Two	Year Three	Year Four	Year Five
Annual Returns					
Labor Cost Savings	$160,000	$160,000	$160,000	$160,000	$160,000
Distribution of Returns					
For Interest	($14,000)	($12,065)	($9,872)	($7,384)	($4,564)
For Income Tax	($18,400)	($19,174)	($20,051)	($21,046)	($22,174)
For ROE	($58,500)	($50,415)	($41,249)	($30,856)	($19,072)
Equals Capital Recovery	$69,100	$78,346	$88,828	$100,713	$114,189
Cumulative Capital Recovery at End of Year	$69,100	$147,446	$236,274	$336,987	$451,176
Capital Invested at Beginning of Year					
Debt	$175,000	$150,815	$123,394	$92,304	$57,054
Equity	$325,000	$280,085	$229,160	$171,422	$105,958
Total	$500,000	$430,900	$352,554	$263,726	$163,013
Income Tax					
EBIT Increase	$160,000	$160,000	$160,000	$160,000	$160,000
Interest Expense	($14,000)	($12,065)	($9,872)	($7,384)	($4,564)
Depreciation	($100,000)	($100,000)	($100,000)	($100,000)	($100,000)
Taxable Income	$46,000	$47,935	$50,128	$52,616	$55,436
Income Tax	$18,400	$19,174	$20,051	$21,046	$22,174

income tax; (3) ROE (return on equity); and (4) recovery of capital invested in the assets. The first three are fixed amounts each year. The fourth is a free floater; these amounts can follow any pattern year to year. But their total over the five years must add to $500,000, which is the amount of capital invested in the assets.

I'll walk down the first year column in some detail; the other four years are simply repeats of the first year. The first claim on the annual return (in this example the labor cost savings for the year) is for *interest*. For year one the interest claim is $14,000: ($175,000 debt balance at start of year × 8.0% interest rate = $14,000 annual interest). The second demand is for *income tax*. The annual labor cost savings increase the company's taxable income each year. Income tax each year depends on the interest for the year, which is deductible to determine taxable income, and on which depreciation method is used for income tax purposes. As shown in Figure 10.2 the straight-line depreciation method is used, which gives $100,000 depreciation deduction each year for five years using a zero salvage value at the end of five years. (The accelerated depreciation method could be used instead.)

The bottom layer in Figure 10.2 shows the calculation of income tax for each year attributable to the investment. The income tax for the year is entered above as the second take-out from the annual labor cost savings. The third take-out from the annual return is for *earnings on equity capital* (see Figure 10.2). The deduction for ROE is based on the ROE goal of 18.0 percent per year. ROE for year one equals $58,500: ($325,000 equity capital at start of year × 18.0% ROE = $58,500 net income).

As mentioned earlier, the $160,000 annual cash returns amount used in Figure 10.2 is just the starting point in the analysis. This amount may not be enough to actually achieve the 18.0 percent annual ROE goal of the business. The purpose of the analysis is to test whether the $160,000 annual returns would be enough to achieve the ROE goal of the business. Of course if the ROE goal of the business had been lower than 18.0 percent, then the deduction for ROE from the annual return would be a smaller amount.

The fourth and final demand on each year's cash return is for **capital recovery**. Capital recovery is the residual amount remaining from the annual return after deducting interest, income tax, and the ROE amount for the year. For year one capital recovery is $69,100 (see Figure 10.2). The amount of capital recovery is not reinvested in additional cash registers; the company has all the cash registers it needs, at least for the time being.

In the future the business may consider replacing the cash registers, or increasing the number of cash registers it uses. But as far as this particular investment is concerned the capital recovery each year simply goes back to the cash balance of the business. The capital leaves this project (the cash registers investment). The business may put the money in another investment, or may increase its cash balance, or may reduce its debt, or may pay a higher cash dividend.

As shown in Figure 10.2 in the first year the company liquidates $69,100 of its investment in the cash registers; this much of the total capital that was originally invested in the assets is recovered and is no longer tied up in this particular investment. Therefore, the amount of capital invested during the second year is reduced by $69,100: ($500,000 initial capital − $69,100 capital recovery = $430,900 capital invested at start of year two). Debt supplies 35 percent of this capital balance and equity the other 65 percent, as shown in the column for year two.

From year to year this investment sizes down, because each year the business recovers part of the original capital invested in the assets. Thus, the annual amounts of interest and ROE earnings decrease year to year, as the total capital invested decreases from year to year. But note that the income tax increases year to year because the annual interest expense deduction decreases.

The cumulative capital recovery at the end of each year is shown in Figure 10.2. At the end of the fifth and final year of the investment, this amount should equal the initial amount of capital invested in the assets, which is $500,000 in this example. As Figure 10.2 shows the cumulative capital recovery falls short of $500,000, however.

Why a Second Pass at the Investment Is Needed

Given the annual returns of $160,000 the cumulative capital recovery at the end of the investment is only $451,176 (see Figure 10.2). But the business has to recover $500,000 capital from the investment, which is the initial amount of capital invested in the cash registers. Thus, the annual returns of $160,000 are not enough. The $160,000 amount of annual returns does not generate enough capital recovery after taking out interest, income tax, and earnings on equity each year—unless the ROE for each year is lowered so that more would be available for capital recovery each year.

Suppose the business goes ahead with the investment and it turns out that the annual returns are only $160,000 per year. In this situation the actual ROE rate earned on the investment would be lower than the 18.0 percent used in Figure 10.2. The precise ROE rate, assuming that the annual returns are $160,000, can be solved with the spreadsheet model. Instead of using the preestablished 18.0 percent rate the ROE rate is lowered until the exact rate is found that makes the total capital recovery over the five years equal to $500,000. (Figure 10.5, the Appendix to this chapter, shows the solution for the exact ROE rate, which is 14.6613%.)

At the $160,000 level of annual returns the cash registers investment is not completely attractive, assuming that the business is serious about earning the annual 18.0 percent ROE rate. Clearly the annual returns have to be higher than $160,000. The manager should ask his or her accountant, or other financial staff person to determine the amount of annual labor cost savings that would justify the investment from the cost of capital viewpoint.

Determining Exact Amounts for Returns

The investment analysis model shown in Figure 10.2 for the cash registers example is the printout of my personal computer spreadsheet program. One reason for using a spreadsheet for capital investment analysis is to do all the required calculations quickly and surely. Another reason is that the factors in the analysis can be easily changed for the purpose of investigating different scenarios for the investment.

So I changed the annual cash returns in order to find the exact amount required to earn an annual 18.0 percent ROE. Other input variables were held the same; only the amount of the annual labor cost savings was changed. With a change in the amount of annual returns the output variables for each year change accordingly—in particular the income tax for each year and the amount of capital invested each year, which in turn change the amounts of interest and earnings on equity for each year. There is a cascade effect on the output variables from changing the amount of annual returns.

Finding the precise answer can use a trial-and-error, or plug-and-chug process that is repeated until the exact amount of future annual cash returns is found that makes total capital recovery $500,000. This may seem to be time consuming, but it's not. Only a few trials, or passes are required to zero in on the exact answer. From Figure 10.2 I already knew that $160,000 was too low. So I bumped the annual returns to $175,000. This proved to be a little too high. After a few trials I converged on the exact amount. Figure 10.3 presents the answer. Annual labor cost savings of $172,463 for five years yield an annual 18.0 percent ROE and recovers exactly $500,000 capital from the investment.

Now comes the hard part. The manager must decide whether the business could, realistically, achieve $172,463 annual labor cost savings. This is the really tough part of the decision-making process. But the manager knows that if the annual labor cost savings turn out to be this amount or higher, then the investment will prove to be a good decision from the cost of capital point of view.

Flexibility of a Spreadsheet Model

As mentioned before, any factor in the analysis can be changed to test how sensitive the annual returns would be to the change. For instance instead of the straight-line method the accelerated depreciation method could be used for income tax. Instead of uniform labor cost savings across the years returns could be set lower in the early years and higher in the later years—or vice versa. The debt to equity

FIGURE 10.3 Exact Amount of Future Returns Required for Investment

Interest Rate	8.0%	
ROE	18.0%	Cost of Capital Factors
Income Tax Rate	40.0%	
Debt % of Capital	35.0%	
Equity % of Capital	65.0%	

	Year One	Year Two	Year Three	Year Four	Year Five
Annual Returns					
Labor Cost Savings	$172,463	$172,463	$172,463	$172,463	$172,463
Distribution of Returns					
For Interest	($14,000)	($11,856)	($9,425)	($6,668)	($3,543)
For Income Tax	($23,385)	($24,243)	($25,215)	($26,318)	($27,568)
For ROE	($58,500)	($49,540)	($39,382)	($27,865)	($14,806)
Equals Capital Recovery	$76,578	$86,824	$98,441	$111,612	$126,546
Cumulative Capital Recovery at End of Year	$76,578	$163,401	$261,842	$373,454	$500,000
Capital Invested at Beginning of Year					
Debt	$175,000	$148,198	$117,810	$83,355	$44,291
Equity	$325,000	$275,225	$218,789	$154,803	$82,255
Total	$500,000	$423,422	$336,599	$238,158	$126,546
Income Tax					
EBIT Increase	$172,463	$172,463	$172,463	$172,463	$172,463
Interest Expense	($14,000)	($11,856)	($9,425)	($6,668)	($3,543)
Depreciation	($100,000)	($100,000)	($100,000)	($100,000)	($100,000)
Taxable Income	$58,463	$60,607	$63,038	$65,794	$68,919
Income Tax	$23,385	$24,243	$25,215	$26,318	$27,568

Tip

Note in Figure 10.3 that the annual depreciation tax deduction amounts differ from the annual capital recovery amounts. For instance, the first year's depreciation tax deduction is $100,000 (using the straight-line method) but the capital recovery for the first year is $76,578. Both the total depreciation over the five years and the total capital recovery over the five years are $500,000. But the two amounts differ year-to-year. This disparity is typical of capital investments, and does not present a problem when using a spreadsheet model for analysis. (The difference between these two factors is much more of a nuisance in using the mathematical analysis techniques discussed in the Chapter 11.)

ratio can be shifted. Of course, the interest rate and ROE target rate can be changed. Once a change is entered the effects of the change are instantly available on screen.

To illustrate an alternative scenario for the cash registers example, assume the following cost of capital situation for the retailer instead of the example examined earlier:

CAPITAL STRUCTURE AND COST OF CAPITAL FACTORS

no debt; 100% equity source of capital

annual interest rate on debt—not applicable

40% income tax rate

18.0% annual ROE objective

In this alternative scenario the business uses no debt capital; all its capital comes from equity sources (capital invested by its shareowners and retained earnings). The ROE target rate is the same as before (18% annual ROE). Figure 10.4 shows the annual returns that would be needed in this situation. The required annual returns would jump to $199,815 compared with $172,463 in the earlier example, an increase of more than $27,000 per year! This is a rather significant increase. The capital structure of the business makes a difference on the future returns needed from an investment.

Leasing versus Buying Long-term Assets

Business managers have opportunities for leasing instead of buying long-term operating assets. Almost any long-term operating asset (trucks, equipment, machinery, computers, telephone systems, etc.) can be leased, either directly from the manufacturer of the asset or indirectly through a third party leasing specialist. The cash registers probably could be leased instead of purchased. Leasing may be very appealing if the business is short of cash.

Perhaps the lessor has a lower cost of capital than the business, in which case the business might be better off leasing rather than investing its own capital in the assets. Then again the lessor's cost of capital may be higher, which means that the lease rents would be higher than the returns needed by the business based on its lower cost of capital rate. Complicating matters is the fact that the term of the lease and pattern of lease rents may differ from the stream of returns generated from the assets.

Also, leases typically offer a purchase option at the end of the lease, at which time the business can purchase the assets. And

FIGURE 10.4 Future Returns Required from Investment for an Alternative Scenario (All Equity; No Debt)

Interest Rate	0.0%				
ROE	18.0%	Cost of Capital Factors			
Income Tax Rate	40.0%	←			
Debt % of Capital	0.0%				
Equity % of Capital	100.0%				

	Year One	Year Two	Year Three	Year Four	Year Five
Annual Returns					
Labor Cost Savings	$199,815	$199,815	$199,815	$199,815	$199,815
Distribution of Returns					
For Interest	$0	$0	$0	$0	$0
For Income Tax	($39,926)	($39,926)	($39,926)	($39,926)	($39,926)
For ROE	($90,000)	($77,420)	($62,576)	($45,059)	($24,390)
Equals Capital Recovery	$69,889	$82,469	$97,313	$114,830	$135,499
Cumulative Capital Recovery at End of Year	$69,889	$152,358	$249,671	$364,501	$500,000
Capital Invested at Beginning of Year					
Debt	$0	$0	$0	$0	$0
Equity	$500,000	$430,111	$347,642	$250,329	$135,499
Total	$500,000	$430,111	$347,642	$250,329	$135,499
Income Tax					
EBIT Increase	$199,815	$199,815	$199,815	$199,815	$199,815
Interest Expense	$0	$0	$0	$0	$0
Depreciation	($100,000)	($100,000)	($100,000)	($100,000)	($100,000)
Taxable Income	$99,815	$99,815	$99,815	$99,815	$99,815
Income Tax	$39,926	$39,926	$39,926	$39,926	$39,926

leases are very complicated legal contracts that generally impose all kinds of conditions and constraints on the lessee. Many leases involve front-end cash outlays by the lessee. In short comparing the purchase of long-term assets against leasing the same assets can be very difficult—like comparing apples and oranges.

But to illustrate certain basic points regarding the lease versus buy decision, suppose the retailer had the opportunity to lease the cash registers instead of buying them. Suppose the lessor quotes monthly rents of $14,372 for five years, which equals a total annual rent of $172,463. I selected this rent amount to equal the amount of the annual labor cost savings for the business to earn 18.0 percent

ROE (see Figure 10.3). Also assume that the business would have the option to purchase the cash registers for a nominal amount at the end of the five-year lease. Thus, the business would end up in the same position as if it had purchased the assets to begin with.

Generally the lessee (the retailer) bears all costs of possession and use of the assets as if it had bought them outright. For example, the retailer would pay the fire and theft insurance on the assets whether they are owned or leased. By leasing the cash registers, the retailer would reduce its annual labor costs by $172,463, but would pay annual lease rents of the same amount. From the financial point of view leasing versus buying is a standoff in this case. The retailer may not have any other investment opportunities that would generate an annual 18.0 percent ROE. So if it has the money, the retailer may prefer to make the investment instead of leasing the cash registers. In this way the business could employ its capital and earn an annual 18.0 percent ROE on the investment.

Leases involve certain other considerations beyond just the financial aspects. For one thing the retailer may prefer not to assume the economic risks of owning the cash registers. In a fast-changing technological environment a business may be reluctant to assume the risks making long-term investments in assets that may become obsolete in two or three years. So a business may shop around for a two- or three-year lease.

The simplest analysis situation for comparing leasing with buying assets is this. Suppose a business has identified a promising opportunity that requires it to acquire certain assets that would generate a stream of future returns for so many years, say $150,000 per year for seven years. (This forecast of future returns may turn out to be too optimistic, of course.) Assume that the business is short of cash and that it has tapped out its capital sources. It would be difficult for the business to raise additional capital. Assume that a leasing specialist is willing to rent the assets to the business for $10,000 per month, or $120,000 per year for five years. At the end of the lease the business would have the option to purchase the assets for a nominal amount.

In this scenario the lease makes sense, keeping in mind the risk that the future returns may turn out to be lower than $150,000 per year. The business would realize a $30,000 gain in its operating profit each year: ($150,000 annual returns from using the assets − $120,000 annual lease rents = $30,000 net gain). This is the simplest way to analyze leases. In actual situations the analysis is much more complicated. In any case a business should determine the stream of future returns from acquiring the assets. If the assets are purchased, the returns provide the money to recover the capital invested in the assets and cover the business's cost of capital along the way. If the assets are leased, the returns provide the money to pay the lease rents.

A Word or Two on Capital Budgeting

In theory a business should assemble all its possible investment opportunities, compare them, and rank-order them. The business should select the one with the highest ROE first, and so on. In allocating scarce capital among competing investment opportunities, ROE is the key criterion. According to this view of the world, the job of the business manager is to ration a limited amount of capital among competing investment alternatives.

The premise of rationing scarce capital resources is why the general topic of **capital investment analysis** is sometimes called **capital budgeting**. The term *budgeting* here is used in the allocation or apportionment sense, not in the sense of overall business management planning and goal setting. The comparative analysis of competing investment alternatives is beyond the scope of this book. Corporate financial management books cover this topic in depth.

Summary

Business managers make many long-term capital investment decisions. The analysis of capital investments hinges on the cost of capital requirements of the business, which depend on the company's mix of debt and equity capital, the cost of each, and the income tax situation of the business. The cost of equity capital is not a contractual rate like interest. Management decides on the ROE (return on equity) objective for the business.

Based on the amount of capital invested a manager can determine the amounts of future returns that will be needed to satisfy the cost of capital requirements of the business. The manager has to judge whether these future returns can be actually achieved. The chapter explains how to apply the cost of capital imperatives of a business in making capital investment decisions. A spreadsheet model is used to analyze and illustrate a prototype capital investment. A spreadsheet model has two important advantages: It is an excellent device for organizing and presenting the relevant information for an investment, and it is a versatile tool for examining different scenarios of an investment.

Analysis is important, to be sure. But we should not get carried away. More important is the ability of managers to find good capital investment opportunities and blend them into the overall strategic plan of the business.

Appendix

FIGURE 10.5 Exact ROE Rate for Cash Registers Capital Investment with $160,000 Annual Returns

Interest Rate	8.0%			
ROE	14.6613%	←	Exact ROE Rate Solved for in This Figure	
Income Tax Rate	40.0%			
Debt % of Capital	35.0%			
Equity % of Capital	65.0%			

	Year One	Year Two	Year Three	Year Four	Year Five
Annual Returns					
Labor Cost Savings	$160,000	$160,000	$160,000	$160,000	$160,000
Distribution of Returns					
For Interest	($14,000)	($11,761)	($9,272)	($6,503)	($3,424)
For Income Tax	($18,400)	($19,295)	($20,291)	($21,399)	($22,630)
For ROE	($47,649)	($40,030)	($31,557)	($22,134)	($11,654)
Equals Capital Recovery	$79,951	$88,913	$98,880	$109,964	$122,291
Cumulative Capital Recovery at End of Year	$79,951	$168,864	$267,744	$377,709	$500,000
Capital Invested at Beginning of Year					
Debt	$175,000	$147,017	$115,898	$81,290	$42,802
Equity	$325,000	$273,032	$215,238	$150,966	$79,489
Total	$500,000	$420,049	$331,136	$232,256	$122,291
Income Tax					
EBIT Increase	$160,000	$160,000	$160,000	$160,000	$160,000
Interest Expense	($14,000)	($11,761)	($9,272)	($6,503)	($3,424)
Depreciation	($100,000)	($100,000)	($100,000)	($100,000)	($100,000)
Taxable Income	$46,000	$48,239	$50,728	$53,497	$56,576
Income Tax	$18,400	$19,295	$20,291	$21,399	$22,630

CHAPTER 11

Discounting
Investment Returns

This chapter is like a bookend with Chapter 10. That chapter explains the analysis of long-term investments in operating assets by businesses. This chapter continues discussing the topic, with one key difference. The time line of analysis in the previous chapter goes like this:

Present   ————————→   Future

Starting with the amount of capital that would be invested today, the analysis looks forward in time to determine the amounts of future returns from the investment that would be needed in order to satisfy the cost of capital requirements of the business.

The time line of analysis in this chapter goes like this:

Present   ←————————   Future

Starting with the amounts of future returns from an investment (which are treated as fixed) the analysis travels backward in time to determine an amount called the **present value (PV)** of the investment. The present value is the most that a business should be willing to invest today to receive the future returns from the investment, based on its cost of capital requirements. The present value is compared with the entry cost of an investment.

Time Value of Money and Cost of Capital

The pivotal idea in this and the previous chapter is the *time value of money*. This term refers not only to money but also more broadly to capital and economic wealth in general. Capital should generate an income, or gain, or profit over the time it is used. The ratio of earnings on the capital invested over a period of time, one year being the standard time period of reference, is the measure for the time value of money. Karl Marx said that capital is "dead labor" and argued that capital should be publicly owned for the good of everyone. I won't pursue this economic philosophy any further. Quite clearly in our economic system capital does have a time value—or a rather a time *cost* depending on whose shoes you're standing in.

The business example in Chapter 10 has the following capital structure and cost of capital factors:

CAPITAL STRUCTURE AND COST OF CAPITAL FACTORS

35% debt and 65% equity mix of capital sources
8.0% annual interest rate on debt
40% income tax rate (combined federal and state)
18.0% annual ROE objective

This business example is continued this chapter. The debt and equity mix and the cost of capital factors differ from business to business, of course. But for a large swath of businesses this scenario is in the middle of the fairway.

Chapter 10 focuses on a decision of a retailer regarding investing in cash registers that would generate labor cost savings in the future. The analysis reveals that $160,000 annual returns from the cash registers investment wouldn't be enough to justify the investment; the annual returns would have to be $172,463. Figures 10.2 and 10.3 illustrate these important points. Assuming that annual returns of $172,463 could be earned for five years by using the cash registers the present value of the investment would be exactly $500,000. The entry cost of the investment is $500,000; this is the initial amount of capital that would be invested in the cash registers.

When the present value exactly equals the entry cost of an investment, the future returns are the exact amounts needed to recover the total capital invested in the assets and to satisfy the business's cost of capital requirements each year during the life of the investment. The present value of an investment is found by *discounting* its future returns.

Back to the Future: Discounting Investment Returns

The first pass in analyzing the cash registers investment by the retailer in Chapter 10 is for a scenario in which the future annual returns would be $160,000 for five years. Relative to the business's cost
of capital requirements this stream of future returns would be too
low. The business would not recover the full $500,000 amount of
capital that would be invested in the cash registers. Looking at it another way, if the business invested $500,000 and realized only
$160,000 labor cost savings for five years, the annual return on equity
(ROE) on this investment would fall short of its 18.0 percent goal.

Now, suppose the seller of the cash registers is willing to dicker
on the price. The $500,000 asking price for the cash registers is not
carved in stone; the seller will haggle over the price. At what price
would the cash registers investment be acceptable relative to the
company's cost of capital requirements? Using the spreadsheet
model explained in Chapter 10, I lowered the purchase price so that
the total capital recovered over the life of the investment equals the
purchase price. I kept the cost of capital factors the same, and I kept
the future annual returns at $160,000. Finding the correct purchase
price required only a few iterations using the spreadsheet model.

Figure 11.1 presents the solution to the question. Suppose the retailer could negotiate a purchase price of $463,868. At this price the
investment makes sense from the cost of capital point of view. The
total capital recovered over the five years is exactly equal to this purchase price. By the way, note that the annual depreciation amounts
for income tax are based on this lower purchase cost.

One important advantage of using a spreadsheet model for capital
investment analysis is that any of the variables for the investment
can be changed in order to explore a variety of questions and to examine a diversity of scenarios. The "what if the purchase price were
only $463,868?" scenario is the one presented in Figure 11.1.

Solving for the present value is called *discounting* the future returns. This analysis technique also is called the **discounted cash
flow (DCF)** method. This analysis method usually is explained in a
mathematical context, which uses equations that are applied to the
future stream of returns.

Spreadsheets versus Equations

The DCF method is very popular. However, I favor a spreadsheet
model to determine the present value of an investment. Spreadsheet
programs are very versatile. Furthermore, a spreadsheet does all the

FIGURE 11.1 Purchase Cost of Cash Registers That Would Justify the Investment Relative to the Business's Cost of Capital Requirements

Interest Rate	8.0%	
ROE	18.0%	Cost of Capital Factors
Income Tax Rate	40.0%	←
Debt % of Capital	35.0%	
Equity % of Capital	65.0%	

	Year One	Year Two	Year Three	Year Four	Year Five
Annual Returns					
Labor Cost Savings	$160,000	$160,000	$160,000	$160,000	$160,000
Distribution of Returns					
For Interest	($12,988)	($10,999)	($8,744)	($6,187)	($3,287)
For Income Tax	($21,695)	($22,491)	($23,393)	($24,416)	($25,576)
For ROE	($54,273)	($45,960)	($36,536)	($25,851)	($13,736)
Equals Capital Recovery	$71,044	$80,550	$91,327	$103,547	$117,401
Cumulative Capital Recovery at End of Year	$71,044	$151,593	$242,921	$346,467	$463,868
Capital Invested at Beginning of Year	Variable solved for in this analysis.				
Debt	$162,354	$137,488	$109,296	$77,332	$41,090
Equity	$301,514	$255,336	$202,978	$143,616	$76,310
Total	$463,868	$392,824	$312,275	$220,947	$117,401
Income Tax					
EBIT Increase	$160,000	$160,000	$160,000	$160,000	$160,000
Interest Expense	($12,988)	($10,999)	($8,744)	($6,187)	($3,287)
Depreciation	($92,774)	($92,774)	($92,774)	($92,774)	($92,774)
Taxable Income	$54,238	$56,227	$58,483	$61,040	$63,939
Income Tax	$21,695	$22,491	$23,393	$24,416	$25,576

irksome calculations involved in investment analysis. Different scenarios can be examined quickly and efficiently, which I find to be an enormous advantage. In business capital investment situations managers have to make several critical assumptions and forecasts. The manager is well advised to test the sensitivity of each critical input factor. A spreadsheet model is an excellent device for doing this.

Even if you are not a regular spreadsheet user, the logic and layout of the spreadsheet presented in Figure 11.1 are important to understand. Figure 11.1 provides the relevant information for the management decision-making phase, and for management follow-through after a decision is made. The year-by-year data points shown in Figure 11.1 are good benchmarks for monitoring and controlling the actual results of the investment as it plays out each year. In short, a spreadsheet model is a very useful analysis tool and is a good way for organizing the relevant information about an investment.

Frankly, another reason for using a spreadsheet model is to avoid mathematical methods for analyzing capital investments. In Chapter 10 not one equation is presented, and so far in this chapter not one equation is presented. In my experience managers are put off by a heavy-handed mathematical approach loaded with arcane equations and unfamiliar symbols. However, in the not-so-distant past personal computers were not as ubiquitous as they are today, and spreadsheet programs were not nearly so sophisticated.

In the old days (before personal computers came along) certain mathematical techniques were developed to do capital investment analysis computations. These techniques have become entrenched in the field of capital investment analysis. Indeed, the techniques and terminology are household words that are used freely in the world of business and finance—such as *present value, discounted cash flow,* and *internal rate of return.* Business managers should have at least a nodding acquaintance with these terms and a general idea of how the techniques are applied.

The remainder of this chapter presents a quick, introductory tour of the mathematical techniques for capital investment analysis. To the extent possible I avoid going into detailed explanations of the computational equations, which I believe have little interest to business managers. These quantitative techniques are just different ways of skinning the cat. I think a spreadsheet model is a better tool of analysis, which reminds me of a personal incident several years ago.

I was shopping for a mortgage on the new house we had just bought. One loan officer pulled out a well-worn table of columns and rows for different interest rates and different loan amount modules. He took a few minutes to determine the monthly payment amount for my mortgage loan. I had brought a business/financial calculator to the meeting. I double-checked his answer and found that it was incorrect. He was somewhat offended and replied that he had been doing these sorts of calculations for many years, and perhaps I had made a mistake. It took me only five seconds to check my calculation. I was right. He took several minutes to compute the amount again and was shocked to discover that his first amount was wrong. I thought better of suggesting that he should use a calculator to do these sorts of calculations.

Discounted Cash Flow (DCF)

To keep matters focused on bare-bone essentials, suppose that a business has no debt (and thus no interest to pay) and is organized as a pass-through entity for income tax purposes. The business does not pay income tax as a separate entity. Its only cost of capital factor is its annual return on equity (ROE) goal. Assume that the business has established an annual 15 percent ROE goal. (Of course, the ROE could be set lower or higher than 15 percent.) Assume that the business has an investment opportunity that promises annual returns at the end of each year as follows:

RETURNS

Year One	$115,000.00
Year Two	$132,250.00
Year Three	$152,087.50

What is the value of this investment to the business today, at the present time? This is called the present value of the investment.

The discounted cash flow (DCF) method of analysis computes the present value as follows:

PRESENT VALUE CALCULATIONS

Year One	$115,000.00 \div (1 + 15\%)^1 =	$100,000
Year Two	$132,250.00 \div (1 + 15\%)^2 =	$100,000
Year Three	$152,087.50 \div (1 + 15\%)^3 =	$100,000
	Present Value =	$300,000

I rigged the future return amounts for each year so that the calculations are easier to follow. Of course, a business should forecast the actual future returns for an investment.

Each future return is *discounted,* or divided by a number greater than one. The future returns represent either increases of cash inflows from making the investment, or decreases of cash outflows (as in the cash registers investment example). Thus, the term discounted *cash flow.*

The divisor in the DCF calculations equals $(1 + r)^n$ – in which r is the cost of capital rate each period, and n is the number of periods until the future return is realized. Usually r is constant period-to-period over the life of the investment, although a different cost of capital rate could be used for each period.

In summary the present value of this investment equals $300,000.

This means that if the business went ahead and put $300,000 capital into the investment and at the end of each year realized a future return according to the above schedule, then the business would earn exactly 15 percent annual ROE on the investment. To check this present value, I used my spreadsheet model. Figure 11.2 shows the printout of the spreadsheet model, as adapted to the circumstances of this investment. At the end of the third year the full $300,000 capital invested is recovered, which proves that the present value of the investment equals $300,000, using the 15 percent cost of capital discount rate.

The DCF method can be used when the future returns from an investment are known or can be predicted fairly accurately. The purpose is to determine the present value (PV) of an investment, which is the maximum amount that a business should invest today in exchange for the future returns. The DCF technique is correct, of course. But it has one problem. Well, actually two problems I should say—one not so serious, and one more serious.

The not-so-serious problem concerns how to do the computations

FIGURE 11.2 Check on the Present Value Calculated by the DCF Method

Interest Rate	0.0%	
ROE	15.0%	Cost of Capital Factors
Income Tax Rate	0.0%	
Debt % of Capital	0.0%	
Equity % of Capital	100.0%	

	Year One	Year Two	Year Three
Annual Returns	$115,000.00	$132,250.00	$152,087.50
Distribution of Returns			
For Interest	$0.00	$0.00	$0.00
For Income Tax	$0.00	$0.00	$0.00
For ROE	($45,000.00)	($34,500.00)	($19,837.50)
Equals Capital Recovery	$70,000.00	$97,750.00	$132,250.00
Cumulative Capital Recovery at End of Year	$70,000.00	$167,750.00	$300,000.00
Capital Invested at Beginning of Year			
Debt	$0.00	$0.00	$0.00
Equity	$300,000.00	$230,000.00	$132,250.00
Total	$300,000.00	$230,000.00	$132,250.00

required by the DCF method. One way is to use a handheld busi-ness/financial calculator. These are very powerful, relatively cheap, and fairly straightforward to use (assuming you read the owner's manual). Another way is to use the financial functions included in a spreadsheet program. (Excel® includes a complete set of financial functions.)

The second problem in using the DCF method is more substantive and has nothing to do with doing the computations for present value. The problem concerns the *lack of information* in using the DCF technique. The unfolding of the investment over the years is not clear from the present value (PV) calculation. Rather than opening up the investment for closer inspection, the PV computation closes it down and telescopes the information into just one number. The method doesn't reveal important information about the investment over its life.

Figure 11.2 presents a more complete look at the investment. It shows that the cash return at the end of year one is split between $45,000 earnings on equity and $70,000 capital recovery. The capital recovery aspect of an investment is very important to understand. The capital recovery portion of the cash return at the end of the first year reduces the amount of capital invested during the second year. Only $230,000 is invested during the second year: ($300,000 initial amount invested – $70,000 capital recovered at end of year one = $230,000 capital invested at start of year two). Business investments are self-liquidating over the life of the investment; there is capital re-covery each period, as in this example.

Managers should anticipate what to do with the $70,000 capital recovery at the end of the first year. (For that matter, managers should also plan what to do with the $45,000 net income.) Will the capital be reinvested? Will the business be able to reinvest the $70,000 and earn 15 percent ROE? To plan ahead for the capital re-covery from the investment, managers need information as pre-sented in Figure 11.2, which tracks the earnings and capital recovery year by year. The DCF technique does not generate this information.

Net Present Value and Internal Rate of Return

Suppose the business has an investment opportunity that would cost $300,000 to enter today. (Recall that in this example the business has no debt and is a pass-through tax entity that does not pay income tax.) The manager forecasts the future returns from the investment would be as follows:

RETURNS

Year One $118,000.00
Year Two $139,240.00
Year Three $164,303.20

The present value and the *net present value* for this stream of future returns is calculated as follows:

PRESENT VALUE CALCULATIONS

Year One $118,000.00 ÷ (1 + 15%)^1 = $102,608.70
Year Two $139,240.00 ÷ (1 + 15%)^2 = $105,285.44
Year Three $164,303.20 ÷ (1 + 15%)^3 = $108,032.02

$$\text{Present Value} = \$315,926.16$$
$$\text{Entry Cost of Investment} = (\$300,000.00)$$
$$\text{Net Present Value} = \$\ 15,926.16$$

The present value is $15,926.16 more of the amount of capital that would have to be invested. The difference between the calculated present value (PV) and the entry cost of an investment is called its **net present value (NPV)**. Net present value is negative when the PV is less than the entry cost of the investment. The NPV has informational value, but it's not an ideal measure for comparing alternative investment opportunities. For this purpose the **internal rate of return (IRR)** of each investment is determined and the internal rates of return for each investment are compared.

The IRR is the precise discount rate that makes PV exactly equal to the entry cost of the investment. In the example the investment has a $300,000 entry cost. The IRR for the stream of future returns from the investment is 18.0 percent, which is higher than 15.0 percent cost of capital discount rate used to compute the PV. The IRR rate is solved for using a business/financial calculator, or by entering the relevant data in a spreadsheet program using the IRR financial function.

Figure 11.3 demonstrates that the IRR for the investment is 18.0 percent. This return on capital rate is used to calculate the earnings on capital invested each year that is deducted from the return for that year. The remainder is the capital recovery for the year. The total capital recovered by the end of the third year equals the $300,000 entry cost of the investment (see Figure 11.3). Thus, the internal rate of return (IRR) is 18.0 percent.

A business should favor investments with higher IRRs in prefer-

FIGURE 11.3 Illustration That Internal Rate of Return (IRR) is 18.0%

Interest Rate	0.0%
ROE	18.0% ← Internal Rate of Return (IRR)
Income Tax Rate	0.0%
Debt % of Capital	0.0%
Equity % of Capital	100.0%

	Year One	Year Two	Year Three
Annual Returns	$118,000.00	$139,240.00	$164,303.20
Distribution of Returns			
For Interest	$0.00	$0.00	$0.00
For Income Tax	$0.00	$0.00	$0.00
For ROE	($54,000.00)	($42,480.00)	($25,063.20)
Equals Capital Recovery	$64,000.00	$96,760.00	$139,240.00
Cumulative Capital Recovery at End of Year	$64,000.00	$160,760.00	$300,000.00
Capital Invested at Beginning of Year			
Debt	$0.00	$0.00	$0.00
Equity	$300,000.00	$236,000.00	$139,240.00
Total	$300,000.00	$236,000.00	$139,240.00

ence to investments with lower IRRs—all other things being the same. A business should not accept an investment that has an IRR less than its *hurdle rate*, that is, its cost of capital rate. Another way of saying this is that a business should not proceed with an investment that has a negative net present value. Well, this is the theory.

Capital investment decisions are complex and often involve many nonquantitative, or qualitative factors that are difficult to capture fully in the analysis. A company may go ahead with an investment that has a low IRR because of political pressures, or to accomplish social objectives that lie outside the profit motive. The company might make a capital investment even if the numbers don't justify the decision in order to forestall competitors from entering its market. Long-run capital investment decisions are at bottom really survival decisions. A company may have to make huge capital investments to upgrade, automate, or expand; if they don't, they may languish and eventually die.

The After-Tax Cost of Capital Rate

So far I have skirted around one issue in discussing discounted cash flow techniques for analyzing business capital investments—*income tax*. DCF analysis techniques were developed long before personal computer spreadsheet programs became available. The DCF method had come up with a way for dealing with the income tax factor, and it did, of course. The trick is to use an *after-tax* cost of capital rate and to separate the stream of returns from an investment and the depreciation deductions for income tax.

An example is needed to demonstrate how to use the after-tax cost of capital rate. The cash registers investment examined in the previous chapter is a perfect example for this purpose. To remind you, the retailer's sources of capital and its cost of capital factors are as follows:

CAPITAL STRUCTURE AND COST OF CAPITAL FACTORS

35% debt and 65% equity mix of capital sources
8.0% annual interest rate on debt
40% income tax rate (combined federal and state)
18.0% annual ROE objective

The *after-tax cost of capital rate* for this business is calculated as follows:

AFTER-TAX COST OF CAPITAL RATE

Debt: $35\% \times [(8.0\%)(1 - 40\% \text{ tax rate})] =$ 1.68%

Equity: $[65\% \times 18.0\%] =$ 11.70%

After-tax cost of capital rate = 13.38%

ROE is an after-tax rate; net income earned on the owners' equity of a business is after income tax. To put the interest rate on an after-tax basis, the interest rate is multiplied by $(1 - \text{tax rate})$ because interest is deductible to determine taxable income. The debt weight (35 percent in this example) is multiplied by the after-tax interest rate; and, the equity weight (65 percent in this example) is multiplied by the after-tax ROE rate. The after-tax cost of capital, therefore, is 13.38 percent for the business.

Recall that the entry cost of investing in the cash registers is $500,000. Assume that the future annual returns from this investment are $172,463 for five years. Figure 10.3 in the previous chapter shows that for this stream of future returns the company's cost of capital requirements are satisfied exactly. Therefore, the present value of the investment must be exactly $500,000, which is the entry cost of the investment. Using the after-tax cost of capital rate to discount the returns from the investment proves this point.

As just calculated, the company's after-tax cost of capital rate is 13.38 percent. Instead of applying this discount rate directly to the $172,463 returns (labor cost savings) from the investment, the annual returns are first converted to an after-tax basis, as if the returns were fully taxable at the 40 percent income tax rate. However, income tax is overstated because the depreciation deduction based on the cost of the assets is ignored. The depreciation tax effect is brought into the analysis as follows.

In this example the straight-line depreciation method is used, so the company deducts $100,000 depreciation each year for income tax. This reduces its taxable income and thus its income tax $40,000 each year: ($100,000 annual depreciation × 40% tax rate = $40,000 income tax savings). The depreciation tax savings are added to the $103,478 after-tax returns each year, which gives a total of $143,478 for each year. These annual amounts are discounted using the after-tax cost of capital rate as follows:

YEAR	PRESENT VALUE CALCULATIONS	
1	$143,478 \div (1 + 13.38\%)^1 =$	$126,546
2	$143,478 \div (1 + 13.38\%)^2 =$	$111,612
3	$143,478 \div (1 + 13.38\%)^3 =$	$\ 98,441
4	$143,478 \div (1 + 13.38\%)^4 =$	$\ 86,824
5	$143,478 \div (1 + 13.38\%)^5 =$	$\ 76,577
	Present Value =	$500,000

The present value calculated in this manner equals the entry cost of the investment. (When the stream of future returns consists of uniform amounts, only one global calculation is required, but I show the calculations for each year to leave a clear trail regarding how present value is calculated.) The company would earn exactly its cost of capital, because the present value equals the entry cost of the investment. This point also is demonstrated in Figure 10.3 in the previous chapter.

As I've said before, I favor a spreadsheet model for capital investment analysis over the equation-oriented DCF method. A spreadsheet model is more versatile and it provides more information for management analysis. Also I think it is a more intuitive and straightforward approach.

Regarding Cost of Capital Factors

Most discourses on business capital investment analysis assume a constant mix, or ratio, of debt and equity over the life of an investment. And the cost of each source of capital is held constant over the life of the investment. Also the income tax rate is held constant. Before spreadsheets came along there were very practical reasons for making these assumptions, mainly to avoid using more than one cost of capital rate in the analysis. Today these constraints are no longer necessary.

If the situation calls for it, the manager should change the ratio of debt and equity from one period to the next, or change the interest rate and/or the ROE rate from period to period. Each period could be assigned its own cost of capital rate, in other words. Sometimes, this is appropriate for particular capital investments. For instance a capital investment may involve direct financing, in which a loan is arranged and tailor-made to fit the specific features of the investment.

One example of direct financing is when a business offers its customers the alternative of leasing its products instead of buying them. The business makes an investment in the assets leased to its customers. The business borrows money to provide part of the capital invested in the assets leased to customers. The leased assets are used as collateral for the loan; and the terms of the loan are designed to parallel the terms of the lease. Over the life of the lease the mix of debt and equity capital invested in the assets changes period to period. Furthermore, the interest rate on the lease loan and the ROE goal for lease investments very likely are different from the cost of capital factors for the company's main line of business.

Summary

This and the previous chapter explain the analysis of business long-term investments in operating assets. The capital to make these investments comes from two basic sources—debt and owners' equity. A business should carefully analyze capital investments to determine whether the investment will yield sufficient operating profit to provide for its cost of capital during the life of the investment. This chapter demonstrates how to use the spreadsheet model developed in the previous chapter for discounting the future returns from an investment to determine its *present value*. The chapter also presents a succinct survey of the commonly used mathematical techniques for analyzing business capital investments.

Discounted cash flow is the broad generic name, or umbrella term, for the traditional equation-oriented capital investment analysis methods. A stream of future cash returns from an investment is discounted to calculate the present value, or the net present value of the investment. Alternatively, the *internal rate of return* that the future returns would yield is determined. The IRR of an investment is compared against the company's cost of capital rate, and with the internal rates of return of alternative investments. These mathematical analysis techniques are explained in the chapter, while keeping the computational equations to a minimum.

The equation-oriented techniques were developed before sophisticated spreadsheet programs were available for personal computers. In my view the spreadsheet model is a better tool of analysis. Spreadsheets are more versatile, easier to follow, and make it possible to display all the relevant information for decision-making analysis and management control. Nevertheless, the traditional capital investment analysis methods probably will be around for some time.

CHAPTER 12

Management Control, Budgeting, and Accounting

Management decisions constitute a plan of action for accomplishing a business's objectives. Establishing the objectives for the period may be done through a formal budgeting process or may be done without a budget. In either case actually achieving the objectives for the period requires *management control*. In the broadest sense management control refers to everything managers do in moving the business toward its objectives. Decisions start things in motion; control brings things to a successful conclusion. Good decisions with bad control can turn out as disastrous as making bad decisions in the first place. Good tools for making management decisions should be complemented with good tools for management control.

Previous chapters concentrate on models of profit, cash flow, and capital investment that are useful in decision-making analysis. This chapter shifts attention to management control and explores how managers keep a steady hand on the helm of the business along its financial voyage, often across troubled waters. The chapter also presents a brief overview of business budgeting. This short summary on budgeting is not an exhaustive treatise on the topic, of course.

This chapter pays particular attention to the important role that accounting plays in management control and budgeting.

Management control and budgeting have many dimensions, but accounting provides essential information for both these management practices.

Management Control: Follow-Through on Decisions

Management control is both preventive and positive in nature. Managers have to prevent, or at least minimize wrong things from happening. Murphy's Law is all too true; if something can go wrong, it will. Equally important, managers have to make sure right things are happening and happening on time. Managers shouldn't simply react to problems; they should be proactive and push things along in the right direction. Management control is characterized not just by the absence of problems but also by the presence of actions to achieve the goals and objectives of the business.

One of the best definitions of the management control process that I've heard was by a former student. I challenged the students in the class to give me a very good but very concise description of management control—one that captured the essence of management control in very few words. One student answered in two words: "watching everything." This pithy comment captures a great deal of what management control is all about.

Management theorists include control in their conceptual scheme of the functions of managers, although there's no consensus regarding the exact meaning of control. Most definitions of management control emphasize the need for *feedback information* on actual performance that is compared against goals and objectives for the purpose of detecting deviations and variances. Based on the feedback information managers take corrective action to bring performance back on course.

Management control is an information dependent process, that's for sure. Managers need actual performance information reported to them on a timely basis. In short feedback information is the main ingredient for management control. And managers need this information quickly. Information received too late can result in costly delays before problems are corrected.

Management Control Information

In general management control information can be classified in three types:

1. Regular periodic *comprehensive coverage reports*, such as the financial statements to managers on the profit performance,

cash flows, and financial condition of the business as a whole and major segments of the business.

2. Regular periodic *limited scope reports* that focus on critical factors, such as bad debt write-offs, inventory write-downs, sales returns, employee absenteeism, quality inspection reports, productivity reports, new customers, and so on.

3. *Ad hoc reports* triggered by specific problems that have arisen unexpectedly, which are needed in addition to regular control reports.

Feedback information divides naturally into either good news or bad news. Good news is when actual performance is going according to plan, or better than plan. Management's job is to keep things moving in this direction. Management control information usually reveals bad news as well—problems that have come up and unsatisfactory performance areas that need attention.

Managers draw on a very broad range of information sources to keep on top of things and to exercise control. For examples, managers monitor customer satisfaction, employee absenteeism and morale, production schedules, quality control inspection results, and so on. Managers listen to customers' complaints, shop the competition, and may even decide that industrial intelligence and espionage are necessary to get information about competitors. The accounting system of a business is one of the most important sources for control information.

Managers are concerned with problems that directly impact on the financial performance of the business, of course—such as sales quotas not being met, sales prices being discounted lower than predicted, product costs higher than expected, expenses running over budget, cash flow running slower than planned, and so on. Or perhaps sales are over quota, sales prices are higher than predicted, product costs are lower than expected, and so on. Even when things are moving along very close to plan managers need control reports to inform them of conformity with the plan.

Control reports should be designed to fit the specific areas of authority and responsibility of individual managers. The purchasing (procurement) manager gets control reports on inventory and suppliers; the credit manager gets control reports on accounts receivable and customers' payment histories; the sales manager gets control reports on sales by product categories and salespersons, and so on.

Periodic control reports are detail rich. For example, the monthly sales report for a territory may include breakdowns on hundreds and perhaps more than a thousand different products and customers. Moving up in the organization, to a brand manager or a division manager for example, the span of management authority and responsibility becomes broader and broader. At the top level (president/chief executive officer), the span of authority and responsibility encompasses the whole business. At the higher rungs on the organizational ladder managers need control information in the form of comprehensive financial and other reports.

Financial statements for management control are much more detailed and are supplemented by many supporting schedules and analyses compared with the profit and cash flow models explained in earlier chapters, which are used primarily for decision-making analysis. For instance management control financial reports include detailed schedules of accounts receivables that are past due, products that have been held in inventory too long, lists of products that have unusually high rates of return from customers (that probably indicate product defects), particular expenses that are out of control relative to last period or the targets for this period, and so on. The profit and cash flow models illustrated in earlier chapters are like executive summaries, compared with the enormous amount of detail in management control reports.

In addition to comprehensive control reports a manager may select one or a few specific factors, or key items, for special attention. I read about an example of this approach a couple of years ago that I still remember. During a cost-cutting drive the chief executive of a business asked for a daily count on the number of company employees. He was told he couldn't get it. Some data were kept by divisions and were hard to gather together in one place. Some were in a payroll database accessible only to programmers. But he persisted, and now the data are at his fingertips whenever he wants them: A specially designed executive information system links personnel data directly to a personal computer in his office. "Management knows I'm watching the count very closely," he said. "Believe me, they don't add staff carelessly."

It's a good idea to identify the few relative critical success factors and keep a close and constant watch on them. Knowing what these factors are is one secret of good management. Product quality is almost always one such key success factor. Customer loyalty is another.

By their very nature management control reports are confidential and are not discussed outside the company. Management control reports contain very sensitive information; these reports disclose the "mistakes" of decisions that were made or how decisions went wrong.

Often unexpected and unpredictable developments upset the apple cart of good decisions. Some degree of inherent uncertainty surrounds all business decisions, of course. Nevertheless, management control reports do have a strong element of passing judgment on managers' decisions and their ability to make good predictions.

The Foundation of Internal Accounting Controls

A business relies heavily on its accounting system to supply essential information for management control. The reliability of accounting information depends heavily on especially designed procedures called **internal accounting controls** that are established by a business and how well these controls are working in actual practice.

Forms and Procedures

Specific forms are required to carry out the activities of the business, and certain set procedures must be followed. One fundamental purpose of these forms and procedures is to eliminate (or at least minimize) data processing errors in capturing, processing, storing, retrieving, and reporting the large amount of information needed in operating a business.

Forms and procedures are not too popular, but without them an organization couldn't function. Without well-designed forms and clear-cut procedures for doing things an organization couldn't function very well, if at all. On the other side of the coin, one danger is that filling out the forms becomes perfunctory and careless and some employees bypass or take shortcuts instead of faithfully following official procedures.

Internal accounting controls also are instituted for a second extremely important reason—to protect against *theft* and *fraud* by employees, suppliers, customers, and managers themselves. Unfortunately, my father-in-law was right. He told me many years ago that based on his experience "there's a little bit of larceny in everyone's heart." He could have added that there's a lot of larceny in the hearts of a few. It's an unpleasant fact of business life that some customers will shoplift, some vendors and suppliers will overcharge or short-count on deliveries, some employees will embezzle or steal assets, and some managers will commit fraud against the business or take personal advantage of their position of authority in the business. Newspapers and the financial press report stories of employee and management fraud with alarming frequency.

In summary internal controls have two primary purposes: (1) to ensure the accuracy, completeness, and timeliness of information collected, processed, and reported by the accounting system; and (2) to deter and detect dishonest, illegal, and any other behavior against the policies of the business by its employees and managers, as well as guarding against such behavior by its customers and others it deals with. This is a tall order, but any business manager you ask about this will attest to the need for effective internal accounting controls.

The ideal internal accounting control is one that ensures the integrity of the information being recorded and processed, that deters or at least quickly detects any fraud and dishonesty, *and is cost effective*. Some controls are simply too costly or are too intrusive of personal privacy, such as a body search of every employee on exit from work, though diamond and gold mines take these precautions, I understand, and a recent article I read in the *New York Times* on General Electric indicated some of its employees must go through a search on exit from work.

Independent CPA Audits and Internal Auditing

The national organization of CPAs, the American Institute of Certified Public Accountants (AICPA), is a good source for useful publications that deal with internal accounting controls.* These are excellent summaries and reflect the long experience of CPAs in auditing a wide range of businesses. The AICPA's guidelines are an excellent checklist for the types of internal accounting controls that a business should establish and enforce with due diligence.

Speaking of CPAs, *financial statement audits* by independent public accountants can be viewed as one type of internal control. Based on their annual audit the CPA firm expresses an opinion on the external financial statements issued by a business. Business managers should understand the limits of audits by CPAs regarding discovering errors and fraud. Auditors are responsible for discovering *material* errors and fraud, which would cause the financial statements to be misleading. However, it is not cost effective to have the outside auditor firm do a thoroughgoing examination that would catch all errors and fraud. It would take too long and cost too much. The first line of defense is the business's internal accounting con-

---

*A good place to start is *Statement on Auditing Standards No. 55*, "Consideration of the Internal Control Structure in a Financial Statement Audit," (American Institute of Certified Public Accountants, Inc., New York, originally issued in 1988 and later amended.) Also, the AICPA has put out an *Audit Guide* on this topic, and the Committee of Sponsoring Organizations of the Treadway Commission issued a series of influential publications dealing with internal control in 1992.

trols. Having an audit by an independent CPA firm provides an independent appraisal and check on its internal controls, but the business itself has the primary responsibility to design and establish effective internal accounting controls.

Many larger business organizations establish an *internal auditing* function in the organization structure of the business. Although the internal auditors are employees of the organization, they are given autonomy to act independently. Internal auditors report to the highest levels of management, often directly to the board of directors of the corporation. Internal auditors monitor and test the organization's internal accounting controls regularly. They also carry out special investigations either on their own or at the request of top management and the board of directors. Different departments and areas of operation are audited on a surprise basis or on a regular rotation basis.

Fraud Problems

Business fraud is like adultery. It shouldn't happen but having done it every attempt is made to hide it, although it often comes out eventually. The same holds for business fraud. Businesses handle a lot of money, have a lot of valuable assets, and give managers and other employees a lot of authority. So it's not surprising that a business is vulnerable to fraud and other dishonest schemes. Fraud, in contrast to theft, involves an element of deception. The guilty person is in a position of trust and authority. The perpetrator of fraud owes a duty to his or her employer, but deliberately violates this duty and covers up the scheme.

Tip

A few years ago several investment banks and other financial institutions revealed huge losses caused by employees making unauthorized trades in financial derivatives. In virtually all of these cases there was a breakdown in important internal controls. Many of these cases violated one of the most important of all internal controls—requiring two or more persons to authorize significant expenditures or taking on major risk exposures. Many of these cases also revealed that another key internal control was violated called the *separation of duties*. The authority for making a decision and carrying it out should always be separated from the accounting and recordkeeping for the decision and its outcome. One person should never do both.

Many books have been written on business fraud. Many seminars and training programs are offered that deal with fraud in the business world. Indeed, developments are underway to make the control and detection of business fraud a professional specialty. Keep in mind that audits and internal accounting controls are not foolproof. A disturbing amount of fraud still slips through these preventive measures. High-level management fraud is particularly difficult to prevent and detect. By their very nature high-level managers have a great deal of authority and discretion. Their positions of trust and power give high-level managers an unparalleled opportunity to commit fraud and the means to conceal it.

One prime example of a high-risk fraud area in business comes to mind. The purchasing agents of a business are vulnerable to accepting bribes, kickbacks, under-the-table payments, or other favors from vendors. A purchasing agent I know very well made me aware of how serious a problem this is. He didn't exactly say that all purchasing agents are corrupt, but he certainly said that the temptation is there and many succumb.

It is argued that business should aggressively prosecute offenders. The record shows, however, that most businesses are reluctant to do this, fearing the adverse publicity surrounding legal proceedings. Many businesses adopt the policy that fraud is just one of the many costs of doing business. They don't encourage it, of course, and they do everything practical to prevent fraud. But in the final analysis the

Tip

Keeping a close watch on cash flows is a good way to catch signs of possible fraud, which is evidently overlooked by most managers. Most fraud schemes and scams go after money. Like Willie Sutton said when asked why he robbed banks: "Because that's where the money is." To get to the money and to conceal the fraud as long as possible an asset or a liability has to be manipulated and misstated by the perpetrator—most often accounts receivable, inventories, and sometimes accounts payable. (Other assets and liabilities may be involved.)

In brief, managers should keep alert to increases in accounts receivable and inventories, as well as accounts payable. Not only do these increases cause negative cash flow effects, but such increases also could signal a suspicious change that is not consistent with changes in sales activity and other facts and information known to the manager.

majority of businesses appear to tolerate some amount of normal loss from fraud.

For an example, suppose an employee or mid-level manager steals inventory and sells the products for cash, which goes into his or her pocket. A good management control reporting system keeps a very close watch on inventory levels and cost of goods sold expense ratios. If a material amount of inventory is stolen, the inventory shrinkage number and/or profit margin figures should sound alarms. The sophisticated thief realizes this and will cover up the missing inventory. Indeed, this is exactly what was done in many fraud cases.

The company's internal controls were not effective in preventing the coverup; the accounting system reported inventory that in fact was not there. Thus, inventory showed a larger increase (or a smaller decrease) than it should have. You might think that managers would be alert to any inventory increase. But in the majority of fraud cases managers did not pursue the reasons for the inventory increase. If they had they might have discovered the inventory theft.

In similar fashion, fraud may involve taking money out of collections on accounts receivable, which is covered up by overstating the accounts receivable account. Other fraud schemes may use accounts payable to conceal the fraud. Managers should keep in mind that the reported profit performance of the business is overstated as the result of undiscovered fraud. This is terribly embarrassing when it is discovered and prior period financial statements have to be revised and restated. But fraud can be disastrous. Furthermore, it may lead to firing the executive who failed to discover the theft or fraud; one responsibility of managers is to prevent fraud by subordinates, and to devise ways and means of making certain that no fraud is going on.

Guidelines for Management Control Reports

The design of effective and efficient management control reports is a real challenge. This section presents guidelines and suggestions for management control reporting. Unfortunately, there is no one best format and system for control reporting. There is no "one size fits all" approach for communicating the vital control information needed by managers, no more than there are simple answers in most areas of business decision-making. One job of managers is to know what they need to know, and this includes the information they should get in their control reports.

Control Reports and Decision-Making

The first rule for designing management control reports is that they should be based on the decision-making analysis methods and models used by managers. This may sound straightforward but it's not nearly as easy as it sounds. This first rule for control reports is implicit in the concept of feedback information, which is discussed at the beginning of the chapter. One problem is that control reports include a great deal of detail, whereas the profit and cash flow models that are best for decision-making analysis are condensed and concise.

Nevertheless, control reports should resonate as much as possible with the logic and format of the models used by managers in their decision-making analysis. For example, the control reports on the actual results of a capital investment decision each period should be structured in the same way that the manager analyzed the capital investment. If the manager used the layout shown in Figure 6.2 or 6.3 for instance, then the control report should be in the same format and include comparison of actual returns with the forecast returns from the investment.

Need for Comparative Reports

More than anything else management control is directed toward achieving profit goals and meeting the other financial objectives of the business. Goals and objectives are not established in a vacuum. Prior period performance is one reference for comparison of course. Ideally, however, the business should adopt goals and objectives for the period that are put into a framework of clearcut benchmarks and standards that actual performance is compared against. Budgeting is one way of doing this, which is discussed later in the chapter.

In practice many companies simply compare actual performance for this period against last period. This is certainly better than no comparison at all; and it does focus attention on trends especially if several past periods are used for comparison and not just the most recent period. However, this approach may sidetrack one of management's main responsibilities, which is to look ahead and forecast changes in the economic environment that will affect the business.

Changes from last period may have been predictable and should have been built into the plan for the current period. The changes between this period and last period don't really present any new information relative to what should have been predicted. The manager should get in a forward planning mode. Chapter 9 explains basic budgeting methods that can be used for this purpose. Based on forecasts of broad average changes for the coming period, profit and cash flows budgets are developed, which serve as the foundation for planning the capital needs of the business during the coming period. One danger of using last period for comparison is that the manager gets into a rear view style of management—looking behind but not ahead.

Management by Exception

One key concept of management control reporting is referred to as *management by exception*. Managers have limited time to spend on control reports and therefore they focus mainly on deviations and variances from the plan (or budget). Departures and detours from the plan are called *exceptions*. The premise is that most things should be going according to plan but some things will not. Managers need to pay the most attention to the things going wrong, or the things off course.

Frequency of Control Reports

A tough question to answer is how frequently to prepare control reports for managers. They cannot wait until the end of the year for control reports, of course, although a broadbased and overall year-end review is a good idea that serves as the platform for developing next year's plan. Daily or weekly control reports are not practical for most businesses, although some companies such as airlines and banks monitor sales volume and other vital operating statistics on a day-to-day basis.

Monthly or quarterly management control reports are the most common. Each business develops its own practical solution to the frequency question; there's no one general answer that fits all companies. The main thing is to strike a balance between preparing control reports too frequently versus too seldom. With computers and other electronic means of communication today, it is tempting to bombard managers with too much control information too often. Sorting out the truly relevant from the less relevant and truly irrelevant information is at the core of the manager's job.

Profit Control Reports

The type of management profit report illustrated in previous chapters, which is based on the profit model introduced in Chapter 1, is a logical starting point for designing reports to managers for profit control. First and foremost, *profit margins* and total *contribution margin* should be the main focus of attention, and should be clear and easy to follow. These two key measures of performance should be reported for each major product or product line (backed up with detailed schedules for virtually every individual product) in management profit performance reports. These are very confidential data, which are not divulged in external income statements, or for that matter very widely within the business organization.

Variable expenses should be divided between those that depend on sales volume versus those that depend on sales revenue, and broken down into a large number of specific accounts. Sales volumes for each product and product line should be reported. Fixed expenses should be broken down into major components—salaries, advertising, occupancy costs, and so on. Sales and/or manufacturing capacity should be reported. Any significant change in capacity due to changes in fixed expenses should be reported.

Management control reports should analyze changes in profit. In particular, the impact of sales volume changes should be separated from changes in sales price, product cost, and variable expenses as explained in earlier chapters (see Chapters 6 and 7). If trade-off decisions were made—for example, cutting sales price to increase sales volume—there should be follow-up analysis in the management control profit reports that track how the decision actually worked out. Did sales volume increase as much as expected?

As the chapter explains later in more detail there is a fringe of negative factors that constantly threaten profit margins and bloat fixed expenses. Each of these negative factors should be singled out for special attention in management profit control reports. Inventory shrinkage, for example, should be reported on a separate line, as should sales returns, unusually high bad debts, and any extraordinary losses or gains recorded in the period (with adequate explanations).

Investment Performance Measures in Control Reports

Management control financial statements should include investment performance measures, which are discussed in Chapters 5 and 10.

> **Tip**
>
> If there is a general fault with internal profit reports for management control purposes, it is in my opinion the failure of the accounting staff to explain and analyze why profit increased or decreased relative to last period, or relative to the budget for the period. Such profit change analysis would be very useful to include in the profit reports. But managers generally are left on their own to do this. The analysis tools discussed in previous chapters are very helpful for this.

Return on assets (ROA) and return on equity (ROE) are two key measures of profit performance relative to the amount of capital invested in assets that definitely should be included in management control reports. Control reports should disclose any significant changes in the financial leverage gain or loss for the period compared against the goal for the period or last period. (Financial leverage is explained in Chapter 4.) If the business falls below its ROE goal, there should be a very clear explanation that pinpoints which factors are to blame.

Sales Price Negatives

When eating in a restaurant, you don't argue about the menu prices, and you don't bargain over the posted prices at the gas pump or in the supermarket. In contrast, sales price negotiation is the way of life in many industries. Many businesses advertise or publish list prices. Examples are sticker prices on new cars, manufacturer's suggested retail prices on consumer products, and standard price sheets for industrial products.

List prices are not the final prices; they are only the point of reference for negotiating the final terms of the sale. In some cases, such as new car sales, neither the seller nor the buyer take the list price as the real price—the list price simply sets the stage for bargaining. In other cases the buyer agrees to pay list price, but demands other types of price concessions and reductions or other special accommodations.

Prompt payment discounts are offered when one business sells to another business on credit. For example a 2 percent discount may be given for payment received within 10 days after the sales invoice date. These are called *sales discounts*. Buyers should view these as penalties for delayed payment. Also, businesses commonly give their customers *quantity discounts* for large orders, and most businesses offer *special discounts* in making sales to government agencies and educational institutions.

Many consumer product companies offer their customers *rebates* and *coupons*, which lower the final net sales price received by the seller, of course. Businesses also make *allowances* or *adjustments* to sales prices after the point of sale because some customers complain about the quality of the product, or when some customers discover minor product flaws after taking delivery. Instead of having the customer return the products the company reduces the original sales price.

Managers must decide how these sales price negatives should be handled in their internal management control reports. One alternative is to report sales revenue net of all such sales price reductions. I don't recommend this method. The better approach is to report sales revenue at established list prices. All sales price negatives should be recorded in sales revenue contra accounts that are deducted from gross (list price) sales revenue.

Figure 12.1 illustrates the reporting sales price negatives to managers. Seven different reductions from sales revenue are shown in this figure. A business may not have all the sales contra accounts shown here but three or four are not unusual. The amounts of each contra account may not be as large as shown (hopefully not).

In the external income statement of the business only net sales revenue ($8,303,000 in this example) is reported, as a general rule. For internal management control reporting, however, gross (list price) sales revenue before all sales price reductions should be—to give managers the complete range of information they need for controlling sales prices. Sales price negatives should be accumulated in contra (deduction) accounts so that managers can monitor each one relative to established sales pricing policies, and so they can make comparisons with previous periods and with the goals (or budget) for the current period.

Inventory Shrinkage

Inventory shrinkage is a serious problem for many businesses, especially retailers. These inventory losses are due to shoplifting by customers, employee theft, and short-counts from suppliers. Many businesses also suffer inventory obsolescence, which means they end up with some products that cannot be sold or have to be sold below cost. When this becomes apparent, inventory should be de-

FIGURE 12.1 Sales Revenue Negatives in Management Control Reports

Gross Sales Revenue, at List Prices		$10,000,000
Sales Price Negatives		
Sales Price Discounts—Normal	($150,000)	
Sales Price Discounts—Special	($200,000)	
Sales Returns	($175,000)	
Quantity Discounts	($275,000)	
Rebates	($650,000)	
Coupons	($165,000)	
Sales Price Allowances	($82,000)	($1,697,000)
Net Sales Revenue		$8,303,000

creased by write-down entries. The inventories asset account is decreased and an expense account is increased.

Inventory losses caused by damage to and deterioration of products being held in inventory and **inventory write-downs** to recognize product obsolescence should be separated from losses due to theft and dishonesty—but sometimes the inventory shrinkage expression is used to include any type of inventory disappearance and loss. Inventory shrinkage of 1.5 percent to 2.0 percent of retail sales is not unusual.

Inventory loss due to theft is a particularly frustrating expense. The business has to buy (or manufacture) these products, and then hold them in inventory, which requires carrying costs, only to have them stolen by customers or employees. On the other hand, inventory shrinkage due to damage from handling and storing products, product deterioration over time, and product obsolescence are normal and inescapable economic risks of doing business.

Internal management control reports definitely should separate inventory shrinkage expense and not include it in the cost of goods sold expense. Inventory shrinkage is virtually never reported as a separate expense in external income statements; it is combined with cost of goods sold or some other expense. However, managers need to keep a close watch on inventory shrinkage, and cannot do so if it is buried in the larger cost of goods sold expense.

Another reason for separating inventory shrinkage in management control reports is that this expense does not behave the same way as cost of goods sold expense. Cost of goods sold expense varies with sales volume. Inventory shrinkage may include both a fixed amount that is more or less the same regardless of sales volume, and the remainder may vary with sales volume.

Strong internal controls help minimize inventory shrinkage. But even elaborate and expensive inventory controls do not eliminate inventory shrinkage. Almost every business tolerates some amount of inventory shrinkage. For instance, most businesses look the other way when it comes to minor employee theft; they don't encourage it, of course, but they don't do anything about it, either. Preventing all inventory theft would be too costly or might offend customers and hurt sales volume. Would you shop in retail stores that carried out body searches on all their customers leaving the store? I doubt it. Many retailers hesitate even to require customers to check bags before entering their stores. On the other hand, closed circuit TV monitors are common in many stores. Retailers are constantly trying to find controls that do not offend their customers. As you know product packages are designed to make it difficult to shoplift the product, such as oversized packages that are difficult to conceal.

In internal management control reports the negative factors just discussed should be set out in separate expense accounts if they are relatively material, or listed separately in a supplementary schedule. Managers may have to specifically instruct their accountants to isolate these expenses. In external income statements these costs are grouped in a larger expense account (such as cost of goods sold, or general and administrative expenses).

Sales Volume Negatives

Sales returns can be a problem, although this varies from industry to industry quite a bit. Many retailers accept sales returns without hesitation as part of their overall marketing strategy. Customers may be refunded their money, or they may exchange for different products. On the other hand, some products such as new cars are seldom returned (even when recalled).

Sales returns definitely should be accumulated in a separate sales contra account that is deducted from gross sales revenue; see Figure 12.1 again. The total of sales returns is very important control information. On the other hand, in external income statements only the amount of net sales revenue (gross sales revenue less sales returns and all other sales revenue negatives) is reported.

Lost sales due to temporary *stock outs* (zero inventory situations) are important for managers to know about. Such nonsales are not recorded in the accounting system. No sales transaction takes place, so there is nothing to record in the sales revenue account. However, missed sale opportunities should be captured and kept track of in some manner, and the amount of these lost sales should be reported to managers even though no sales actually took place. Managers need a measure of how much additional contribution margin could have been earned on these lost sales.

Customers are willing to back order the products, or sales can be made for future delivery when customers do not need immediate delivery, which are called sales *backlogs*. Information about sales backlogs should be reported to managers, but not as sales revenue, of course. If a customer refuses to back order or will not wait for future delivery the sale may be lost. As a practical matter it is difficult to keep track of lost sales. The manager may have to rely on other sources of information, such as complaints from customers and the company's sales force.

Key Sales Ratios

Many retailers keep an eye on sales revenue per employee and sales revenue per square foot of retail space. Most retailers have rough rules, such as $300/$400 sales per square foot of retail space, or $300,000 sales per employee. These amounts vary widely from industry to industry. Trade associations collect data from their members and publish industry averages. Retailers can compare their performances against local and regional competition, as well as national averages. Hotels and motels carefully watch their occupancy rates, which is an example of a useful ratio to measure actual sales against capacity.

When sales ratios are lagging the business probably has too much capacity—too many employees, too much space, too many machines, and so on. The obvious solution is to reduce the fixed operating costs of the business. However, reducing these fixed expenses is not easy, as you probably know. Employees have to be fired (or temporarily laid off); major assets have to be sold; contracts may have to be broken, and so on. Downsizing decisions are extremely difficult to make. For one thing they are an admission of the inability of the business to generate enough sales volume to justify their fixed expenses. Nonetheless, part of the manager's job is to make these painful decisions.

The tendency is to put off the decision, to delay the tough choices that have to be made. In an article in the *Wall Street Journal* the former CEO of Westinghouse observed that one of the biggest failings of U.S. chief executives is of procrastinating—that executives are reluctant to face up to making these decisions at the earliest possible time.

In Closing

I would like to show you examples of management control reports. But control reports are highly confidential; companies are not willing to release them outside the business. In some situations control reports contain proprietary information that a business is not willing to give out without payment (such as customer lists). Management control reports are like income tax returns in this regard—neither is open for public inspection.

However, you may be able to get your hands on one type of management control report—those that are required in a franchise contract between the franchisee and the parent company that owns the franchise name. These contracts usually require that certain accounting reports be prepared and sent to the home office of the company that operates the chain. These reports are full of management control information that is very interesting. Perhaps you could secure a blank form of such an accounting control report.

Last, I should point out that management control reports vary a great deal from business to business. Compare in your mind, if you would, the following types of businesses—a gambling casino, a grocery store, an auto manufacturer, an electric utility, a bank, a hotel, and an airline. Each type of business is unique in the types of control information its managers need. The comments above offer general observations and suggestions for management control reports, without going into the many details for particular industries.

Brief Overview of Budgeting

Chapter 9 explains basic methods for building a profit and cash flow budget. These two budget plans set the stage for determining the capital needs of the business during the coming period. The company's managers should plan ahead for how much more capital will be needed and decide on the strategy for securing money from debt and equity sources. Planning for capital needs is one important purpose of budgeting. There are many other purposes, of course. The technical aspects and detailed procedures of a comprehensive budgeting system are beyond the scope of the book; fundamentals are the focus in the following discussion.

Reasons for Budgeting

Management decisions taken all together should constitute an integrated and coordinated strategy and overarching plan of action for achieving the profit and financial objectives of a business. Decisions are like the blueprint for a building; control should be carried out in the context of the decision blueprint. Budgeting is one very good means of integrating management decision-making and management control, akin to constructing a building according to its blueprint.

Decisions are made explicit in a budget, which is the concrete plan of action for achieving the profit and financial objectives of the business according to a timetable. Actual results are then evaluated against budget period-by-period, line-by-line, and item-by-item. Variances have to be explained. They serve as the catalyst for taking corrective action where needed, or for revising the plan as needed.

No budgeting doesn't necessarily mean that there is no management control. Budgeting is certainly helpful but not absolutely essential for management control. Many businesses do little or no budgeting, yet they make a good profit and remain solvent and financially healthy. They depend on the management control reports to track their actual profit performance, financial position, and cash flows. But they have no formal or explicit budget against which to compare actual results. More than likely they use last year as the reference for comparison.

The master budget is made up of the separate profit and other budgets for each organizational unit—such as sales territories, departments, product lines, branches, divisions, and subsidiaries. Each subunit's budget is like a building stone in a large pyramid that leads up to the master budget at the top. Starting at the bottom end, sales and expense budgets dovetail into larger-scale profit budgets, which in turn are integrated with cash flow and financial condition (balance sheet) budgets.

The larger the organization, the more likely you'll find a formal and comprehensive financial budgeting process in place. And the more bureaucratic the organization, the more likely it uses a budgeting system. The budget is one primary means of *communication* and authorization down the line in the organization. The budget provides the key benchmarks for evaluating performance of managers at all levels. Actual is compared against budget, and significant variances are highlighted, which are investigated and reported up the line. Managers are rewarded for meeting or exceeding the budget, and they are held accountable for unfavorable variances.

A complete budget plan requires a profit budget (income statement) and cash flow budget for the coming period, and a budgeted financial condition report (balance sheet) at the end of the period. As explained in previous chapters the financial condition of the business is driven mainly by the profit-making operations of the business. Capital expenditures for replacements and expansions of long-term operating assets of the business must be included in the cash flow budget and the budgeted year-end financial condition. A total financial plan in which a profit budget is integrated with the financial condition and cash flow budgets is a very convincing package when you're applying for a loan or renewing an existing line of credit. It shows that the company's total financial plan has been thought out.

Costs and Disadvantages of Budgeting

There are persuasive reasons for and advantages of budgeting. On the other side of the coin, budgeting is costly and may lead to a lot of game playing and dysfunctional behavior. Some reasons for budgeting are not highly applicable to smaller businesses, and even to mid-sized businesses. Smaller businesses do not need budgets for communication and coordination purposes, which are much more important in larger organizations in which top management is distant from its far-flung, day-to-day operations.

Profit budgeting depends heavily on the ability of managers to forecast changes in the key factors that drive profit—in detail and with reasonably good accuracy. Nothing is so counterproductive and more discouraging than an unrealistic profit budget built on flimsy sales projections. If no one believes the sales budget numbers, the budget process becomes a lot of wasted motion or, worse, an exercise in hypocrisy.

The profit budget should be accepted as realistically achievable by those managers responsible for meeting the objectives and goals of the profit plan, and to serve as the benchmarks against which actual performance will be compared. If budget goals are too unrealistic, managers may engage in all sorts of manipulations and artificial schemes to meet their budget profit targets. There are enormous pressures in a business organization to make budget, even if managers think the budget is not fair and realistic.

Then there are always unexpected developments—events that simply cannot be foreseen at the time of putting together a budget. The budget should be adjusted for such developments, but making budget revisions is not easy; it's like changing horses in the middle of the stream. Once adopted, budgets tend to become carved in stone. Higher levels of management quite naturally are suspicious that requests for budget adjustments may be attempts to evade budget goals or may be excuses for substandard performance. Budgeting works best in a stable and predictable environment.

As mentioned above, management control deals with a thousand and one details. Control deals with detail, detail, and more detail. Day-to-day, and month-to-month the manager has to pay attention to an avalanche of details. Keeping all the details in perspective is a challenge, to say the least. Control reports comparing actual with budget should not let the details take over, causing managers to lose sight of the overall progress toward the profit goal.

The whole point of budgeting, but easy to lose sight of, is to achieve profit and other financial objectives. Budgeting is not an end but a means. Detailed expense and cost reporting is required—so that the manager can keep close watch on the total effect on the key expense and cost factors that were forecast in the profit budget. Often managers ask for reams of detailed expense and cost reports but they do not necessarily read all the detail.

Summary

Managers do not simply make decisions and then assume that their decisions put into motion everything that has to be done to achieve the goals of the business. Managers must follow through and exercise management control throughout the period. There is no such thing as putting a business on automatic pilot. Managers have to watch everything. Management control depends on feedback information on actual performance, which managers compare against the plan.

Management control begins with a solid foundation of internal accounting controls. These forms and procedures are absolutely essential to ensure the reliability of the information recorded by a business's accounting system. Internal accounting controls also serve a second duty—to deter and detect fraud and other dishonest behavior. Most fraud can be traced to the absence or breakdown of internal accounting controls. These controls should be enforced vigilantly. Many larger business organizations use internal auditors to evaluate and improve their internal accounting controls, as well as to perform other functions.

The chapter discusses guidelines for management control reports. These reports should resonate with the decision-making analysis and models used by managers. These reports should provide the most relevant benchmarks against which actual performance is compared. Control reports contain a great amount of detail, but key factors and variances should be highlighted and not be lost in the avalanche of details. Control reports should focus on several negative factors that adversely affect sales prices, sales volume, and expenses.

Budgeting provides useful yardsticks and standards for management control. But budgeting is done for more than just control purposes. Budgeting is a broader management practice that encompasses strategic planning, communication throughout the organization, motivation of managers, and more. The brief overview in the chapter looks at the reasons for budgeting, as well as the disadvantages inherent in it.

CHAPTER 13

Selecting Accounting Methods

Most business managers don't get involved in choosing accounting methods; they leave these decisions to the controller (chief accountant) of the business. This chapter argues that managers should get involved in selecting accounting methods. Managers should have a basic understanding of which alternative methods are permitted under generally accepted accounting principles (GAAP), without going into all the technical details of the methods.

Once a certain accounting method is selected, a business sticks with the method for some time, more or less indefinitely. A business keeps its accounting methods on a consistent basis from year to year, except in unusual circumstances. A business has to make a significant change in how it operates, or it takes some cataclysmic event for a business to change its accounting methods. The federal income tax law discourages accounting method changes without very good reasons for doing so. In short, choosing an accounting method is like getting married without much chance of a divorce.

This chapter focuses on two important expenses for which a business has to choose between alternative accounting methods—*cost of goods sold* and *depreciation*. Each choice makes a difference in the amount of expense recorded and thus in bottom-line net income for the period. As just mentioned the choice for each accounting method is carved in stone and cannot be easily changed. Nevertheless, both methods can be tweaked, or to use a harsher term, manipulated by a savvy manager to make the method produce a result more to his or her liking. How managers manipulate these two accounting methods is examined in Chapter 14, which explains tricks and techniques for massaging the numbers, cooking the books, and touching up financial statements.

Determining Cost of Goods Sold Expense and the Cost Value of Inventories

The cost of products sold to customers usually is a company's largest single expense, commonly being 50 percent to 70 percent of sales revenue. In passing I should mention that many businesses sell *services* instead of products; examples are airlines, telephone utilities, rental companies, and movie studios. Service businesses do not invest in inventories of products that are held for sale. (Well, some service companies also sell products such as popcorn by movie theaters and boxes by moving companies.) Gross margin and the profit lines below gross margin depend on which accounting method is used to measure cost of goods sold expense.

Clearly managers have a stake in how profit is measured; they should understand clearly how the biggest deduction against sales revenue is determined. In my opinion the chief executive should decide which accounting method to use for the company's cost of goods sold expense. This decision also can have a major impact on the amount for the inventories asset account that is reported in the company's balance sheet.

The cost of goods (products, merchandise) that are purchased or manufactured is first put into the *inventories* asset account. The cost remains in this asset account and is not removed and charged to cost of goods sold expense until the products are sold. In this way the cost of products sold is matched with the sales revenue of the products sold to determine *gross margin* (also called *gross profit*). This is a basic feature of the *accrual basis of accounting*, which is explained in further detail in Chapter 2. The amount of cost that is taken out of the inventories account and put into the expense account depends on which cost removal method is used.

Three basic methods are widely used to determine cost of goods sold expense for products that are sold from inventory (from stock). All three have theoretical support. All three methods are acknowledged interpretations of the general accounting principle that the cost of products sold to customers should be matched against the revenue from the sales in order to correctly measure gross margin for the period. There's no disagreement about this. The disagreement concerns exactly how to determine the cost of goods sold when there is more than one acquisition cost in the inventories account. If the purchase or manufacturing cost of a product remained constant and never changed over time, the business wouldn't have to make a choice. But as you know, product costs do change over time so making a choice is unavoidable.

The only situation in which a business does not have to choose from different acquisition costs for products sold is when each product sold is unique and is not homogeneous with similar products. If a product is unique and significantly different from similar products then the *specific identification method* should be used—each separate product has its own unique cost. I bought a Honda Accord auto recently; I had no options to choose from (except its color). In contrast, most car buyers can choose from a large number of options; given the large number of option combinations that are available, every auto is unique and has a unique cost. The auto dealer has to keep track of the cost of each separate car and charge this cost to expense when the car is sold. Used cars are like this also; each has a separate cost.

Most businesses sell from a stock of homogeneous products; the products are identical and interchangeable. The problem is that the acquisition cost per unit of the product varies from one batch to the next. A specific example is needed to demonstrate the accounting problem and to contrast the differences among the three methods on gross margin and ending inventory cost. Suppose a company sold 4,000 units of a particular product during the year just ended. (It doesn't make any difference whether the business manufactures this product or is a retailer that purchases the product for resale.) The company started the year with 1,000 units, which is the carryforward quantity of this product from last year.

Businesses do not let their inventory level drop to zero—unless a product is being phased out or because of circumstances beyond their control. The company in this example replaces products as they are sold during the year. Accordingly, the company replaced the 4,000 units sold; the product is a steady seller and the business did not want to increase or decrease its inventory level of this product. Thus, the business ended the year with exactly the same number of units it started with, which is 1,000 units. This example avoids the complications of changes in inventory quantities in order to focus on the root cause of the accounting problem.

The company made four acquisitions of products during the year, each being a batch of 1,000 units. The size of each batch manufactured or purchased may vary, of course. Businesses do not necessarily acquire products in equal-sized lots during the year. In summary, the company started the year with 1,000 units, sold 4,000 units, replaced the 4,000 units sold, and ended the year with 1,000 units.

Figure 13.1 presents the facts of the example. As you see, product cost drifted up over the year. Each successive acquisition cost the business $5,000 more than the one before. Before proceeding, I'd like to get your opinion on this accounting problem. How would you divide the $550,000 total cost between the 4,000 units sold and the 1,000 units not sold and on hand in inventory at year-end? (See Figure 13.1 again.) No fair sitting on the fence.

I believe that you would agree that the $550,000 total cost of the 5,000 units that was put into the inventories assets account should be divided, or allocated between cost of goods sold expense for the 4,000 units sold during the year and the inventories asset at year-end for the 1,000 units not yet sold. (These units will be sold and will generate sales revenue next year.) I'm sure that you wouldn't charge the entire $550,000 of all 5,000 units against the sales revenue for only 4,000 units sold during the year.

If you were the chief executive of this business, how would you instruct your accountant to divide the $550,000 total cost? Instead of making this decision you could let the company's controller make the decision. Too often managers simply sit on the sidelines and go along with the method recommended by their accountants. However, I think managers should analyze the situation and decide them-

FIGURE 13.1 Example for Deciding on Cost of Goods Sold Expense and Cost Value of Ending Inventory

Product Batches	Quantity	Cost
Beginning Inventory	1,000 units	$100,000
First Acquisition	1,000 units	$105,000
Second Acquisition	1,000 units	$110,000
Third Acquisition	1,000 units	$115,000
Fourth Acquisition	1,000 units	$120,000
Totals	5,000 units	$550,000
Goods Sold	4,000 units	???
Ending Inventory	1,000 units	???

selves which is the best method for recording this major expense of the business.

Like other management decisions this one comes down to certain basic questions: What are the alternatives? What are the consequences of each alternative? Which alternative is best relative to the company's goals and strategy? If you were in a room with 9 other business executives I doubt that all 10 of you would come to the same decision. The 10 of you probably would split into three camps on this question, which we turn to next.

Three different accounting methods could be used to determine the cost of goods sold expense for the period, and the cost value to leave in the inventories asset account at the end of the period. These three are the following:

1. *Average cost* method

2. *Last-in, first-out (LIFO)* method

3. *First-in, first-out (FIFO)* method

Each method is explained in the following sections.

Average Cost Method

My guess is that most business managers, not all but probably a majority, would intuitively choose the **average cost method**. The argument for this method is that $\frac{4}{5}$ of the goods were sold, so $\frac{4}{5}$ of the $550,000 total cost of goods that were available for sale should be charged to cost of goods sold expense and $\frac{1}{5}$ should be allocated to the cost of the ending inventory of the product. Therefore:

AVERAGE COST METHOD

($550,000 × $\frac{4}{5}$) = $440,000 cost of goods sold expense

($550,000 × $\frac{1}{5}$) = $110,000 cost value of ending inventory

The logic is that gross margin (profit) is being measured for the whole year, so all costs for the year should be pooled and each unit should share and share alike—whether the unit was sold or not sold (still in ending inventory). Put another way, the average cost per unit is $110 ($550,000 total cost ÷ 5,000 total units = $110 average cost per unit). This average cost is multiplied by the 4,000 units sold to calculate the $440,000 cost of goods sold expense. The ending inventory is assigned a cost value of $110,000, or 1,000 units in ending inventory times the $110 average cost per unit.

The average cost method has a lot of intuitive appeal, and makes a lot of common sense. However, you might be surprised to hear that

DETERMINING COST OF GOODS SOLD EXPENSE AND THE COST VALUE

this method runs a distant third in popularity. Much more likely a business would select one of the two other accounting methods for determining its cost of goods sold expense.

Last-In, First-Out (LIFO) Method

The **last-in, first-out**, or **LIFO** method works in reverse chronological order to determine the cost of goods sold expense for the period, and leaves the oldest acquisition cost in the inventories asset account. To determine the cost of goods sold expense, LIFO first selects the cost of the most recent acquisition batch, then the second most recent batch, and continues backward until the cost for the number of units sold is accumulated. The LIFO in this example grabs the cost of the four batches acquired during the year for the cost of goods sold expense of the 4,000 units sold during the year. To illustrate, the cost of goods sold expense is determined as follows:

COST OF GOODS SOLD BY LIFO METHOD

Fourth Acquisition (1,000 units)	$120,000
Third Acquisition (1,000 units)	$115,000
Second Acquisition (1,000 units)	$110,000
First Acquisition (1,000 units)	$105,000
Cost of Goods Sold (4,000 units)	$450,000

The term *last-in* refers to the most recent, or latest acquisition. The term *first-out* refers to charging cost to expense before turning to the cost of another acquisition. Working backward, or in the reverse order in which the acquisitions were made, the cost each acquisition is accumulated until the cost for the 4,000 units sold during the period is reached.

The theoretical underpinning for the LIFO method is that when products are sold they are replaced in order to continue in business, and that the most recent (last-in) costs are nearest to the costs of replacing the products sold. Acquisition costs increased during the year. So the LIFO method selects the batches with the highest costs. In periods of increasing costs LIFO maximizes the cost of goods sold expense and minimizes gross margin. In other words during periods of increasing costs LIFO is a conservative accounting method because it maximizes the cost of goods sold expense and minimizes gross margin. The LIFO method also minimizes the cost value of the inventories asset account that is reported in a business's balance sheet at the end of the period.

The cost of the beginning inventory batch of 1,000 units of product, which is $100,000 in this example as shown in Figure 13.1, becomes the cost value for ending inventory. The actual products on hand at year-end are *not* those that were sitting in inventory at the start of the year. The products on hand in ending inventory are most likely from the most recent acquisition (the one that cost $120,000). The actual flow of products out of inventory seldom follows a last-in, first-out sequence. The earliest, or first products acquired usually are the first ones sold and delivered to customers. This is of no concern; the LIFO method ignores the actual physical flow of products. LIFO retrieves the most recent (last-in) batches for determining the cost of goods sold expense for the year—and the cost of inventories be damned, as it were.

The LIFO method has the result that the inventories asset account equals the residual amount of cost after removing the costs of the most recent batches for determining the cost of goods sold expense for the period. In other words the LIFO method leaves the oldest costs in the inventories asset account. After several years of using LIFO a company's inventory reminds me of the story of Dorian Gray looking in the mirror. The actual inventory is young, but its reported cost in the balance sheet is old, perhaps very old.

My favorite example of this LIFO effect is found in the financial statements of Caterpillar, the manufacturer of bulldozers and other heavy equipment. For several years the company has included a footnote to its financial statements explaining that if it had used the first-in, first-out method instead of the LIFO method that it has used for many years, the cost value of its inventories would be about $2.0 billion higher in its balance sheet. This is a huge difference, even for a business the size of Caterpillar.

LIFO produces predictable effects when product costs steadily increase year to year—that is, cost of goods sold expense is maximized and inventory cost gets older and older. Keep in mind, however, that this is only one of several different scenarios. The manufacturing costs of some products actually decline over the years. Some products have very short life cycles—new models replace the old models every year or so. Therefore, the product cost that remains in inventory does not stay there very long to get very old and out of date. And if product costs remain relatively stable and don't change too much over several years the choice of accounting method makes little difference. Although the Caterpillar case comes to mind again, over 40 or 50 years even a small amount of product cost inflation each year can accumulate to a big gap between the LIFO-based cost of inventories, compared with the most recent acquisition costs of the product.

The First-In, First-Out (FIFO) Method

The LIFO method selects costs in reverse chronological order, as just explained. In contrast the **first-in, first-out**, or **FIFO** method takes costs in their chronological order for determining cost of goods sold expense for the period. The FIFO method in this example selects the beginning inventory batch and the first, second, and third acquisition batches to make up the total cost for the 4,000 units sold during the year. The sum of these four batches is $430,000, which is shown as follows:

COST OF GOODS SOLD BY FIFO METHOD

Beginning Inventory (1,000 units)	$100,000
First Acquisition (1,000 units)	$105,000
Second Acquisition (1,000 units)	$110,000
Third Acquisition (1,000 units)	$115,000
Cost of Goods Sold (4,000 units)	$430,000

The first batches of products acquired are the first to be charged out to cost of goods sold expense by the FIFO method. And the cost of the most recent acquisition batch remains as the cost value in the inventories asset account. During periods of cost inflation, as in this example, FIFO minimizes the cost of goods sold expense and maximizes gross margin. And the cost value for inventories in the balance sheet at the end of the period is reported at the most recent, or highest costs of the products.

One reason for using FIFO is to be consistent with the actual flow of products as the products are taken out of inventory and delivered to customers—that generally follows a first-in, first-out sequence in most businesses.

Which Method to Use?

Suppose you're the chief executive of the business in this example. At year-end you review the profit performance of every product the business sells. Assume that the sales revenue from the 4,000 units of product sold during the year in the example is $645,000. The key question is: How much gross margin did you earn on this product for the year? Well, the answer depends on which accounting method you use. The gross margin by each method and the cost of ending inventories is summarized as follows:

	LIFO	Average Cost	FIFO
Sales Revenue	$645,000	$645,000	$645,000
Cost of Goods Sold	−$450,000	−$440,000	−$430,000
Gross Margin	$195,000	$205,000	$215,000
Ending Inventories Cost	$100,000	$110,000	$120,000

Sales revenue is the same across all the methods; the business set its sales prices and sold 4,000 units that generated $645,000 sales revenue for the year. Only the cost of goods sold expense and ending inventories amounts differ among the three methods. In this example gross margin by FIFO is $20,000 higher than LIFO, a spread of more than 10 percent, and the cost value of ending inventories by the FIFO method is 20 percent higher than by LIFO.

The merits of each accounting method can be debated until the cows come home. Personally, I think the proper method is the one that is most consistent with the sales pricing policy of the business. In other words, I need to know how a business goes about setting its sales prices before I can decide on the most appropriate cost of goods sold expense accounting method for the business.

Suppose that the business in the example sets its sales prices as follows. It starts with the purchase (or manufacture) cost of a batch of products. The company marks up the cost per unit to set sales price, which is a common approach used by many businesses. It holds this sales price constant until all units are sold from the batch, and then moves on to the next batch and repeats the process. Many factors other than product cost affect sales prices, of course. Nevertheless, absent other pressures on sales prices many businesses set their target sales prices in this manner, although their benchmark sales prices may be just the point of departure. A business may increase or lower their final sales prices because of competition and other economic pressures.

For the product in this example suppose the company in fact uses a first-in, first-out approach to set sales prices; it marks up product cost 50 percent to set sales prices and is able to actually sell each batch of products at the sales prices set by this mark-up. Therefore, the company's sales revenue for the year from this product is determined as follows (see Figure 13.1 for cost data):

50% MARK-UP ON COST TO SET SALES PRICES

$100,000 cost of beginning inventory × 150% = $150,000

$105,000 cost of first acquisition × 150%   = $157,500

$110,000 cost of second acquisition × 150% = $165,000

$115,000 cost of third acquisition × 150%   = $172,500

Sales Revenue   = $645,000

Note that a 50 percent mark-up on cost means that gross margin is one-third of sales price. For each $2.00 of cost the business adds $1.00 of mark-up for $3.00 of sales price. The $1.00 mark-up, or gross margin equals one-third of sales price.

Suppose the business sets its sales prices in this manner. In this situation I would definitely favor the FIFO method. Gross margin by the FIFO method equals exactly one-third of sales revenue: [$215,000 gross margin ÷ $645,000 sales revenue = $\frac{1}{3}$ exactly]. Both the average cost method and LIFO would result in a gross margin ratio lower than $\frac{1}{3}$, but this is inconsistent with the company's sales pricing method.

Regardless of how they set sales prices, many businesses adopt the LIFO method—despite the fact that this method yields the lowest gross margin and the lowest ending inventory cost in periods of rising costs. One reason is *conservatism*. Most companies, it appears, prefer to err on the downside and not be accused of overstating profits and the cost values of their assets. Historically there was a strong preference for conservatism in financial statements, but I'm not so sure about this today. By and large businesses, especially public corporations whose capital stock shares are traded on public markets, seem to use much more aggressive accounting methods for measuring profit.

Another reason for LIFO could be to minimize the amount of net income that is subject to a profit-sharing or profit-based bonus plan—although employees and managers wouldn't like this, of course. Another reason might be to hide profit during periods of labor problems or union contract bargaining. Perhaps a business needs to appear to be in need of more profit, and thus is justified to raise its sales prices or to lay off employees.

In many cases the main reason for using LIFO is simply to minimize taxable income. LIFO is allowed for federal income tax purposes. Looking back at the comparison among the three methods, note that the LIFO method reduces taxable income by $20,000 compared with the FIFO method in this example for one product. Income tax rates on business have remained relatively stable over the past several years, However, if income tax rates were forecast to go up in the future, it could be better to use FIFO and report higher taxable income this year while tax rates are lower than they will be in the future.

Cash flow from profit is also a very important reason to minimize taxable income by using the LIFO method. A business could be in a very tight cash position and need to hang on to every dollar of cash for as long as possible. So a company would elect LIFO to delay paying income tax. Even if not strapped for cash, a business can invest the temporary tax savings from using LIFO and earn a return on the investment. If inflation is forecast to continue in the future, then a business could delay paying its income taxes as long as possible and pay in the cheaper dollars of the future.

Depreciation Dilemmas

Most businesses invest in long-term assets such as buildings, building improvements, machines, equipment, tools, office furniture, computers and computer peripheral equipment, vehicles, and so on. The generic name for these are *fixed assets*, although the more formal account title that is generally used in a statement of financial condition (balance sheet) is *property, plant, and equipment.* Chapter 2 explains that the cost of fixed assets is allocated to each year of their useful economic lives by an accounting method called *depreciation*. It is definitely against generally accepted accounting principles (GAAP) to charge the cost of a fixed asset entirely to expense in the year of its purchase or construction, well, unless the amount involved is immaterial such as the cost of a screwdriver that may last several years.

A business keeps *two accounts* for its fixed assets—one for the original cost of the assets and a second, contra account called *accumulated depreciation*, the balance of which is deducted from the balance in the cost account. (Figure 5.2 in Chapter 5 presents a bal-

---

Tip

Please keep in mind as you read this chapter the cash flow aspects of depreciation. Recording depreciation does not require a cash outlay. Therefore, to determine cash flow from profit (or to be technically correct, cash flow from operating activities) the amount of depreciation is a positive cash flow factor. The cash inflow from sales revenue for the year, in part, recovers a fraction of the original capital invested in fixed assets. In rough terms the depreciation recovery can be compared with taking money out each year from a savings account (capital invested in fixed assets) and putting the money into a checking account.

ance sheet example, which shows how these two accounts are reported.) The *book value* of fixed assets equals their original cost less the accumulated depreciation that has been recorded since acquisition. Depreciation accounting methods are not quite as cut-and-dried as suggested in earlier chapters. This section explains some of the practical problems in determining the cost of fixed assets that will be depreciated, and compares two alternative methods of determining the amount of annual depreciation expense.

As just mentioned fixed assets are long-term investments by a business. Over the years of their use the company has to recover through sales revenue the amount of capital invested in these assets. A business does not hold fixed assets for the purpose of selling them later for more than they paid for the fixed assets. At the end of their useful lives fixed assets are sent to the junk pile or sold for their salvage value. Well, this general statement is true except for land and buildings (real estate).

Machinery, equipment, tools, and vehicles do not appreciate in value over the years of their use. The clock is ticking on the usefulness of these fixed assets; midnight strikes when the assets reach the end of their physical lives, or when economic obsolescence makes replacing the assets a cheaper alternative than keeping them. Land and buildings are different kettles of fish. The cost of land is not depreciated. Land is a property right that entitles the owner to occupy a certain space. In this sense land is an asset that never wears out—although a flood or earthquake could damage or destroy the property. But the building and improvements on the land do wear out over time; they gradually lose their economic usefulness to the business.

The cost of buildings is depreciated, even though the market value of the buildings may actually appreciate over time. It can be argued that the cost of a building should not be depreciated when its market value increases. But GAAP says to depreciate the cost of buildings, no matter what. This is one thing to keep in mind about depreciation—market value appreciation is not considered. For example, buildings are depreciated even though their market value may appreciate. A second thing to keep in mind is that the amount of depreciation expense recorded each period depends on which costs are included and which are not included in the total cost of fixed assets.

Costs That May or May Not Be Capitalized (Included in Total Cost of Fixed Assets)

The proper amount of total cost to record in a fixed asset account is open to interpretation; actual practice varies regarding whether to include certain types of costs of acquiring fixed assets and making them ready for use. Suppose a business buys several new delivery trucks. The total purchase invoice cost paid to the dealer for the fleet of trucks is *capitalized*, that is, recorded as an increase in the fixed asset account for these long-term operating resources. The term *capitalized* comes from the idea of making a capital investment. The amount of sales taxes paid by the business is also capitalized; sales taxes are a direct and inseparable add-on cost of the trucks. To this point there is no argument; the cost of the trucks includes the purchase invoice cost and sales taxes paid by the buyer. Beyond these two direct costs, however, accounting theory and actual accounting practice often diverge.

Suppose the business paints its new trucks with the company's name, address, telephone number, and logo. Also the business installs special racks and fittings in the trucks. In theory these additional costs should be capitalized and included in the cost basis of the fixed assets. These additional costs are not directly part of the purchase; these are postpurchase costs, mainly to prepare the fixed asset for how the business will use them. These additional costs should be capitalized because the costs improve the value-in-use of the trucks, and these costs like the purchase cost should be allocated over the years of their use through depreciation accounting.

When purchasing many long-lived operating assets a business incurs additional costs that should be added to the cost basis, but in fact may not be. Accounting theory says to capitalize these costs. As a practical matter, however, only the purchase cost plus other direct costs of purchase are capitalized. Any additional costs are recorded as expenses immediately, instead of being depreciated over the useful lives of the fixed assets.

There are countless examples of such additional costs. A business may paint several signs on a new building it just moved into. It may fumigate the entire building before moving in. It may upgrade the lighting in several areas. After purchasing new machines or new equipment a business usually incurs costs of installing the assets and preparing them for use. Such additional costs should be capitalized according to accounting theory.

In actual practice, however, the additional costs are usually not recorded in a company's fixed assets. Instead the costs are charged to expense in the period incurred. One reason is to deduct these costs immediately for income tax purposes, that is, to minimize current taxable income in the year the costs are incurred. (A business should be very careful regarding what the Internal Revenue Service tolerates in this regard.) Another reason for not capitalizing such costs is simply that of practical expediency. It is much easier to charge such costs to expense rather than adding them to the fixed asset cost.

While on the topic of practical expediency, I should mention that most businesses buy an assortment of relatively low-cost tools and equipment items—examples are hammers, power saws, drills, floor-cleaning machines, dollies, pencil sharpeners, lamps, and so on. The costs of these assets, since they will be used several years, should be capitalized and depreciated over their expected useful lives. Keeping a separate depreciation schedule for each screwdriver or pencil sharpener is ridiculous, of course. The federal income tax law allows a certain amount spent for fixed assets (other than buildings and property held for investment) to be charged off to expense in the year of purchase, instead of capitalized and depreciated—this amount was $25,000 in the year 2003.

Most businesses set minimum dollar limits below which costs of fixed assets are not capitalized but are charged directly to expense. This is accepted practice; CPA auditors tolerate this practice as long as a business is consistent one year to the next. The only question concerns the materiality of such costs. The CPA auditors, as well as the Internal Revenue Service, might object if the aggregate of these non-capitalized costs were extraordinarily high in one year.

In any case, business managers should understand the financial statement effects of not capitalizing the additional costs associated with buying fixed assets and not capitalizing the costs of small tools and equipment. To illustrate, suppose a business purchased new fixed assets during the year. The sum of the invoice prices plus sales taxes for all these assets was $1,400,000 for the year. The $1,400,000 is capitalized; the business records this cost in its fixed asset accounts. If it didn't the company's CPA auditors would object in the strongest possible terms, and the IRS could accuse the business of income tax evasion (which is a felony).

In addition to the direct costs of the new fixed assets suppose the business spent $120,000 during the year to prepare the new fixed assets for use such as the costs are described above, and the business spent another $20,000 for small tools and inexpensive equipment items. The $140,000 total expenditures could have been properly capitalized. But, consistent with previous years, the company recorded the amount to expense.

To simplify assume that the various fixed assets are depreciated over 7 years, and that the business uses the **straight-line depreciation method**. (As will be discussed shortly, many businesses use an accelerated depreciation method instead of the straight-line method.) The effects of capitalizing only the direct costs versus capitalizing all costs are compared as follows:

ANNUAL EXPENSES IF ONLY DIRECT ACQUISITION COSTS ARE CAPITALIZED

Year 1: [$200,000 depreciation + $140,000] = $340,000 total expense

Years 2–7: $\dfrac{\$1,400,000}{7 \text{ years}}$ = $200,000 depreciation expense

ANNUAL EXPENSES IF ALL COSTS ARE CAPITALIZED

Years 1–7: $\dfrac{\$1,540,000}{7 \text{ years}}$ = $220,000 depreciation expense

If the business chooses alternative (1) then the total expense in the first year is $120,000 higher than alternative (2): [$340,000 – $220,000 = $120,000]. But, thereafter, the annual depreciation expense is $20,000 less for the following six years. If all costs are capitalized then every year bears the same amount of expense, or $220,000 depreciation expense. Total expenses over the entire seven years are the same either way. It's year-by-year that expenses are different.

Accelerated versus Straight-line Depreciation Methods

Most business buildings last 50, 75, or more years. Yet under the federal income tax law the cost of nonresidential buildings used by a business can be depreciated over 39 years. Automobiles and light trucks used by businesses last 10 years or longer, but can be depreciated over 5 years under the tax law. I've been in business offices that bought their furniture when Harry Truman was President but under the income tax law this type of fixed asset can be depreciated over just 7 years.

In brief, the federal income tax law permits business fixed assets to be depreciated over a shorter number of years than the actual useful lives of the assets. This is the deliberate economic policy of Congress to encourage capital investment in newer, technologically superior resources to help improve the productivity of U.S. businesses.

Accelerated depreciation deductions are higher and tax payments are lower in the early years of using fixed assets. Thus, the business has more cash flow available to reinvest in new fixed assets—both to expand capacity and to improve productivity. This accelerated depreciation philosophy has become a permanent feature of the income tax law, and is not likely to change anytime soon.

The federal income tax law regarding depreciation of fixed assets has effectively discouraged any realistic attempt of estimating the useful lives of a company's long-lived operating resources. This is a fact of business life, like it or not. The shortest lives permitted for income tax are selected by most businesses for reporting depreciation expense in their financial statements. The schedule of these short, or accelerated useful lives are found in the section of the income tax law named the Modified Accelerated Cost Recovery System, or MACRS for short. (Alternatively, the income tax code permits businesses to adopt longer useful life estimates than the MACRS schedules.)

MACRS also allows the *front-end loading method* of depreciation, instead of a level and equal amount of depreciation each year (called the *straight-line method*). More depreciation is allocated to the early years and less in the later years. The annual depreciation amounts walk down the stairs, each year being less than the year before. Like the LIFO accounting method for cost of goods sold expense, I seriously doubt whether accelerated depreciation would be used by many businesses if this method were not allowed for income tax.

Managers and investors should keep in mind that, with rare exceptions, the fixed assets of a business are overdepreciated—not in the actual wearing out or physical using up sense, but in the accounting sense. The reported book values of a company's fixed assets (original cost less accumulated depreciation) are understated. In short a company's fixed assets are written off too fast. Book values shrink much quicker than they should.

In summary a business has two basic alternatives regarding how to record depreciation expense on its fixed assets:

1. Adopt the *accelerated income tax approach*—use the shortest useful lives and the front-end loaded depreciation allocation allowed by the tax code; or

2. Adopt more *realistic, longer useful life estimates* for fixed assets and allocate the cost in equal amounts to each year— *straight-line depreciation.*

For an example assume that a business pays $120,000 for a new machine. Under MACRS this asset falls in the 7-year class. Alternatively, the business could elect to use a 12-year useful life estimate, which we'll assume to be realistic for this particular machine.

Figure 13.2 compares the annual depreciation amounts determined by the *double-declining accelerated depreciation schedule* permitted by MACRS in the left columns, with the $10,000 annual depreciation amount according to the straight-line method in the right columns. (Only one-half year depreciation can be deducted in the year of acquisition under the income tax law.)

FIGURE 13.2 Comparison of Accelerated versus Straight-line Depreciation Methods

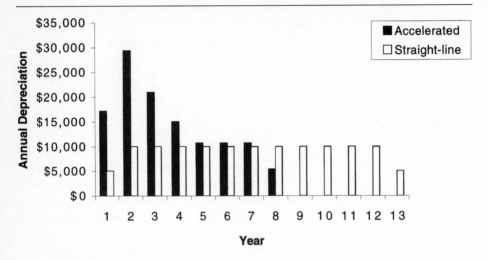

Suppose the machine actually is used for 12 years. Therefore, this asset adds value to the operations of the business every year of its use. The value added in some years may be more than in other years. It's virtually impossible to determine exactly how much sales revenue any one machine is responsible for—or any particular fixed asset for that matter. Nevertheless, it bothers me that the accelerated depreciation method does not charge the last 5 years of using the machine with any expense. What do you think?

Although accelerated depreciation has obvious income tax advantages, there are certain disadvantages. For one thing the book (reported) values of a company's long-term operating assets are lower. When a company is borrowing money, a lender looks at the company's assets as reported in its balance sheet. The lower book values of its fixed assets caused by using accelerated depreciation may, in effect, lower the debt capacity of a business (the maximum amount it can borrow).

Managers and investors are very much interested in whether a business was able to improve its profit performance over last year. Ideally, when a profit increase is reported, the increase should be due to real causes—better profit margins on sales, gains in operating efficiency, higher sales volumes, and so forth. Spurious increases in profit can be misleading. Profit trends are difficult to track if there are drop-offs in annual depreciation expense, which is precisely the result of using the accelerated depreciation (see Figure 13.2 again). The straight-line method has one advantage: depreciation expense is constant year to year on the same fixed assets.

Other Critical Accounting Choices

A business has to decide on many basic accounting methods, in addition to selecting methods for its cost of goods sold and depreciation expenses. It's not possible here to dig into the details of these other accounting methods. Instead, a brief overview will have to suffice.

- The *timing for recording sales revenue* is a troublesome issue for many companies. The general rule is to record sales revenue when the sale has been completed and goods and services have been delivered to customers. However, this exact point of finality for a sale is open to different interpretations when a business has to provide follow-up services to its customers, and when a sale is tentative and not completely signed, sealed, and delivered in every respect.

- A business has to decide whether and how to look ahead and record certain *expenses that emanate from sales but don't show up until weeks or months after the sale*—examples include *bad debts* (uncollectible accounts receivable from sales on credit), *warranty and guarantee work*, and possible *product recalls*.

- Most businesses that sell products must decide how often to take the time and trouble to determine inventory shrinkage expense (the cost of products that have been stolen by customers and employees and the loss from products that have lost value due to deterioration and damage); also, they have to determine decreases in the sales value of their inventories that should be recorded as an expense according to the lower of cost or market write-down rule.

- A business has to determine how to accumulate *vacation and sick pay of employees*, which is recorded in an accrued expenses payable liability.

- A business has to make decisions regarding several variables that are put into the equations for recording the *cost of the retirement plans* for employees.

- A business has to keep alert for *impairments in the values of its operating assets*, and decide how to determine the amount of write-down when assets become impaired.

I could catalog additional accounting choices that a business has to make. But I think you get a good idea from the list above. What I advise you to do is this: Ask the chief accountant (controller) to prepare a list of the critical accounting choices facing the business. The chief executive officer, president, and other high-level managers should review this list, ask for clear explanations of which alternative accounting methods are acceptable for each, which method presently is being used, and whether the accounting methods are conservative or aggressive for measuring profit and presenting the financial condition of the business.

Summary

The chapter advocates that managers should be involved in selecting the critical accounting methods used to measure profit and to present the financial condition of the business. Two key accounting choices are examined in the chapter:

- The method for recording cost of goods sold and cost of ending inventories, which in most situations comes down to choosing between *first-in, first-out (FIFO)* or *last-in, first-out (LIFO)*.

- The policy for *capitalizing the costs of fixed assets* and the decision regarding how to allocate this cost over the useful lives of the resources, which comes down to choosing between the conservative *accelerated depreciation* method or the *straight-line* method that uses a longer useful life estimate and allocates a uniform amount to each year.

In my opinion the cost of goods sold method should be the one that most closely corresponds with the sales pricing policies and practices of a business. If a business uses the FIFO sales pricing approach, which many businesses do, then the FIFO cost of goods sold method measures gross margin (profit) in a manner consistent with the company's sales pricing. Choosing between the accelerated and the straight-line method for depreciation is heavily influenced by income tax considerations. Accelerated depreciation saves income tax in the short run, but has certain disadvantages that managers should be aware of.

In any case managers should be aware of which accounting methods are used to measure their company's profit, as well as whether these methods produce conservative or more liberal profit numbers.

CHAPTER 14

Touching-Up the Financials, Short of Fraud

This chapter discusses sensitive topics. In fact I had pangs of conscience in writing this chapter. Books on financial analysis generally avoid these topics, giving the impression that such things don't happen. But they do, which any experienced accountant or manager will admit (probably off the record). The topics I discuss in this chapter are sleight of hand techniques that business managers use to manipulate financial statement numbers, especially bottom-line net income. These techniques are called variously *massaging the numbers, cooking the books, creative accounting, profit management,* or by other pejorative terms. I've selected the term *touching-up the financials* as you see in the chapter title.

Note also the last part of the chapter title—short of fraud. This is included as a warning that these manipulations to make a business's profit and financial statements look better can get out of hand and lead to financial fraud. Managers are on a slippery slope when engaging in these practices. It's easy to slide off the edge into legal trouble, to say nothing about the ethics of doing these things. I discuss these accounting tricks not to encourage their use, of course, but for the main purpose of giving you a better understanding of the limitations and arbitrary nature of financial statements.

The late sportscaster Howard Cosell was well known for his remark "Tell it like it is." Many business managers seem to have the attitude that accountants tell it like it is in financial statements. They seem to think that the accountant holds a mirror to the economic reality of the business and that financial statements are a reflection of this economic reality. This is far from the truth. Just as politicians put a spin on developments, businesses exercise spin control on their financial statements. Their CPA auditors generally tolerate these practices, although if a business is too heavy-handed, its auditor will intercede.

Nudging the Bottom Line: An Example to Start With

Suppose the chief accountant (controller) of a business has just prepared the final draft of its annual financial statements, and submits them for top-level management review and approval. It's standard practice for the CEO and other top-level managers, as well as the board of directors, to review the financials before they are released to the shareowners of the business. Assume that the CEO is quite disappointed with the bottom-line net income figure she sees in the income statement. She had already promised the shareowners that net income would be higher than this amount. So, she suggests to the controller that additional sales be recorded in order to improve gross margin for the year.

This scenario is based on an actual audit I worked on many years ago. The company sold products that it installed on the customer's premises. Some minor follow-up work was done a week or two after the products were installed. The business had followed the practice of waiting until the follow-up work was done to record a sale as completed, at which time the sales revenue was recorded—even though the follow-up work involved only minor technical adjustments to the products. But this year the CEO asked the controller to identify those sales that were virtually completed at the end of the year and record the sales revenue for these particular sales. The controller identified several sales that were virtually completed and were waiting only minor follow-up work at the end of the year. These sales in progress were recorded in the current year instead of waiting until next year to record the sales revenue.

Figure 14.1 presents the financial statement effects of moving forward the time for recording sales revenue. Only the *changes* in the balance sheet and income statement are shown in Figure 14.1—not the entire financial statements. I don't recall the exact numbers involved, so I have to use hypothetical figures for the additional amounts of sales revenue and cost of goods sold expense.

FIGURE 14.1 Profit and Balance Sheet Effects of Recording Additional Sales for the Year

BALANCE SHEET			INCOME STATEMENT	
ASSETS		**LIABILITIES**	**Sales Revenue**	$894,000
Accounts Receivable	$894,000			
Inventories	($615,000)	**OWNERS' EQUITY**	Expenses	$615,000
		Retained Earnings $279,000	Net Income	$279,000

In Figure 14.1 the gross margin increase is $279,000. The business operated as a partnership and did not pay income tax as a separate entity. So recording additional gross margin increased net income the same amount.

As shown in Figure 14.1, recording additional sales revenue increased accounts receivable; recording additional cost of goods sold expense decreased inventories; the additional gross margin increased net income; and the additional net income increased retained earnings (an owners' equity account). Therefore, the company's balance sheet looked better: Total assets increased $279,000 and the balance in its retained earnings was higher the same amount. However, the main purpose was to boost net income.

Since the net income increase was a material amount, our audit firm insisted that this change in its accounting method for recording sales revenue had to be disclosed in a footnote to the financial statements, which the business agreed to do. But the footnote did not divulge how much lower net income would have been had the change not been made.

Not all businesses have such latitude in choosing the timing for recording their sales revenue. Wal-Mart and other retailers either make a sale or they don't—although, customers generally can return products so a retailer could argue that its sales are not final until sometime after the sales are made. In any case, there are many businesses that can control the exact point in time for recording their sales revenue. They can cherry pick those sales that are in the process of being finalized at the end of the year, and either record these sales in the current year or delay recording the sales until the following year.

Management Input for End-of-Year Adjusting Entries

The annual accounting cycle of a business consists of two broad phases: (1) the routine recording of transactions and activities of the business during the year according to its established accounting methods and procedures; and (2) the *end-of-period* **adjusting entries** that are necessary to complete the accounting process. To illustrate:

Recording Transactions
and Activities during Year

End-of-Year
Adjusting ⟶ Financial
Entries

Release of
Financial
Statements

Several important accounting decisions are postponed until the end of the year. It's standard practice to wait until the close of the year to make final decisions about several expenses, and these decisions require *management input.*

At the close of the year the accountant prepares a listing of all accounts called the *trial balance,* to make sure the books are in balance (that debits equal credits). The trial balance serves as the point of departure for making *end-of-period adjusting entries.* These important entries are made in order to bring the accounts up to date for preparing financial statements (and income tax returns). The accounts are still on trial, in a court trial as it were. The books haven't gone to the jury yet for final decisions.

The chief accountant consults with the CEO and other top-level managers on many accounting issues in order to make the necessary end-of-period adjusting entries. Most of these final entries involve the amounts of expenses to record for the period. The following sections discuss some of the major accounting areas in which management input is critical. Managers can tilt their information input one way and thereby control the amount of expense recorded for the period.

Inventory Write-downs

The end-of-year adjusting entry to write-down inventory is a prime example of how a manager can directly affect the amount of profit recorded for the year. At the close of the year the accountant prepares a list of slow-moving products that have been in inventory longer than normal holding periods. The question is whether these products will have to be sold below regular sales prices, or perhaps below cost to move the goods off the shelves. When products cannot be sold at their normal gross margins, or will have to be sold below cost, the **lower of cost or market** accounting rule requires that the inventories asset account should be written-down. This is an accounting procedure required by generally accepted accounting principles (GAAP). An expense for loss of inventory value is recorded, which decreases profit for the period, of course.

The sales manager and purchasing manager provide critical information to the accountant in deciding whether to write down certain products in inventory, and by how much. Obviously the managers can influence the amount of expense to be recorded. For example, assume that a business has in inventory certain products that will have to be sold below normal sales prices and in some cases below cost. Assume that the pessimistic estimate is that inventories should be written down $125,000 but a more optimistic estimate is that the inventory write-down should be $75,000. Suppose the decision is made to adopt the pessimistic estimate.

The financial results of the inventory write-down decision are shown in Figure 14.2 (income tax effects are ignored). If the optimist estimate had been used for the inventories, write-down profit would have been $50,000 higher (before income tax), and inventories and the retained earnings would have been $50,000 higher.

I once knew a shady character who was the sole owner of a retail clothing store. At year-end he wrote down his ending inventory—but by a much higher amount than could be justified under the lower of cost or market rule. He did this to minimize his taxable income from the business. He called this the annual inventory knockdown. He owned all the stock shares of the corporation, so he did not have to worry about how his financial statements would look to outside shareowners. However, he did have trouble explaining the financial statements to his bank when applying for a loan. In my view he crossed the line and was on thin ice. Later I noticed in the newspaper that the Internal Revenue Service had filed a lien against his assets for unpaid income taxes.

Bad Debts

Another example where management input provides essential information for the amount of an expense concerns accounts receivable from credit sales that probably will not be collected from customers. These are called *bad debts*. Accounts receivables that cannot be collected should be written off and charged to bad debts expense. At

FIGURE 14.2 Profit and Balance Sheet Effects of Recording Write-down of Inventories

BALANCE SHEET		INCOME STATEMENT	
ASSETS	**LIABILITIES**	Sales Revenue	
Inventories ($125,000)			
	OWNERS' EQUITY	Expenses	$125,000
	Retained earnings ($125,000)	Net Income	($125,000)

the end of the year the accountant prepares a list of overdue customers' accounts receivable. The credit manager and sales manager scrutinize this list and decide which of these overdue accounts should be written off.

Instead of the direct write-off method, just described, a business may use the *allowance method* to record bad debts expense. Based on its past experience a business establishes a baseline percent of total credit sales that will eventually turn out to be uncollectible. This estimate may end up being too high or too low, of course. Anyway, the accountant multiples the total amount of credit sales for the year by the estimated bad debts percent to record bad debts expense for the period. In either case—the direct write-method or the allowance method—management input determines the amount of bad debts expense for the period.

Suppose a business uses the direct write-off method for recording its bad debts expense. Its overdue customer accounts receivable are analyzed at the end of the year, to identify which of these customers' accounts probably will not be collected. The most pessimistic estimate is that $65,000 will not be collected, but a more optimistic estimate is that only $25,000 will prove to be uncollectible. Only time will tell, of course. The accountant can't make an entry until the manager makes a decision. Suppose the optimistic estimate is used. The effects of recording bad debts expenses based on the optimistic estimate are shown in Figure 14.3 (before income tax).

If the pessimistic estimate had been used, then profit would have been $40,000 lower (before income tax), and accounts receivable and retained earnings would have been lower the same amount. I worked on an audit in Lincoln, Nebraska, many years ago that I still remember. The business hardly ever had to write off a customer's account. (The business was very careful regarding which customers it extended credit to.) As I recall the business wrote off only $3,000 bad debts in the year of the audit. Yet the business recorded a very high amount of bad debts expense for the year because it used the

FIGURE 14.3 Profit and Balance Sheet Effects of Recording Bad Debts Expense

BALANCE SHEET		INCOME STATEMENT
ASSETS	LIABILITIES	
		Sales Revenue
Accounts Receivable ($25,000)		
	OWNERS' EQUITY	Expenses $25,000
	Retained Earnings ($25,000)	Net Income ($25,000)

allowance method based on a very high bad debts percent. When using the allowance method a business creates a contra asset account and the balance in this negative account is deducted from accounts receivable—just like accumulated depreciation is deducted from fixed assets.

Based on its past record of bad debts the business clearly was using an unrealistically high percent for bad debts. I put a note about this in the audit working papers, pointing out that the company's bad debts expense was materially overstated and that the book value of its accounts receivable was seriously understated. The partner in charge of the audit replied that this was an acceptable conservative accounting practice—and that was the end of that. The client did not change its bad debts expense, even though its accounts receivable asset was understated several hundred thousand dollars.

Management Input for Other Expenses

Business managers provide critical information input for several other end-of-period adjusting entries. The accountant needs management input for recording *accrued employee vacation and sick pay,* for recording the *cost of employee retirement plans,* and for recording *accruals for guarantee and warranty costs* for products already sold by the business—to name only three accounting areas needing management input. The manager can tilt his or her estimate up or down, and thereby shift the amount of expense up or down for the period.

Managers prefer to be consistent year to year in making estimates for the accountants in recording end-of-year adjusting entries. Nonetheless, managers have a range of discretion in making these estimates—and therefore they can nudge the amount of profit recorded for the period in either direction. In many situations managers are under pressure to achieve preset profit objectives for the period. Providing input for the end-of-period accounting adjusting entries is a convenient way for managers to close the gap and reach the profit goal for the period.

Management Intervention

Considerably before the end of the year managers have a good fix on how the profit number will turn out. They receive monthly and quarterly profit reports. Suppose the profit picture doesn't look too good for the year. A manager can intervene in the normal course of operations of the business for the purpose of boosting profit. These actions go beyond providing information to the accountant in the process of making end-of-period adjusting entries. Management intervention is when a manager deliberately takes an action that he or she knows will help (or hurt) profit for the period. There is no legitimate operational reason for the action; it's done to make profit come out better (or worse). One such maneuver is *deferred maintenance.*

Deferred Maintenance

Suppose a business normally spends $25,000 per month on routine repairs and maintenance of its buildings, machinery, equipment, and other fixed assets. Virtually all fixed assets require regular upkeep, minor repairs, tune-ups, replacement of parts, and so on. These expenditures keep the assets in good working order and extend their useful lives. Repairs and maintenance expense is recorded when cash outlays are actually made for this work. So a manager may do the following: Instead of authorizing the normal maintenance work for the month the manager could order that no maintenance work be done that month. Thus, the repairs and maintenance expense for the month would be avoided. The practice of skipping normal repair and maintenance work for a period is called deferred maintenance.

The effects of skipping a month of repairs and maintenance are shown in Figure 14.4. Expenses would be $25,000 lower, which means net income would be $25,000 higher (ignoring income tax). Cash would be $25,000 higher because the business skipped a month of disbursements for repairs and maintenance expenses; and its retained earnings would be $25,000 higher.

Deferred maintenance is a well known and evidently a commonly used tactic to inflate profit. But it can be dangerous because the operating efficiency and working order of the company's fixed assets may be put in jeopardy. Eventually deferred maintenance catches up with a business, may lead to substantial costs for overhauls and major repair work on its fixed assets, or cause other serious problems. For example a business may not replace tiles on the roof of its ware-

FIGURE 14.4 Profit and Balance Sheet Effects of Deferred Maintenance

BALANCE SHEET			INCOME STATEMENT	
ASSETS	LIABILITIES			
Cash $25,000			Sales Revenue	
	OWNERS' EQUITY		Expenses	($25,000)
	Retained Earnings $25,000		Net Income	$25,000

house building. Later a heavy rainstorm causes the roof to leak that causes serious water damage to its inventory.

A similar profit manipulation tactic is to delay training programs for employees. Or a manager may defer spending on advertising. These tactics reduce expenses in the short run, but may have serious long-term consequences. In general any expense that is recorded on the cash basis is an eligible candidate for the deferred maintenance tactic.

LIFO Liquidation Gain

The last-in, first-out (LIFO) method for recording the cost of goods sold expense and the cost of inventory is explained in Chapter 13. One feature of this method is not explored in that chapter however—using LIFO to manipulate the cost of goods sold expense for the period. A manager could deliberately allow the inventory level of a product to fall below its normal level. As the result, in recording the cost of goods sold expense for the period the accountant has to reach back into one or more of the old cost layers of the product. The costs in the old layer(s) probably are substantially lower than current costs of the product. In this way the cost of goods sold expense would be artificially depressed and profit would be inflated for the period. The boost in profit from doing this is called a **LIFO liquidation gain**.

I'll use an extreme example to explain how a LIFO liquidation gain works, which I admit is not entirely realistic but it does serve to dramatize the point. I mention in Chapter 13 that Caterpillar has used the LIFO method for many years. In a footnote to its financial statements the company discloses that the current value of its inventories is about $2.0 billion (yes, that's billion) higher than the LIFO-based cost reported for its inventories asset account in its balance sheet.

Suppose that during the year 2003 Caterpillar's unionized labor force goes out on a general strike and the company has to shut down its manufacturing operations. Assume the strike continues a long time and the company is not able to resume its manufacturing operations until the following year. By the end of the year assume that Caterpillar had reduced its inventories to virtually zero. It sold all the products that it had in inventory at the start of the strike, and the company was not able to manufacture replacement products, as it normally would have. If it had been able to manufacture products during the year the cost of the products sold would have been about $2.0 billion more than the LIFO-based costs in its inventories account. Since no products were manufactured to replace the units sold during the year, the accountant had no choice but to go back and pull out the very old LIFO-based costs from the inventories account to record the cost of goods sold expense for the year. Thus, cost of goods sold in 2003 would be the costs from 20, 30, and 40 years ago.

As a consequence Caterpillar's cost of goods sold expense would be $2.0 billion lower compared with current manufacturing costs. This $2.0 billion reduction in its normal cost of goods sold expense would be a LIFO liquidation gain. I doubt such a strike would completely shut down its manufacturing operations, although Caterpillar has a history of labor problems.

A business could force the recording of a LIFO liquidation gain on some of its products in order to increase its profit for the year. It could deliberately reduce inventory quantities below normal levels for several products simply by not replacing all the goods sold during the year. Toward the end of the year the manager could delay the production or purchase of these products, thus causing their inventory quantities to fall to abnormally low levels. This would force the accountant to dig back into the old cost layers of the products. These old LIFO costs are less than the current replacement cost of the products, so cost of goods sold expense would be artificially depressed and gross margin would get a shot in the arm.

Aside from the deliberate reduction in inventory levels to force a LIFO liquidation gain, the same effect happens when a product reaches the end of its life cycle. These occurrences are not driven by the profit manipulation motive, but the result is the same. Please refer back to Figure 13.1 in Chapter 13 for the product example discussed in that chapter. The LIFO cost for the 1,000 units in ending inventory is $100,000 in this example. Now move forward in time to several years later. At this point assume that the product has reached the end of its life cycle.

The company maintained its inventory level of this product at 1,000 units, so the accountant never had to use any of the $100,000 cost for recording cost of goods sold expense during the years. During the year just ended the company sold the last 1,000 units of this product; these units were not replaced because the product was phased out. The LIFO cost of these 1,000 units is still $100,000. The most recent batch of 1,000 units of this product cost $175,000 (product cost continued to increase over the years).

Because the product was being discontinued the business dropped its normal sales price of the product. To move the goods out the door, the business sold the 1,000 units for $175,000, which is the cost of the most recent acquisition. Relative to the most recent acquisition cost there is a zero gross margin on the final sale. However, the final sale results in recording $75,000 gross margin: [$175,000 sales revenue − $100,000 LIFO cost of products sold = $75,000 gross margin]. This one-time nonrecurring effect is a LIFO liquidation gain. Taxable income is also $75,000 higher as a result of phasing out the product.

The lesson of this example is that by using the LIFO method a business only defers, or puts off the recording gross margin—both in its annual income statements and in its annual income tax returns. Eventually, when the end of a product's life cycle is reached and the business liquidates its inventory of the product, gross margin that would have been recorded along the way by the first-in, first-out (FIFO) method (or the average cost method) catches up with the business and the gross margin has to be recorded. Managers should be aware of the eventual LIFO liquidation gain that will happen at the end of a product's life cycle (assuming that the products are sold at sales prices higher than the old LIFO costs of the products).

In summary, businesses that use LIFO have some gross margin in reserve, or on the shelf and ready to be recorded at any time. There is nothing to prohibit a business from manipulating profit by the partial liquidation of its LIFO-based inventories. For whatever reason suppose a business had a material amount of LIFO liquidation gain in the year. This type of gain is nonrecurring in nature and therefore should be disclosed in a footnote to the business's externally reported financial statements, or as extraordinary (one-time) gain in its income statement. These disclosure requirements may discourage the use of LIFO liquidation gains as a means for manipulating profit, compared with the abundance of other methods that do not have disclosure requirements attached to them.

Opportunities of Manufacturers to Inflate Profit

Businesses that manufacture the products they sell have a unique way to pump up profit, which is not available to retailers or service businesses. The product cost of retailers is the *purchase* cost. In contrast, the product cost of a manufacturer is a built-up amount consisting of *four cost components*:

1. *Raw materials* (parts and materials purchased from other businesses).

2. *Direct labor* (employees that work directly on the production line).

3. *Variable manufacturing overhead costs* (indirect production costs that fluctuate in proportion to production output levels).

4. *Fixed manufacturing overhead costs* (indirect production costs that are fixed in amount for the year and do not fluctuate with production output levels).

Manufacturing processes require many different indirect production costs that cannot be matched or identified with particular products during the manufacturing process. These indirect manufacturing costs generally are referred to as **overhead costs**. Some overhead costs vary with total production output, such as electricity that powers machinery and equipment. In contrast, many production overhead costs are fixed for the year.

Manufacturing businesses have to commit to a certain level of fixed manufacturing costs for the year that do not vary with actual production output. Examples of fixed manufacturing costs are property taxes on the production plant, fire insurance on the building, plant security guards and nurses on fixed salaries, fixed salaries of production managers, depreciation of production machinery and equipment, air conditioning and air treatment systems that have to be kept running regardless of production levels, and so on.

Fixed manufacturing overhead costs are incurred by a business to provide *production capacity*. Suppose a manufacturer's annual production capacity is 120,000 units. Its total annual fixed manufacturing costs provide the physical facilities and human resources to produce a maximum of 120,000 units under normal and practical operating conditions. Assume the following facts for a manufacturing business for the year. To simplify the analysis, assume the company manufacturers just one product.

INFORMATION FOR MANUFACTURING BUSINESS EXAMPLE

Production capacity	120,000 units
Sales volume	100,000 units
Production output	100,000 units
Fixed manufacturing overhead costs	$3,960,000

Tip

The combined cost of raw materials and direct labor in manufacturing products is called *prime* cost. Direct labor plus manufacturing overhead costs (both fixed and variable) is called *conversion* cost. Conversion cost is the measure of *value added* by the manufacturing process. Generally speaking the best opportunity for making profit lies in the conversion cost area, although the efficient use of raw materials also is important.

Note that the company's output for the year is below its annual production capacity. Few manufacturing businesses run at full capacity. This business produced 100,000 units during the year just ended, which is 83 percent of its capacity. This is not unusual. Most manufacturers operate in the 80 percent to 90 percent range of their annual production capacities, although this statistic varies from industry to industry.

Note also that sales volume equals production output for the year: The business sold 100,000 units and manufactured 100,000 units during the year. So its inventory level of the product did not change. Chapter 13 explains that a business can select either the FIFO or LIFO method to determine cost of goods sold. This business uses the LIFO method.

Because the business manufactured 100,000 units and sold 100,000 units during the year, all its manufacturing costs of the year are charged to cost of goods sold expense. (By the way, the business could have forced a LIFO liquidation gain if it had produced only, say, 90,000 units during the year; the accountant would have had to reach into old cost layers for the other 10,000 units sold during the year.)

In this scenario the business manufactured 100,000 units. Therefore, the amount of fixed manufacturing overhead cost included in product cost per unit is computed as follows.

FIXED MANUFACTURING OVERHEAD COST COMPONENT IN PRODUCT COST

$$\frac{\$3{,}960{,}000 \text{ fixed manufacturing overhead costs for year}}{100{,}000 \text{ units produced}} = \$39.60 \text{ per unit}$$

Product cost also includes the costs of raw materials, labor, and variable manufacturing overhead. Assume these other components of product cost are $60.00 per unit. Thus total product cost per unit is $99.60: ($60.00 variable manufacturing costs + $39.60 fixed manufacturing costs = $99.60 product cost per unit). The company's cost of goods sold expense for the year is $9,960,000: ($99.60 product cost per unit × 100,000 units sold = $9,960,000 cost of goods sold expense).

The cost of goods sold expense for the year includes $39.60 per unit of fixed manufacturing overhead costs. In other words all the $3,960,000 fixed manufacturing overhead costs is charged to cost of goods sold expense. But what if the business had manufactured more units that it sold during the year?

Suppose the business had manufactured 110,000 units during the year just ended, thus increasing its inventory level 10,000 units (110,000 units production output − 100,000 units sold = 10,000 units inventory increase). In this alternative scenario the fixed manufacturing overhead costs per unit would be:

FIXED MANUFACTURING OVERHEAD COST COMPONENT IN PRODUCT COST (IF PRODUCTION OUTPUT IS 110,000 UNITS FOR THE YEAR)

$$\frac{\$3{,}960{,}000 \text{ fixed manufacturing overhead costs for year}}{110{,}000 \text{ units produced}} = \$36.00 \text{ per unit}$$

In this scenario cost of goods sold expense is charged with only $3,600,000 of the company's total fixed manufacturing overhead costs for the year: (100,000 units sold × $36.00 fixed manufacturing overhead costs per unit = $3,600,000 included in cost of goods sold expense). The increase in inventory would absorb the other $360,000 of the annual fixed manufacturing overhead costs: (10,000 units increase in inventory × $36.00 fixed manufacturing overhead costs per unit = $360,000).

Figure 14.5 shows the effects on its financial statements (before income tax) of manufacturing more units than are sold during the year. The business's profit would be $360,000 higher (before income tax). Inventories would be $960,000 higher: ($96.00 product cost per unit × 10,000 units added to inventory = $960,000 increase in cost of inventories). Cash would be $600,000 lower due to the variable costs of producing an additional 10,000 units (assuming all these costs were paid in cash during the year, which is approximately correct). No pun intended, but the business could manufacture an additional $360,000 of profit by producing 10,000 more units than it sold during the year.

When production outstrips sales for the year, some of the year's fixed manufacturing overhead costs are shifted to future years because the increase in inventories absorbs a proportionate share of these costs for the year. In other words if inventories had not increased, all the fixed manufacturing overhead costs would have been

FIGURE 14.5 Profit and Balance Sheet Effects of Producing More Units Than Were Sold During Period

BALANCE SHEET				INCOME STATEMENT	
ASSETS		LIABILITIES		Sales Revenue	
Cash	($600,000)				
Inventories	$960,000	OWNERS' EQUITY		Expenses	($360,000)
		Retained Earnings	$360,000	Net Income	$360,000

expensed in the year, which is the situation for the first scenario in which 100,000 units are produced. Security analysts keep a sharp eye on any material increases in inventories by manufacturing businesses. They know the profit effect from an increase in inventories.

Growing businesses need to build up their inventories in anticipation of higher sales volume next year. However, even rapidly expanding companies may produce too many products, or more than what's needed for the higher sales volume next year. It's possible that a large inventory build up could be in anticipation of a long strike looming in the near future, which will shut down production for many months. Or perhaps a company predicts serious shortages of raw material during the coming months. There are such legitimate reasons for a large inventory build up, but these situations are unusual.

Window Dressing

The discussion to this point in the chapter has focused on profit manipulation techniques. A business also is concerned about how its *solvency* looks in its balance sheet. Solvency refers to the ability of a business to pay its liabilities when they come due for payment. Insolvency means that a business is not able to pay its liabilities on time, which can lead to very serious consequences, of course. The analysis of short-term solvency focuses on the current assets and current liabilities of a business. Also lenders and shareowners look at the cash balance of a business.

Suppose that a business has been operating with a very low cash balance, virtually on the ragged edge as a matter of fact. It has to wait to see how much cash is collected each day before deciding which bills can be paid. At the end of its most recent year, December 31, the balances of its current assets and current liabilities are shown in Figure 14.6. Its low cash balance would stick out like a sore thumb. The business probably would do something to avoid reporting such a low cash balance. One thing it might do is called **window dressing**.

The business could hold its cash receipts journal open in order to record additional cash collections from customers during several days in January of the following year, and record these cash receipts as if the money had been received December 31. Suppose that during these early days in January the business receives $400,000 cash collections from customers. The business records these receipts as if the money had been collected December 31. Thus, two of its current assets would be reported at different amounts, which are shown in Figure 14.7.

FIGURE 14.6 Year-End Balances of Current Assets and Current Liabilities (before Window Dressing)

Current Assets		Current Liabilities	
Cash	$85,000	Accounts Payable	$875,000
Accounts Receivable	$2,250,000	Accrued Expenses Payable	$795,000
Inventories	$2,390,000	Income Tax Payable	$78,500
Prepaid Expenses	$115,000	Short-term Notes Payable	$750,000
Total Current Assets	$4,840,000	Total Current Liabilities	$2,498,500

The company's cash balance is $400,000 higher and its accounts receivable balance is $400,000 lower from doing window dressing. Clearly the cash position of the business looks better. Would the company's CPA auditors tolerate this legerdemain? Well, in my experience the answer is yes—up to a point. The auditors probably would allow a business to touch up its cash balance, as long as the books were not held open too long.

Window dressing can be done for other reasons as well. Based on the balances of current assets and current liabilities in Figure 14.7 (after window dressing was done to improve its cash balance), the company's *current ratio* is as follows.

COMPUTATION OF CURRENT RATIO

$$\frac{\$4,840,000 \text{ current assets}}{\$2,498,500 \text{ current liabilities}} = 1.94 \text{ current ratio}$$

Most businesses prefer a current ratio of 2.0 or higher; in fact the company's bank loan may have a proviso that the business must maintain its current ratio at or above 2.0. To achieve a current ratio of 2.0 the business could hold its books open for a few more days. Suppose that during these additional days the business collects an additional $175,000, which increases cash and decreases accounts

FIGURE 14.7 Year-End Balances of Current Assets and Current Liabilities (after Window Dressing)

Current Assets		Current Liabilities	
Cash	$485,000	Accounts Payable	$875,000
Accounts Receivable	$1,850,000	Accrued Expenses Payable	$795,000
Inventories	$2,390,000	Income Tax Payable	$78,500
Prepaid Expenses	$115,000	Short-term Notes Payable	$750,000
Total Current Assets	$4,840,000	Total Current Liabilities	$2,498,500

receivable this amount. The business writes checks for this amount to pay some accounts payable, as if the checks had been written on December 31. So cash would be reduced $175,000 and accounts payable would be reduced the same amount. The balances of its current assets and current liabilities after this second phase of window dressing are shown in Figure 14.8.

The company's current ratio is now computed as follows.

COMPUTATION OF CURRENT RATIO

$$\frac{\$4,665,000 \text{ current assets}}{\$2,323,500 \text{ current liabilities}} = 2.01 \text{ current ratio}$$

Of course, a business does not disclose in the footnotes to its financial statements (or anywhere else in its annual financial report) that it has used window dressing to improve its solvency appearance. Lenders, as they consider making a loan to a business, should be aware that the business may have engaged in window dressing, which means that the numbers for some current assets and current liabilities may be rigged to look better than they actually were at the close of the period.

Window dressing also is done for anther reason: to improve cash flow from profit for the year. By holding its books open and recording additional cash collections from customers as if the money was received by the close of the year, a business reports more cash flow from profit in its statement of cash flows. Cash flow from profit is receiving more and more attention in financial statement analysis, so managers may be tempted to use window dressing to improve cash flow from profit for the year. On the other hand holding the cash journal open after the end of the year for this purpose comes very close to financial statement fraud, which is discussed next.

Financial Statement Fraud

Several techniques for touching up financial statements, discussed above, are mainly for the purpose of manipulating the amount of

FIGURE 14.8 Year-End Balances of Current Assets and Current Liabilities (Two Phases of Window Dressing)

Current Assets		Current Liabilities	
Cash	$485,000	Accounts Payable	$700,000
Accounts Receivable	$1,675,000	Accrued Expenses Payable	$795,000
Inventories	$2,390,000	Income Tax Payable	$78,500
Prepaid Expenses	$115,000	Short-term Notes Payable	$750,000
Total Current Assets	$4,665,000	Total Current Liabilities	$2,323,500

profit recorded for the year. I mentioned at the outset of the chapter that in using these devices business managers are on a slippery slope. Sometimes, these manipulations are desperate measures used as a last resort to buy more time for a business that is in dire straits. But the business may end up in bankruptcy proceedings, and nasty lawsuits may be filed against the business and its executives.

Defending these manipulations in a court of law may prove difficult. The judge or jury may conclude that the business executive committed financial fraud. The shareowners and lenders that suffered losses may be entitled to collect damages against the executive. On the other hand the manipulations may never come to light, especially if the business avoids bankruptcy. Lenders and shareowners may never discover that such things were done to make the financial statements look better. Even if they do find out about the manipulations, they may not be able to prove that they suffered losses that are directly attributable to the financial statement accounting gyrations.

A business has a fiduciary duty to its lenders and shareowners, which includes providing financial statements that are truthful and not misleading. Financial statement fraud is a violation of this duty. However, drawing a line between accounting that puts the best face on the financial statements versus out-and-out fraud is not clear-cut. There are not many bright lines that separate cosmetic techniques from fraudulent shenanigans. I use the term *touching up* to describe the financial statement manipulations explained in the chapter. My father-in-law prefers the term *fluffing the pillows*. Other terms are closer to fraud, such as *cooking the books* and *massaging the numbers*.

Financial statement fraud is a complex area of law. Nevertheless, deliberately preparing false and misleading financial statements is a clear case of fraud. A student once asked for my advice about regarding buying a business (his father was putting up the money). Instead of a normal income statement the student showed me a copy of the business's income tax return for the most recent year. The student asked my advice on a fair price for the business. Instead I told him that the numbers in the tax return looked suspicious. He was very surprised, and asked why. I told him that the gross margin ratio on sales revenue was too high for this type of business.

I recommended that he should ask the owner of the business for permission to have a CPA auditor look over the books and inspect the inventory of the business. When I next saw the student I asked him if he bought the business. He said that when he suggested having a CPA go in and inspect the books, the owner changed his mind and the business was not for sale. I suspect that the owner had simply made up fictitious numbers for sales revenue and cost of goods sold expense, in order to make the business look more profitable than it was. I explained to the student how easy it would be to take a blank copy of a tax return and simply enter numbers for sales revenue and expenses. The student was shocked that someone would do such a thing.

Some managers push the envelope pretty far in manipulating their financial statements. It reminds me of driving faster than the speed limit. Everyone knows that going 67, or even 70 in a 65-mile speed zone probably won't result in a speeding ticket. But some people drive much faster, gambling that they won't get caught. Likewise some businesses go way beyond the speed limit in manipulating their financial statements, gambling that they won't be caught. And often they don't get caught. But sometimes they do.

Financial statements are not like testimony under oath in a court of law, where the witness swears to tell the truth, the whole truth, and nothing but the truth. Managers have a vested interest in the profit performance and other information reported in the financial statements of their business. Businesses are bound by generally accepted accounting principles in preparing their financial statements. Nonetheless, these guidelines still leave managers a good deal of discretion regarding the amount of profit recorded for a period.

Tip

Many small business owners do what is called *skimming*. They do not record all the sales revenue of the business. Instead some of the cash collected from sales is put directly into their pockets and is not recorded as sales revenue in the accounts of the business. Therefore, sales revenue is understated in the income statement. The cost of the products sold is recorded as an *expense*, however. Thus, gross margin and bottom-line net income is understated. Sales skimming is a common type of income tax evasion by small business owners, which can lead to serious penalties and even imprisonment.

The opposite of skimming is *money laundering*. Cash from illegal sources is put into a business and recorded as normal sales revenue. Of course, this overstates the sales revenue, profit, and taxable income of the business. But the cash inflow is made to look legitimate, or clean—which is the whole point.

Summary

This chapter presents a survey of commonly used techniques to manipulate the amount of its profit and improve the solvency appearance of a business. Managers provide key input to accountants for making end-of-year adjusting entries. Managers make estimates for bad debts, inventory write-downs, and for operating liabilities; they can shade their estimates toward the high side or low side, and thus directly control the amount of certain expenses for the period.

Managers can intervene in the operations of the business for the purpose of controlling certain expenses. A prime example is deferred maintenance, in which normal expenditures for routine repairs and maintenance work on fixed assets is not done in order to avoid a certain amount of expense for the period.

Manufacturing businesses can increase production output not because they need more products in inventory but in order to reduce the amount of fixed manufacturing overhead cost included in product cost, which reduces the cost of goods sold expense for the period.

Window dressing is done to improve the solvency appearance of a business. Additional cash collections that are actually received after the close of the year are recorded as if they were received by the last day of the year—to improve the cash balance reported in the balance sheet, and to improve the cash flow from profit for the year.

I hope you don't get the impression from the chapter that profit manipulation is rampant and out of control. But these tactics are not uncommon, unfortunately. Many articles in accounting journals and newsletters lament the *poor quality of earnings* in financial reports, by which is meant that there is far too much management manipulation and interference in the accounting process of many businesses.

In the last analysis the reliability of accounting information in financial statements depends on the integrity and high-mindedness of business executives who are not willing to tolerate management interference in the accounting process. But keep in mind that managers are under intense pressure to achieve the profit goals of the business. The fact that some managers resort to accounting tricks should not surprise you.

Glossary of Key Terms

accelerated depreciation *Accelerated* means two things: (1) the estimate useful life of the fixed asset being depreciated is shorter than a realistic forecast of its probable actual service life; and (2) more of the total cost of the fixed asset is allocated to the first half of its useful life than the second half (i.e., there is a front-end loading of depreciation expense).

accounting equation [Assets = Liabilities + Owners' Equity] This equation reflects the two-sided nature of a business entity; all the assets of a business entity are subject to two types of claims and come from two basic sources of capital—liabilities and owners' equity. This equation is the foundation for double-entry bookkeeping, which uses a scheme for recording changes in the accounts of a business as either debits or credits, such that the total of accounts with debit balances equals the total of accounts with credit balances. Also the accounting equation serves as the basic framework for the statement of financial condition, or balance sheet.

accounts payable These are short-term, noninterest-bearing liabilities of a business that arise in the course of its activities and operations. A business buys many things on credit; the purchase cost of goods and services are not paid for immediately. This liability account records the amounts owed for purchases on credit that will be paid in the short run, which generally means one month or two months at the outside.

accounts receivable   These are short-term, noninterest-bearing debts owed to a business by its customers who bought goods and services from the business on credit. Generally these debts should be collected within a month or two at the most. In a balance sheet this asset is listed immediately after cash. (If a business has short-term, marketable investments this asset is listed after cash and before accounts receivable.) Accounts receivable are viewed as a near-cash type of asset, which will be turned into cash in the short run. A business may not collect all of its accounts receivable. *See* **bad debts.**

accounts receivable turnover ratio   This is the ratio of annual sales revenue divided by the year-end balance of accounts receivable. Technically, to calculate this ratio the amount of annual credit sales should be divided by the average accounts receivable balance, but this information is not readily available from external financial statements. For reporting internally to managers, this ratio should be refined and fine-tuned to be as accurate as possible.

accrual basis of accounting   Frankly, *accrual* is not the most descriptive term in the world. Accrual means much more than that a simple cash receipts and cash disbursement basis of accounting is needed by almost all businesses. Accrual means that a *complete basis* of accounting is used to record the activities of the business and to measure profit for a period. The accrual basis recognizes that (1) a business buys and sells on credit (so accounts payable and accounts receivable are recorded); (2) a business purchases or manufactures products that are held in inventory for some time before they are sold (so the inventories account is recorded); (3) long-term economic resources are bought and used over many years (so fixed assets are recorded and depreciation spreads out the costs over the several years of their use); (4) that some liabilities accumulate over time (so accrued expenses payable is recorded); and so on. Most accounts you see in a balance sheet are the result of the accrual basis of accounting. To comprehend the profit reported by a business, you need a basic understanding of the accrual basis of accounting. In particular, you cannot equate revenue reported in an income statement with cash inflow nor expenses with cash outflow. Life is not so simple in the world of business accounting.

acid test ratio   The sum of cash, accounts receivable, and short-term marketable investments (if any) is divided by total current liabilities to compute this ratio. Suppose its short-term creditors were to pounce on a business and would not roll over the debts owed to them by the business. In this rather extreme scenario the acid test ratio would reveal whether its cash and near-cash assets would be enough to pay off its short-term current liabilities. This ratio is an extreme, or acid, test, which is not likely to be imposed on a business. This ratio is very relevant when a business is in an involuntary liquidation situation, or is in bankruptcy proceedings.

adjusting entries   These key entries are recorded at the end of the period to bring the accounts of a business up-to-date and in particular to record certain expenses (and some revenue as well) that are not recorded during the period. One prime example is the end-of-period adjusting entry to record depreciation expense for the period. Business managers provide very important input to the accountant for making these final entries of the period. In fact a manager can heavily influence the amount of the expense for the period by minimizing or maximizing his or her estimates and forecasts that are required in making several end-of-period adjusting entries.

asset turnover ratio   This is a broad gauge ratio computed by dividing annual sales revenue by total assets. It is a rough measure of the sales generating power of assets. The idea is that assets are used to make sales, and the sales should lead to profit. The more important test is not sales revenue on assets but the profit earned on assets, which is measured by the *return on assets (ROA) ratio*.

average cost method   One of the basic methods to determine the cost of goods sold expense during a period, and the cost of ending inventory. The costs of products acquired during a period (including the cost of beginning inventory) are pooled, and the average cost is computed for the pool. This average cost is used for products sold during the period and for products still in inventory at the end of the period.

bad debts   This term refers to accounts receivable from credit sales to customers that a business will not be able to collect. Of course in hindsight the business shouldn't have extended credit to these particular customers. Since these amounts owed to the business will not be collected, they are written off: The accounts receivable asset account is decreased by the estimated amount of uncollectible receivables and the bad debts expense account is increased this amount. These write-offs can be done by the direct write-off method; no expense is recorded until specific accounts receivable are identified as uncollectible. Or the allowance method can be used based on an estimated percent of bad debts for credit sales during the period. Under this method a contra asset account is created and the balance of the account is deducted from the accounts receivable asset account.

balance sheet   This is the term often used instead of the more formal and correct term—*the statement of financial condition*. This financial statement summarizes the assets, liabilities, and owners' equity of a business at a moment in time. It is prepared at the end of each profit period, and whenever else it is needed. It is one of the three primary financial statements of a business, the other two being the income statement and the statement of cash flows. When the book value of something is determined (such as book value per share of capital stock), the values reported in the balance sheet are the amounts used to determine book value.

basic earnings per share (EPS)   This important ratio equals the net income for a period (usually one year) divided by the number of capital stock shares issued by a business corporation. This ratio is so important for publicly owned business corporations that it is included in the daily stock trading tables published by the *Wall Street Journal*, the *New York Times*, and other major newspapers. Despite being a rather straightforward concept, there are several technical problems in calculating earnings per share. *Two* EPS ratios are needed for many businesses—basic EPS that uses the actual number of capital shares outstanding, and diluted EPS that takes into account additional shares of stock that may be issued for stock options granted by a business and other stock shares that a business is obligated to issue in the future. Also, many businesses report not one but two net income figures—one before extraordinary gains and losses that were recorded in the period, and a second net income after deducting these nonrecurring gains and losses.

big bath   This street-smart term refers to the practice of many businesses of recording very large lump-sum asset write-offs and recording large amounts for pending liabilities that are triggered by business restructurings, massive employee layoffs, disposals of major segments of the business, and other major traumas in the life of a business. Businesses have been known to use these occasions to record every conceivable asset write-off and/or liability write-up that they can think of, in order to clear the decks for the future. In this way a business avoids recording expenses in the future, and its profits in the coming years will be higher. The term is derisive, but investors seem very forgiving regarding the excesses of this accounting device.

book value *and* book value per share   Generally, this term refers to the balance sheet value of an asset (or less often of a liability). The term emphasizes that the amount recorded in the accounts, or on the books of a business is the value being used. For example, the total of the amounts reported for owners' equity in its balance sheet is divided by the number of stock shares of a corporation to determine its book value per share (of stock).

bottom line. *See* **net income.**

breakeven point *or* volume   The annual sales volume level at which contribution margin equals total annual fixed expenses. The breakeven point is only a point of reference, not the goal of a business of course. It is computed by dividing total fixed expenses by unit margin. The breakeven point is useful in analyzing profit behavior and operating leverage.

capital budgeting   This term refers to analysis procedures for ranking investments given a limited amount of total capital that has to be allocated among the various capital investment opportunities of a business. The term sometimes refers to analysis techniques, such as calculating present value, net present value, and the internal rate of return.

capital expenditures   This term refers to investments by a business in its long-term operating assets, such as land and buildings, heavy machinery and equipment, and other economic resources used in the operations of a business. The term *capital* is used to emphasize that these are relatively large amounts and that a business has to raise capital for these expenditures from debt and equity sources.

capital investment analysis   This term refers to various techniques and procedures that are used to determine or to analyze future returns from an investment of capital, in order to evaluate the capital recovery pattern and periodic earnings of the investment. The two basic methods for capital investment analysis are: (1) spreadsheet models (which I strongly prefer); and (2) mathematical equations for calculating the present value or internal rate of return of an investment. Mathematical methods suffer from a lack of information that the decision maker should consider; a spreadsheet model supplies all the needed information and has other advantages as well.

capital recovery   This term refers to recouping, or regaining invested capital over the life of an investment. The pattern of capital recovery period-by-period is very important. In brief, capital recovery means the return *of* capital—not the return *on* capital, which refers to the rate of earnings on the amount of capital invested during the period. The returns from an investment have to be sufficient to provide for both recovery of capital and an adequate rate of earnings on unrecovered capital period-by-period. Sorting out how much capital is recovered each period is relatively easy if you use a spreadsheet model for capital investment analysis. In contrast using a mathematical method of analysis does not provide this period-by-period capital recovery information, which is a major disadvantage.

capital stock   These are ownership shares issued by a business corporation. A business corporation may issue more than one class of capital stock shares. One class may give voting privileges in the election of the directors of the corporation and the other class does not. One class (called preferred stock) may entitle a certain amount of dividends per share before cash dividends can be paid on the other class (usually called common stock). Stock shares may have a minimum amount that they have to be issued for (called the par value) or stock shares can be issued for any amount (called no par stock). Stock shares may be traded on public markets such as the New York Stock Exchange or over the Nasdaq network. There are about 10,000 or so stocks traded on public markets (although estimates vary on this number). In this regard I find it very interesting that there are more than 8,000 mutual funds that invest in stocks.

capital structure *or* capitalization   These terms refer to the sources of capital that a business has tapped for money to invest in its assets—in particular the mix of its interest-bearing debt and owners' equity. In a more sweeping sense the terms also include appendages and other features of basic debt and equity instruments of a business. Such things as stock options, stock warrants, and convertible features of preferred stock and notes payable are included in the more inclusive sense of the terms.

capitalization of costs   When a cost is recorded originally as an increase to an asset account it is said to be capitalized. This means that the outlay is treated as a capital expenditure, which becomes part of the total cost basis of the asset. The alternative is to record the cost as an expense immediately in the period the cost is incurred. Capitalized costs refer mainly to costs that are recorded in the long-term operating assets of a business, such as buildings, machines, equipment, tools, and so on.

cash burn rate   A relatively recent term that has come into use, which refers to how fast a business is using up its available cash when its cash flow from operating activities is negative instead of positive. This term most often refers to a business struggling through its start-up or early phases that has not yet generated enough cash inflow from sales to cover its cash outflow for expenses (and perhaps never will).

cash flow   Well, this term is obvious but at the same time elusive. The term obviously refers to cash inflows and outflows during a period. But the specific sources and uses of cash flows are not clear in this general term. The statement of cash flows, which is one of the three primary financial statements of a business, classifies cash flows into three types: from operating activities (sales and expense operations), from investing activities, and from financing activities. Sometimes, the term *cash flow* is used as shorthand for cash flow from profit (i.e., cash flow from operating activities).

cash flow from operating activities. *See* **cash flow from profit.**

cash flow from profit   This equals the cash inflow from sales during the period minus the cash outflow for expenses during the period. Essentially this equals net income if net income had been accounted for on the cash basis of accounting. Keep in mind that the accrual basis of accounting is required by generally accepted accounting principles to measure net income. Starting with the amount of accrual-basis net income adjustments are made for changes in accounts receivable, inventories, prepaid expenses, and operating liabilities—and depreciation expense is added-back (as well as any other noncash outlay expense) to arrive at cash flow from profit, which is labeled *cash flow from operating activities* in the externally reported statement of cash flows. Chapter 2 presents a better format for internal reporting of operating cash flow to managers.

cash flow statement. *See* **statement of cash flows.**

contribution margin   This is an intermediate measure of profit equal to sales revenue minus cost of goods sold expense and minus variable operating expenses—but before fixed operating expenses are deducted. Profit at this point contributes toward covering fixed operating expenses, and interest and income tax expenses as well.

cost of capital   This refers to the interest cost of debt capital used by a business plus the amount of profit that the business should earn for its equity sources of capital to justify the use of the equity capital during the period. Interest is a contractual and definite amount for a period, whereas the profit that a business should earn on the equity capital employed during the period is not. A business should set a definite objective of earning at least a certain minimum return on equity (ROE), and compare its actual performance for the period against this goal.

current assets   Current refers to cash and those assets that will be turned into cash in the short run. Five types of assets are classified as current: cash, short-term marketable investments, accounts receivable, inventories, and prepaid expenses—and they are listed in this order in the balance sheet.

current liabilities   Current means that these liabilities require payment in the near term. Generally these include accounts payable, accrued expenses payable, income tax payable, short-term notes payable, and the portion of long-term debt that will come due during the coming year.

current ratio   This ratio is calculated to assess the short-term solvency, or debt-paying ability of a business. It equals total current assets divided by total current liabilities. Some businesses remain solvent with a relatively low current ratio, and others could be in trouble with an apparently good current ratio. The general rule is that the current ratio should be 2:1 or higher, but take this with a grain of salt because current ratios vary widely from industry to industry.

debt to equity ratio   This is a widely used financial statement ratio to assess the overall debt load of a business. It equals total liabilities divided by total owners' equity. Both numbers for this ratio are taken from a business's latest balance sheet. There is no standard, or generally agreed maximum ratio, such as 1:1 or 2:1. Every industry is different in this regard. Some businesses, such as financial institutions, have very high debt to equity ratios. In contrast many businesses use very little debt relative to their owners' equity.

deferred maintenance   This is a classic profit manipulation tactic in which the normal repair and maintenance work that should be done during a period is not done, in order to reduce the expense and improve profit performance.

depreciation (expense)   Depreciation refers to the generally accepted accounting principle of allocating the cost of a long-term operating asset over the estimated useful life of the asset. Each year of use is allocated a part of the original cost of the asset. Generally speaking either the accelerated method or the straight-line method of depreciation is used. (There are other methods, but they are relatively rare.) Useful life estimates are heavily influenced by the schedules allowed in the federal income tax law. Depreciation is not a cash outlay in the period the expense is recorded—just the opposite. The cash inflow from sales revenue during the period includes a sliver to reimburse the business for the use of its fixed assets. In this respect depreciation is a source of cash.

diluted earnings per share (EPS). *See also* **basic earnings per share**   This measure of earnings per share takes into account any additional stock shares that may be issued in the future for stock options and as may be required by other contracts a business has entered into, such as convertible features in its debt securities and preferred stock. Both basic earnings per share and, if applicable, diluted earnings per share are reported by publicly owned business corporations. Often the two EPS figures are not far apart, but in some cases the gap is significant. Privately owned businesses do not have to report earnings per share.

discounted cash flow (DCF)   This refers to a capital investment analysis technique that discounts or reduces future cash returns from an investment for the cost of capital on the amount of capital invested each period. Present value is the amount remaining after discounting the future returns. Present value is subtracted from the entry cost of the investment to determine the net present value. The net present value is positive if the present value is more than the entry cost, which signals that the investment would earn more than the cost of capital rate. If the entry cost is more than the present value, the net present value is negative, which means that the investment would earn less than the business's cost of capital rate.

dividend payout ratio   This ratio is computed by dividing cash dividends for the year by the net income for the year. It's simply the percent of net income distributed as cash dividends for the year.

dividend yield ratio   This ratio equals the cash dividends paid by a business over the most recent 12 months (called the trailing 12 months) divided by the current market price per share of the stock. This ratio is reported in the daily stock trading tables in the *Wall Street Journal* and other major newspapers.

double-entry accounting. *See* **accrual basis of accounting.**

earnings before interest and income tax (EBIT)   This measure of profit equals sales revenue for the period minus cost of goods sold expense and all operating expenses—but before deducting interest and income tax expenses. It is a measure of the operating profit of a business, before considering the cost of its debt capital and income tax.

earnings per share (EPS). *See* **basic earnings per share** *and* **diluted earnings per share (EPS).**

extraordinary gains and losses   These are nonrecurring, or one-time unusual gains or losses that are recorded by a business during the period. The amount of each of these gains or losses, net of the income tax effect, is reported separately in the income statement. Net income is reported before and after these gains and losses. These gains and losses should not be recorded very often but in fact many businesses record them every other year or so, which causes much consternation in the investment community.

financial leverage   The equity (ownership) capital of a business serves as a lever for securing debt capital (borrowing money). In this way a business increases the total capital available to invest in its assets and can make more sales and more profit. The strategy is to earn operating profit, or earnings before interest and income tax (EBIT) on the capital supplied from debt that is more than the interest paid on the debt capital. A financial leverage gain equals the EBIT earned on debt capital minus the interest on the debt. A financial leverage gain augments earnings on equity capital. A business must earn a rate of return on its assets (ROA) that is greater than the interest rate on its debt to make a financial leverage gain. If the spread between its ROA and interest rate is unfavorable, a business suffers a financial leverage loss.

financial reports *and* **statements**   *Financial* means having to do with monetary value and economic wealth. *Statement* means a formal presentation. Businesses prepare three primary financial statements: the statement of financial condition, or balance sheet; the statement of cash flows; and, the income statement. These three key financial statements constitute the core of the periodic financial reports that are distributed outside a business to its shareowners and lenders. Financial statements are prepared according to *generally accepted accounting principles* (GAAP), which are the authoritative rules that govern the measurement of net income and the reporting of profit-making activities, financial condition, and cash flows. Internal financial statements, although based on the same profit accounting methods, report more information to managers for decision-making and control. Sometimes, financial statements are called simply *financials*.

financing activities   This is one of the three classes of cash flows reported in the statement of cash flows. This class includes borrowing money and paying debt, raising money from shareowners and the return of money to them, and dividends paid from profit.

first-in, first-out (FIFO)   This is one of the popular accounting methods to measure cost of goods sold during a period and the cost of ending inventory. It's both an expense measurement and an asset valuation method; you can't separate these two aspects of FIFO. The first costs of purchasing or manufacturing products are the first costs charged out to record cost of goods sold expense. Thus, the most recent costs of acquisition remain in the inventories asset account (until the goods are sold sometime later). To examine a simple example suppose a business bought two units of a new product during the year. The first unit cost $100 and the second unit, which was purchased sometime later, cost $105. The business sold one of the two units. FIFO assigns $100 to cost of goods sold expense and $105 to the cost of ending inventory. *See* **last-in, first-out (LIFO)**, which uses the same facts but gives different results.

fixed assets   This is the informal term used for the variety of long-term operating resources used by a business in its operations—including real estate, machinery, equipment, tools, vehicles, office furniture, computers, and so on. In balance sheets the title for these assets typically is property, plant, and equipment. The term *fixed assets* captures the idea that the assets are relatively fixed in place and are not held for sale in the normal course of business. The cost of fixed assets, except land, is depreciated, which means the cost is allocated over the estimated useful lives of the assets.

fixed expenses or costs These are expenses or costs that remain the same in amount, or are fixed over the short run and do not vary with changes in sales volume or sales revenue or other measures of activity of a business. Over the longer run, however, these expenses and costs are raised or lowered as the business grows or declines. Fixed operating costs provide capacity to carry on operations and make sales. Fixed manufacturing overhead costs provide production capacity. Fixed expenses are a key pivot point for the analysis of profit behavior, especially for determining the breakeven point and in analyzing strategies for improving profit performance.

free cash flow Generally speaking this term refers to cash flow from profit. The underlying idea is that a business is free to do what it wants with its cash flow from profit. However, a business usually has many ongoing commitments and demands on this cash flow, so it may not be all that free in deciding what do with the cash. **Warning:** This term is not officially defined anyplace and different persons use the term with different meanings. If you come across the term, pay particular attention to how the author or speaker is using the term.

generally accepted accounting principles (GAAP) This refers to the body of authoritative rules for measuring profit and preparing financial statements that are included in financial reports by a business to its outside shareowners and lenders. The development of these guidelines has been an ongoing evolving process for more than 70 years. Congress passed a law in 1934 that bestowed primary jurisdiction over financial reporting to shareowners by publicly owned businesses to the Securities and Exchange Commission (SEC). But the SEC has largely left the development of GAAP to the private sector. Presently the Financial Accounting Standards Board is the primary (but not the only) authoritative body that makes pronouncements on GAAP. One caution: GAAP are like a moveable feast. New rules are issued fairly frequently, old rules are amended from time to time, and some rules established years ago are discarded on occasion. Professional accountants have a heck of time keeping up with GAAP, that's for sure.

gross margin (*also called* gross profit) This first line measure of profit equals sales revenue less cost of goods sold. This is profit *before* operating expenses and interest and income tax expenses are deducted. Financial reporting standards require that gross margin be reported in external income statements. Gross margin is a key variable in the management profit model for analyzing profit behavior. Gross margin doesn't apply to service businesses that don't sell products.

income statement   This is the financial statement that summarizes sales revenue and expenses for a period, and reports one or more profit lines for the period. It is one of the three primary financial statements of a business. The bottom-line profit figure is called net income, or net earnings by most businesses. Externally reported income statements disclose less information compared with internal management profit reports, but both are based on the same profit accounting principles and methods. Keep in mind that profit is not known until accountants complete the recording of sales revenue and expenses for the period (as well as any extraordinary gains and losses in the period). Profit measurement depends on the reliability of the accounting system and the choices of accounting methods by a business. **Caution:** A business may engage in certain manipulations of their accounting methods and managers may intervene in the normal course of operations for the purpose of improving the amount of profit recorded in the period.

internal accounting controls   This broad term refers to forms and procedures established by a business, which go beyond what would be required for the record keeping function of accounting, that are designed to prevent errors and fraud (a broad term covering embezzlement, employee theft, shoplifting, etc.). For instance, two common internal controls are requiring a second signature by someone higher in the organization to approve a transaction in excess of a certain dollar amount, and of giving customers printed receipts as proof of sale. Other examples of internal control procedures are restricting the entry and exit routes of employees, requiring all employees to take their vacations and assigning another person to do their jobs while they are away, surveillance cameras, surprise counts of cash and inventory, and rotation of duties. Internal controls should be cost effective; the cost of a control should be less than the potential loss that is prevented. The guiding principle for designing internal accounting controls is to deter and detect errors and dishonesty. However, the best internal controls in the world cannot prevent high-level management fraud.

internal rate of return (IRR)   The exact discount rate that makes the present value (PV) of the cash returns from a capital investment equal to the initial amount of capital invested. If IRR is higher than the company's cost of capital rate, the investment is an attractive opportunity; if less, the investment is substandard from the cost of capital point of view.

inventory shrinkage This is the generic term for the loss of products from inventory due to shoplifting by customers, employee theft, damaged and spoiled products that are thrown away, and errors in recording the purchase and sale of products. A business has to make a physical count and inspection of inventory to determine this loss.

inventory turnover ratio This ratio equals the cost of inventories divided by the cost of goods sold expense for period. The ratio depends on how long products are held in stock on average before they are sold. Managers should closely monitor this ratio.

inventory write-down This term refers to making an entry, usually at the close of a period, to reduce the cost value of the inventories asset account in order to recognize loss of value due to products that cannot be sold at their normal mark ups or will be sold below cost. A business compares the recorded cost of products held in inventory against the sales value of the products. Based on the lower of cost or market rule, an entry is made to record the inventory write-down and an expense.

investing activities This is one of the three classes of cash flows reported in the statement of cash flows. This class includes capital expenditures for replacing and expanding the fixed assets of a business, proceeds from disposals of its fixed assets, and other long-term investment activities of a business.

last-in, first-out (LIFO) One of the popular accounting methods to measure cost of goods sold during a period and the cost of ending inventory. It's both an expense measurement and an asset valuation method; you can't separate these two aspects of LIFO. The last, or most recent costs of purchasing or manufacturing products are the first costs charged out to record cost of goods sold expense. Thus, the oldest costs of acquisition remain in the inventories asset account. To examine a simple example suppose a business bought two units of a new product during the year. The first unit cost $100 and the second unit, which was purchased sometime later, cost $105. The business sold one of the two units. LIFO assigns $105 to cost of goods sold expense and $100 to the cost of ending inventory. See **first-in, first-out (FIFO)**, which uses the same facts but gives different results.

LIFO liquidation gain   This refers to a situation in which a business that uses the LIFO method sells more units of a product than are replaced during the period. Thus, the inventory quantity of the product is decreased. To record the cost of goods sold expense for the number of units sold but not replaced, the accountant has to take costs from one or more of the layers recorded in the LIFO-based inventory account. These costs may be quite old and usually the costs are lower than current replacement costs. The difference between the older LIFO cost and the current replacement cost of the product times the number of units sold but not replaced creates a LIFO liquidation gain. A business may force this result to improve its recorded profit for the year.

lower of cost or market   This is a required accounting method that should be applied to the ending inventories of a business. The cost of each product is compared against is current replacement cost and its probable sales value. If its replacement cost or sales value is less, then the product should be written down to the lower amount and an expense is recorded to recognize the loss of value. This accounting rule is more complicated than this concise explanation, but the gist of the method is as explained here. A business manager should make sure that the accountant has applied this test to ending inventories.

management profit and control reports   These are the reports to various managers within a business organization that do not circulate outside the business. These reports are strictly for internal use. These reports contain very confidential information. The level of detail and range of information in these reports is quite different from the external income statement reported by the business to its outside shareowners and creditors.

market capitalization (*or* market cap)   This equals the current market value per share of capital stock multiplied by the total number of capital stock shares outstanding of a publicly owned business. This value often differs widely from the book value of owners' equity reported in the company's balance sheet.

negative cash flow   This term means that the cash flow from the operating activities of a business is negative, so its cash balance decreased from its sales and expense activities for the period. When a business is operating at a loss instead of making a profit, its cash outflows for expenses could be more than its cash inflow from sales. Even when a business makes a profit for the period, its cash inflow from sales could be considerably less than the sales revenue recorded for the period, thus causing a negative cash flow for the period. **Caution:** This term also is used for certain types of investments in which the net cash flow from all sources and uses is negative. For example, investors in rental real estate properties often use the term to mean that the cash inflow from rental income is less than all cash outflows during the period, including loan payments on the mortgage loan on the property.

net income (*also called the* bottom line, earnings, net earnings, net operating earnings)   This equals sales revenue for a period less all expenses for the period; also any extraordinary gains and losses for the period are included in this final figure for profit. Everything is taken into account to arrive at net income, which is popularly called the *bottom line*. Net income is clearly the single most important number in business financial reports.

net present value (NPV)   Equals the present value (PV) of a capital investment minus the initial amount of capital that is invested, or the entry cost of the investment. A positive NPV signals an attractive capital investment opportunity; a negative NPV means that the investment is substandard. Internal rate of return (IRR) is the discount rate that makes NPV equal to zero.

net worth   Generally, this term refers to the book value of owners' equity as reported in a business's balance sheet. The term *net* comes from the accounting equation: [Assets = Liabilities + Owners' Equity]. If liabilities are subtracted from assets the equation becomes: [Assets – Liabilities = Owners' Equity]. In this version of the accounting equation Owners' Equity is the net worth of assets after liabilities are deducted.

operating activities   This is the term used in official pronouncements on generally accepted accounting principles to connote the revenue producing and expense activities of a business. The term is broad and inclusive; it was chosen to embrace all types of activities engaged in by profit-motivated entities toward the objective of earning net income. A bank, for instance, earns net income not from sales revenue but from loaning money on which it receives interest income. Interest income is the main revenue of banks.

operating cash flow. *See* **cash flow from profit.**

operating leverage   A relatively small percent increase or decrease in sales volume causes a much larger percent increase or decrease in profit because fixed expenses do not change with small changes in sales volume. Sales volume changes have a lever effect on profit. This effect should be called sales volume leverage, but in practice it is called operating leverage.

operating liabilities Operating liabilities are the short-term liabilities generated by the profit-making activities of a business. Most businesses have three types of operating liabilities: accounts payable from inventory purchases and from incurring expenses; accrued expenses payable for unpaid expenses; and income tax payable. These short-term liabilities of a business are not interest bearing, although if not paid on time a business may be assessed a late payment penalty that is in the nature of an interest charge.

operating profit. *See* **earnings before interest and income tax (EBIT).**

overhead costs Overhead generally means *indirect*, in contrast to direct costs. Indirect means that a cost cannot be matched or coupled in any obvious or objective manner with particular products, or specific revenue sources, or an organizational unit. For manufacturers overhead costs refer to indirect costs in making products, in addition to direct costs of raw materials and labor. Manufacturing overhead costs include both *variable* costs, such as electricity, gas, and water that vary with total production output, and *fixed* costs that do not vary with increases or decreases in actual production output. Fixed manufacturing costs provide production *capacity*, which may not be fully used during the year. Some idle capacity is normal; thus, a part of the total annual fixed manufacturing overhead cost is absorbed in the product cost of the units manufactured during the year instead of being charged off directly to expense in the period.

owner's equity This term refers to the capital invested in a business by its shareowners and the profit earned by the business that has not been distributed to its shareowners, which generally is called retained earnings. Owners' equity is one of the two basic sources of capital to a business, the other being borrowed money, or debt. The book value, or value reported in a balance sheet for owners' equity is not the market value of the business. Rather, the balance sheet value reflects the historical amounts of capital invested by the owners over the years in the business plus the accumulation of yearly profits that were not paid out to the owners as cash dividends.

present value (PV)   This is the calculated amount from discounting the future cash returns from a capital investment. The discount rate usually is the cost of capital rate for the business. If PV is more than the initial amount of capital that has to be invested the investment is attractive; if less, better investment alternatives should be looked for. In other words, if PV is more than the initial cash outlay to enter the investment then the earnings rate, or internal rate of return (IRR) from the investment is higher than the discount rate and the net present value (NPV) is positive. If PV is less, then the IRR is less than the discount rate and NPV is negative.

price/earnings (P/E) ratio   This key ratio equals the current market price of a capital stock share divided by the earnings per share (EPS) for the stock. The EPS used in this ratio may be the basic EPS for the stock, or its diluted EPS—you have to check to be sure about this. A low P/E may signal an undervalued stock or may reflect a pessimistic forecast by investors for the future earnings prospects of the business. A high P/E may reveal an overvalued stock or reflect an optimistic forecast by investors. The average P/E ratio for the stock market as a whole varies considerably over time—in my memory from a low of about 8 to a high of about 25. This is quite a range of variation, to say the least.

product cost   This is a key factor in the profit model of a business. Product cost is purchase cost for a retailer or wholesaler (distributor), whereas a manufacturer has to accumulate three different types of production costs to determine product cost: direct materials, direct labor, and manufacturing overhead. The cost of products (goods) sold is deducted from sales revenue to determine gross margin (also called gross profit), which is the first profit line reported in an external income statement and in an internal profit report to managers.

profit   The general term profit is not precisely defined; it may refer to net gains over a period of time, or cash inflows less cash outflows for an investment, or earnings before or after certain costs and expenses are deducted from income or revenue. In the world of business profit is measured by the application of generally accepted accounting principles (GAAP). In the income statement the final, or bottom-line profit is called net income, which equals revenue (plus any extraordinary gains) less all expenses (and less any extraordinary losses) for the period. Internal management profit reports include several profit lines: gross margin, contribution margin, operating profit (earnings before interest and income tax), and earnings before income tax. External income statements report gross margin (also called gross profit), and often report one or more other profit lines, although practice varies from business to business in this regard.

profit and loss statement (P&L statement). *See* **income statement.**

profit module   This concept refers to a separate source of revenue and profit within a business organization, which should be identified for management analysis and control. A profit module may focus on one product, or a cluster of products. Profit in this context is not the final, bottom-line net income of the business as a whole. Rather, one or more other measures of profit are used for management analysis and decision-making purposes–such as gross margin, contribution margin, or operating profit (earnings before interest and income tax).

profit ratios   These ratios are based on sales revenue for a period. A measure of profit is divided by sales revenue to compute a profit ratio. For example gross margin is divided by sales revenue to compute the gross margin profit ratio. Dividing bottom-line profit (net income) by sales revenue gives the profit ratio that is generally called return on sales.

property, plant, and equipment. *See* **fixed assets.**

quick ratio. *See* **acid test ratio.**

return on assets (ROA) ratio   Although practice is not uniform for calculating this ratio, generally it equals operating earnings (before interest and income tax) for a year divided by the total assets that are used to generate the earnings. ROA is the key ratio to test whether a business is earning enough on its assets to cover its cost of capital requirements. ROA is used for determining financial leverage gain (or loss).

return on equity (ROE) ratio   This key ratio equals net income for the year divided by owners' equity, and is expressed as a percent. ROE should be higher than a business's interest rate on debt because the owners take more risk.

return on investment (ROI)   This is a very general concept that refers to some measure of income, or earnings, or profit, or gain over a period of time divided by the amount of capital invested during the period. It is almost always expressed as a percent. For a business an important ROI measure is its return on equity (ROE), which is computed by dividing its net income for the period by its owners' equity during the period.

return on sales. *See* **profit ratios.**

revenue-driven expenses   These operating expenses vary in proportion to changes in total sales revenue (total dollars of sales). Examples are sales commissions based on sales revenue, credit card discount expenses, and rents and franchise fees based on sales revenue. These expenses are one of the key variables in the management profit model explained in the book. These expenses are not disclosed separately in externally reported income statements. Segregating these expenses from other types of expenses that behave differently is essential for management decision-making analysis.

Securities and Exchange Commission (SEC)   This is the federal agency that oversees the issuance of and trading in securities of public businesses. The SEC has broad powers, and can suspend the trading in securities of a business. The SEC also has primary jurisdiction in making accounting and financial reporting rules, but over the years it has largely deferred to the private sector for the development of generally accepted accounting principles.

solvency   This term refers to the ability of a business to pay its liabilities on time when they come due for payment. A business may be insolvent, which means that it is not able to pay its liabilities and debts on time. The current ratio and acid test ratio are used to evaluate the short-term solvency of a business.

spontaneous liabilities. *See* **operating liabilities.**

statement of cash flows   This is one of the three primary financial statements that a business includes in its periodic financial reports to its outside shareowners and lenders. This financial statement summarizes the business's cash inflows and outflows for the period according to a threefold classification: (1) cash flow from operating activities (which I prefer to call cash flow from profit); (2)

cash flow from investing activities; and (3) cash flow from financing activities. Frankly, the typical statement of cash flows is difficult to read and decipher; it includes too many lines of information and is fairly technical compared with the typical balance sheet and income statement. I strongly favor a different approach and format for reporting cash flow from profit internally to managers.

statement of changes in stockholders' equity   Although called a statement, this is more in the nature of a supporting schedule that summarizes in one place various changes in the owners' equity accounts of a business—including the issuance and retirement of capital stock shares, cash dividends, and other transactions affecting owners' equity during the period. This statement (schedule) is very helpful when a business has more than one class of stock shares outstanding and when a variety of events occurred during the year that changed its owners' equity accounts.

statement of financial condition. *See* balance sheet.

straight-line depreciation method   This is the depreciation method that allocates a uniform amount of the cost of long-lived operating assets (fixed assets) to each year of use. It is the basic alternative to the accelerated depreciation method. When using the straight-line method a business may adopt a longer life estimate for depreciating a fixed asset compared with the accelerated method (though not necessarily in every case). Both methods are allowed for income tax.

sunk cost   A sunk cost is one that has been paid and cannot be undone or reversed. Once the cost has been paid it is irretrievable, like water over the dam, or sunk. Usually the term refers to the book value of an asset that has lost its value in the operating activities of a business. Examples are the costs of products in inventory that cannot be sold and fixed assets that are no longer usable. The book value of these assets should be written-off to expense. Such costs should be disregarded in making decisions about what to do with the assets (except that the income tax effects of disposing of the assets should be taken into account).

times interest earned   A ratio to test the ability of a business to make the interest payments on its debt, which is calculated by dividing annual earnings before interest and income tax by the interest expense for the year. There is no particular rule for this ratio, such as 3 or 4 times interest, but obviously the ratio should be higher than one.

unit margin   This equals the profit per unit sold of a product after deducting product cost and variable expenses of selling the product from the sales price of the product. Unit margin equals profit before fixed operating expenses are considered and before interest and income tax are deducted. Unit margin is one of the key variables in the management profit model explained in the book.

unit-driven expenses   Those expenses vary in close proportion to changes in total sales volume (total quantities of sales). Examples of these types of expenses are delivery costs, packaging costs, and other costs that depend mainly on the number of products sold or the number of customers served. These expenses are one of the key factors in the management profit model explained in the book. These expenses are not disclosed separately in externally reported income statements. Segregating these expenses from other types of expenses that behave differently is essential for management decision-making analysis. **Note:** The cost of goods sold expense depends on sales volume and is a unit-driven expense. But product cost (i.e., the cost of goods sold) is such a dominant expense that it is treated separately from other unit-driven operating expenses.

variable expenses   These are expenses that change with changes in either sales volume or sales revenue, in contrast to fixed expenses that remain the same over the short-run and do not fluctuate in response to changes in sales volume or sales revenue. *See* **revenue-driven expenses** and **unit-driven expenses.**

weighted-average cost of capital   The term *weighted* means that the proportions of debt capital and equity capital of a business are used to calculate its average cost of capital. This key benchmark rate depends on the interest rate on its debt and the return on equity (ROE) goal established by a business. Often this return on capital rate is applied on an after-tax basis, so the interest rate is converted to an after-tax basis. A business should earn at least this minimum rate of return on assets (ROA) on the capital invested in its assets. The weighted-average cost of capital is used as the discount rate to calculate the present value (PV) of specific investments.

window dressing   This refers to holding the books open after the close of the accounting period in order to record additional cash collections as if these cash receipts had been collected on the last day of the accounting period. This is done to improve the cash balance and the solvency appearance of a business. Also, window dressing may be done to improve the cash flow from profit for the period, or the current ratio of a business. It is a very questionable practice but seems to be tolerated, within limits. In contrast to profit manipulation techniques (which are explained in Chapter 14), window dressing does not affect the profit figure for the period.

Index